WITHDRAWN

WORKING FORENSICS

A Competitor's Guide
Second Edition

M'Liss Hindman   *Jacque Shackelford*   *Kathryn Schlottach*

TYLER JUNIOR COLLEGE

KENDALL/HUNT PUBLISHING COMPANY
4050 Westmark Drive   Dubuque, Iowa 52002

OESTERLE LIBRARY, NCC
NAPERVILLE, IL 60540

Copyright © 1991, 1993 by Kendall/Hunt Publishing Company

ISBN 0-8403-8873-X

All rights reserved. No part of this publication may be reproduced, stored in a retrieval system, or transmitted, in any form or by any means, electronic, mechanical, photocopying, recording, or otherwise, without the prior written permission of the copyright owner.

Printed in the United States of America
10 9 8 7 6 5 4 3

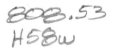

TABLE OF CONTENTS

PREFACE (A Note For Coaches) vii
READ ME FIRST (A Note For The Students) ix
THE NEED TO WIN xii

SECTION I: THE BASICS 1

    WHAT IS FORENSICS AND WHY SHOULD YOU DO IT? 3
    CRITERIA FOR TOURNAMENT PARTICIPATION 4
    EVENT RULES 7
    HOW DO I CHOOSE EVENTS? 9
    A BRIEF OVERVIEW OF WHAT'S INVOLVED 12
    TRADITIONS 14
    THE CARE OF COACHES 16
    HOUSE RULES 18
    BEFORE YOU TURN THE PAGE - A Bridge Before Section II 19

SECTION II: PREPARED SPEAKING EVENTS - GENERAL INFORMATION 21

    HOW TO WRITE A SPEECH - A Brief Overview 22
    THE 8 STEP PROCESS 23
    THE SPEAKER' FIRST SOJOURN INTO THE LIBRARY 27
    IF YOU WERE A SPEECH TOPIC, WHERE WOULD YOU HIDE? 28
    CRITERIA FOR SPEECH TOPICS 29
    EFFECTIVE SPEECH DELIVERY 30
    VISUAL AIDS 32
    WHAT JUDGES LOOK FOR IN SPEAKING EVENTS 34

    PREPARED SPEAKING EVENTS - DESCRIPTIONS & WORKSHEETS 35

    PHASE ONE - COMMITMENT 36
    INFORMATIVE SPEAKING 37
    WORKSHEETS FOR INFORMATIVE 38
    PERSUASIVE SPEAKING 49
    WORKSHEETS FOR PERSUASIVE 50
    SPEAKING TO ENTERTAIN 61
    WORKSHEETS FOR SPEAKING TO ENTERTAIN 62
    COMMUNICATION ANALYSIS 74
    WORKSHEETS FOR COMMUNICATION ANALYSIS 76

SECTION III: LOW-PREPARATION SPEAKING EVENTS 87

    PHASE ONE - COMMITMENT 88
    EXTEMPORANEOUS SPEAKING (GENERAL INFORMATION) 89
    EXTEMPORANEOUS SPEAKING WORKSHEETS 94
    SETTING UP AND MAINTAINING AN EXTEMP FILE 102
    HELPFUL PUBLICATIONS FOR EXTEMPORANEOUS SPEAKING 105
    EXTEMP GAMES 106

  IMPROMPTU SPEAKING (GENERAL INFORMATION) 108
  IMPROMPTU SPEAKING WORKSHEETS 110
  IMPROMPTU GAMES 120
  SOME ORGANIZATIONAL HELP FOR SPEECHES 122

SECTION IV: INTERPRETATION EVENTS - GENERAL INFORMATION 127

  HOW TO DO INTERPRETATION 128
  AN APPROACH TO LITERATURE INTERPRETATION IN GENERAL 129
  FINDING AND SELECTING INTERPRETIVE MATERIAL 131
  SELECTION CRITERIA FOR LITERATURE 132
  THE INTERPER'S FIRST SOJOURN INTO THE LIBRARY 134
  LITERARY MERIT 135
  HOW TO CUT 137
  THE PHYSICAL SCRIPT/BINDER 140
  INTRODUCTIONS AND TRANSITIONS FOR INTERP EVENTS 144
  CREATING CHARACTERS FOR INTERPRETATION 146
  FOCUS IN INTERPRETATION 148
  WHAT JUDGES LOOK FOR IN INTERPRETIVE EVENTS 152

  INTERPRETATION EVENTS - DESCRIPTIONS & WORKSHEETS 153

  PHASE ONE - THE COMMITMENT 154
  PROSE INTERPRETATION 155
  PROSE INTERPRETATION WORKSHEETS 156
  POETRY INTERPRETATION 167
  POETRY INTERPRETATION WORKSHEETS 168
  DRAMATIC INTERPRETATION 181
  DRAMATIC INTERPRETATION WORKSHEETS 183
  DUO DRAMATIC INTERPRETATION 193
  PICKING A PARTNER 194
  DUO INTERPRETATION WORKSHEETS 195
  PROGRAM ORAL INTERPRETATION 205
  PROGRAM ORAL INTERPRETATION WORKSHEETS 207

SECTION V: SURVIVAL SKILLS 219

  WHY SURVIVAL SKILLS 220
  TIME MANAGEMENT 221
  YOUR LIFE MANAGER: THE PORTABLE CALENDAR 223
  BACK-TIMING & YOUR CALENDAR 225
  TAKING STEPS TO WRITE A TERM PAPER 226
  FINAL EDIT CHECK LIST 229
  TIPS FOR IMPRESSING INSTRUCTORS 230
  HINTS FOR DOING BETTER IN CLASS 231
  A FEW HINTS ABOUT TESTS 233

SECTION VI: GETTING READY TO GO TO TOURNAMENT 235

    SOME NOTES ON MEMORIZING 236
    PRACTICE PRACTICES 240
    A HEALTHY COMPETITOR IS A HAPPY COMPETITOR 246
    FOOD AND FORENSICS 251
    PRE-TRAVEL CHECKLIST 252
    PACKING LIKE A PROFESSIONAL COMPETITOR 254
    EMERGENCY SUPPLIES 256
    ROOMIES 257
    ON THE ROAD 259

SECTION VII: AT THE TOURNAMENT 263

    TOURNAMENT BEHAVIOR 264
    MAKING IT TO OUT ROUNDS 270
    WHAT HAPPENS IF YOUR NAME IS NOT ON THE WALL 272
    ETHICAL CONCERNS 274
    USING BALLOTS AS A LEARNING TOOL 275

SECTION VIII: STATE OF MIND 277

    MENTAL TOUGHNESS 278
    THE FRAMEWORK OF WINNING: ATTITUDE 280
    WHEN DREAMS COME TRUE - THE FORENSIC GOD 282
    TOUGH TALK 284

APPENDIX FOR COACHES 287

    COLLEGIATE FORENSIC ORGANIZATIONS 288
    NOTE TO COACHES: HOW TO USE THESE FORMS 291
    FORENSICS SIGN-UP & PROGRESS SHEET 293
    COACHING SCHEDULE 294
    PREPARATION SCHEDULE 295
    STUDENT/COMPETITOR ACADEMIC STATUS REPORT 296
    FORENSIC PERSONAL EVALUATION 298

THE LEXICON 301

INDEX 335

FOREWORD

It has been three years since I had the pleasure of writing the foreword to the first edition of this book; and in that time, I have used it to teach scores of students what forensics has to offer. Yet looking back I cannot help but feel a twinge of guilt for the ease brought to my teaching by this comprehensive pedagogical tool. And in this second edition, these gifted educators have taken a previously polished band and made a symphony out of it. Careful attention to changing rules and details remind us educators how important it is to stay abreast of our ever-changing field. Once again these writers have made our quest to remain up-to-date appear so simple. As a guide, this triptych warns us of new potholes and ever-present hazards in our road ahead; but in so doing it consolidates our paths and focuses our teaching goals.

Why we as members of the forensic community need such a guide is also obvious. In an era when time may well be our most valued commodity, forensic educators find themselves answering and re-answering the same introductory questions over and over and over again. What professors Hindman, Shackelford, and Schlottach have done is answer those questions for us. They continue to refine what I believe is the only continuously updated comprehensive guide to intercollegiate forensics.

Equally impressive is the scope of their project. Designed not only for the beginning coach, but also for the competitor at each stage of the educational process, they have developed a working (and I agree with their fundamental use of the word) text to guide the user through all phases of the creation of a public address speech, a literary performance, and a limited preparation speech. The work sheet is a hands on, here-are-things-you-may-not-have-thought-of approach to forensics and invites all of us to acquaint/reacquaint ourselves with everything from structure to literary merit, from limited preparation games to documentation, from source citations to imagery, from putting together a manuscript book to choosing a methodology for a communication analysis.

As a teacher of performance, I find myself fascinated with the authors abilities to pen some of the critical issues involved in developing a believable literary interpretation: the development of subtext, the clarity of character interplay, the writing of the introduction, the focus -- literally the whole package. The corollary to the accessibility of the performance events is the ease with which they open the door to all the public speaking events: from how to create and manipulate the structure to how to cite that specific piece of documentation, from how to draw in the audience to how to leave a lasting impression -- once again tieing a neat bow around a perfect package.

This guide is just that -- a guide to make the forensic world more accessible to new members of our community. And what I find most pronounced is the zeal of these three writers and coaches dedicated to providing a flashlight for those waiting to enter what may first seem labyrinthine -- the world of intercollegiate forensics.

I encourage you to let them be your guides as I continue to do.

Peter Pober - Director of Forensics
University of Texas - Austin
June 1993

PREFACE
A Note for Coaches

Long ago, in a forensic program far, far away, war broke out. Not a guns and bullets war, but a war, nonetheless. The forensic coaches were fighting for enough time to meet classes, meetings, administrative tasks, play schedules, family and personal commitments--in other words, the ever increasing time demands of typical forensic coaches.

The forensic students, in ever increasing numbers, were bringing with them their own time demands: jobs, families, classes, personal commitments--in other words, more complicated lives than ever before to be merged with a forensic schedule. The war was being fought on two fronts -- domestic and forensic. In addition, the young stressed-out warrior-students were asked to compete in tournaments that had tougher competitors, higher standards, and an ever increasing array of dazzling talent.

Life in the world of forensics was getting harder and harder. Time was winning. What could be done? How could the increased demand ever be met? How could coaches be subdivided into tiny enough increments to provide the students with the training that they needed while battling the clock?

An answer to these desperate questions gave birth to the handouts that grew into a book of sorts--the student guide. You see, on analyzing the problem, we found that, as coaches, we spent much of our time answering the same questions for each student. So, one answer to the problem of more time was to provide the answers in writing to those questions that could be answered generically. The handouts provided "coaching" that could be done by the students on their own, in a form that would allow them to do just that. A student could move ahead, in a directed way, at their own pace and come to a coach when they were ready for hands-on coaching. Then, we could maximize the effectiveness of the time that we were able to spend with a student, safe in the knowledge that each was prepared to gain the most from each coaching session.

When the questions could be answered by the student guide, we sent the student there first. If there was still a problem, we could answer individually. This proved to be a great time saver, and it freed us to spend more time actually coaching and less time being an information dispenser. The student guide was born of necessity and has been tested and refined over a period of years. After a while, we found that our colleagues were hungry for copies of the handouts and so our student guide grew into a book.

This is our guide, developed for our students. It has solved problems for us. We sincerely hope that it will help you and your students. We know that there are many of you who have systems of your own that are successful for you, and that many of your answers are as valid as ours. We did not design this book to take the place of competent coaching, but to enhance that time that you spend coaching students.

We have written this book based on our strongly held belief that forensics is an educational experience for students designed to teach life skills like confidence and perseverance.

Some have called our writing style "casual". We prefer to think of it as "readable". We have designed this book to be used primarily by students. They seem more comfortable with a less formal voice. We know that forensic competitors, by and large, are the brightest and best students in school. We try never to underestimate their intelligence and ability, even when we speak in our more "casual" style.

We have included a list of forensic organizations and some guides for coaches in the appendix. We feel that these forms may enable you to put into practice some further time savers for coaching.

In writing what we refer to as The Last Edition, we have listened carefully to what student and coaches have told us. In additon, we wanted to change some things. The result, we believe, is much more clearly defined. We have reorganized much of the material. Whenever possible, we have gotten rid of assumption and given more rationale for what students are asked to do. We have addressed delivery more directly. However, it is also implicit in many of the worksheets. The low-prep events and communication analysis have been almost completely revamped. Many sections have been significantly added to, such as the section on health. At times references or advice still remain vague or are given to multiple suggestions. These were done intentionally because of the wide range of regional differences. Overall, we believe that this new edition is much simpler and easier to read. BUT, we have maintained our right to enjoy oursleves -- so the dumb jokes are still evident.

We would be remiss in our duty if we failed to say thank you to some special people for helping us. We would like to acknowledge some of the students who made <u>special</u> contributions to our coaching styles over the years-- some by their good behavior and some by their bad behavior. We learned from them all.

So a special thank you to *Nick, Cheree, Cela, Sheri, Steve, Kay, Wayne, David, Vernon, Mike, Rick, Rhonda, Russell, Benard, Faith, Connie, Cheryl, Diana, James, Cindi, Joan, Mitch, Marla, Beth, Mary, Doug, Pam, Amy, Joe, Dex, Jetta, Mark, Doug, Jean, Jeanine, Tim, Tom, Will, Lee, Mike, Sandy, Robyn, Robin, Andy, James, Scott, Scott, Scott (our expert on diet), Jonathon, Cliff, Rusty, Lovenia, Julia, Jill, Anja, Shea, Damon, Carol, Tim, Keith, Marty, Lisa Bell, Laura, Lori, Jonas, Drake, Danny, Chad, Becky, Mary, Bonnie, Troy, Marquette, Spencer, Luke, Sharon, Chris, Jason, Nathan, Christa* and hundreds and hundreds more. We love each of you.

We would like to acknowledge and give a special thanks to our three husbands: Glenn, Robert, and David, who have remained supportive throughout this entire endeavor.

A special thanks to Becky Faulds who has done everything that anyone asked, from coaching to typing.

And to Robin Utay and Chris Shackelford who provided the cover design and art work, we send a double thank you.

READ ME FIRST
A Note for the Students

The title, **WORKING FORENSICS: A Competitor's Guide**, expresses our philosophy. Forensics is work, but there are ways to "work" the system to your advantage. There are many paths that will get you where you want to be. We have written this book for students to use in that endeavor. It is not your usual text book--it gives no definitive answers. ***It is to be used as a guide***. We seldom tell you the way to do anything. We point out many ways and leave you and your coach to make the decisions about the way **you** will go.

Frankly, we love forensics because of what it does for students. What it does, is gives students life-skills in a way that no other type of competition, that we know, can. So, in an effort to make the forensic process work more smoothly, we wrote this book. We tried to make this book "`user friendly`" for the forensics competitor--novice and experienced alike. Before you begin, we want to tell you how to use the book to better advantage.

First of all, **DO NOT TAKE ALL OF OUR COMMENTS AS GOLDEN RULES**. We do not pretend to know everything or a **perfect** way to get you where you want to be. But we do know some shortcuts and a method or two that have proven successful. This book does not want to take the place of your coach. Every coach has methods unique to them. When in doubt, ask your coach. When we are not in agreement with them, follow the lead of your coach. Keep in mind that they can hear you perform and speak, but we cannot.

You should also consider that there are regional differences of which your coach is aware and you are not. Every region of the country does not do every thing in exactly the same way (i.e. opening folders, style of transitions, visual aid use, etc.) Relax. Do not worry that your 'style' may be "wrong". Here again, you can trust your coach to guide you correctly.

In an effort to make the book more readable, we have inserted our own humor. Forgive us, if it bothers you. Our students have been our guinea pigs for quite a few years and on more than one occasion told us when the pages were boring or unreadable. We have often tried to repair such holes with the best band-aid we know -- laughter. We want you to look forward to using the book, and in order to do that you have to want to keep reading. We have found that a bit of humor makes the reading go down a little easier.

The book is arranged in a more or less chronological order. We loosely based the order on the order in which new competitors ask for information. Take a look at the **TABLE OF CONTENTS**.

You will find sections in the book called **COMPANION READING**. It is just that. It is not busy-work; it should be read. You will also find sections in which we ask you to write something down. **PLEASE DO IT**. It works better that way. If you don't write it down, you do not necessarily have to feel guilty. But, don't blame us when it turns out to be "...about as helpful as a pocket with a hole in it."

We know that many of you will choose to read only certain sections. For that reason, many things have been repeated. Certain seasoned competitors may already have learned many of the lessons (or parallel ones). However, even though they may not need to complete all the worksheets, they may still find helpful information and hints in them.

We have chosen not to include any information on debate. Debate deserves a book of its own. Nor have we included interpreters theatre, or the acting events, or improvisation. This was not an accident. We selected the more frequently used/universal IE events.

Our lexicon is much more than a list of words and definitions. It is a helpful quick guide to information. Much of this information does not appear in the text. It could prove to be a divergent kind of light reading, or a learning reference for both common and uncommon terms used in the world of forensics.

REMEMBER THAT, MOST OF ALL, WE WANT YOU TO HAVE FUN.

Through all of the positive growth, and the hard work there should always be a large healthy element of fun. We feel that fun is an outgrowth of working forensics, which is like an intriguing travel through personal growth, research and expansion of talent. We are pleased to serve as one of your guides and hope you enjoy the journey.

The Need to Win

When an archer is shooting for nothing

He has all his skill.

If he shoots for a brass buckle

He is already nervous.

If he shoots for a prize of gold

He goes blind

Or sees two targets--

He is out of his mind.

His skill has not changed.

But the prize divides him.

He cares.

He thinks more of winning

Than of shooting--

And the need to win drains him of power.

Thomas Merton

Thomas Merton: <u>The Way of Chuang Tzu</u>. *Copyright 1965 by the Abbey of Getthsemanie. Reprinted by permission of New Directions Pub., Corp., New York, N.Y.*

I.

THE BASICS

WHAT IS FORENSICS AND WHY SHOULD YOU DO IT?

Students frequently ask, "What is forensics? Is it a Coroners Club? What do you do with the dead bodies?" As we use it, the term refers to competitive speaking and interpreting. But it is so very much more! It offers students fun filled weekends filled with high drama; little sleep; an educational ride or two on luxury school vans; fast food; the opportunity to meet other aggressive, motivated and often charismatic students from around the country. It usually offers excused absences from class; the opportunity to grow as a person and as a performer; the opportunity to strengthen your skills, to receive one-on-one coaching, to become a winner -- a person who feels comfortable and good about who they are and about their abilities.

It is fun. Any time college students from different campuses who have common interests meet, fun happens. It is also an intense, involving activity that demands your time, concentration and energy. It will ask you to rearrange your life. It will demand your best effort. In return, it will give you life-time skills such as poise, confidence, time management, the ability to handle pressure, the ability to communicate more effectively, and it will give you the self esteem that makes you function when other people freeze. It is not uncommon for former students to report that forensic training was the crucial element that made an interview work, that got them a job, that helped them audition successfully, that gave them the tools to successfully close a big deal or meet a difficult problem effectively.

You SHOULD do forensics if.....

1. speech and/or theater competition appeals to you.

2. you want to invest time in acquiring communication skills.

3. you feel it is a wise investment of time.

4. you know you have talent, but don't know how to develop it -- or a part of it -- such as auditioning skills.

5. you want to be more poised, confident, and self assured.

6. you have done competition before and liked it.

7. you are looking for a fun filled time in which you make life-long friends and you don't mind trading hard work to get them.

You SHOULD NOT do forensics if....

1. you _need_ a trophy to define who you are or to prove that you have talent. You will only frustrate yourself and your coach. Trophies are _not_ the measure of self-worth.

2. you think it will be easy.

3. you are doing it because your best friend is doing it.

4. you are doing it only because you think it will "look good on my resume".

CRITERIA FOR TOURNAMENT PARTICIPATION

All students who compete in forensics usually must meet certain criteria. Even though the particular criteria may vary from school to school and coach to coach, there are some things that generally apply to all competitors before they are allowed to compete. They might include:

1. *Interpretive material competition-ready:*
   All material with introduction and any needed transitions should be cut to time, scripted, and in the folder.

2. *Speeches competition- ready:*
   All prepared speeches should be cut to time, scripted, and have visual aids done. Although rules often say that manuscripts are allowed, having the speech memorized is preferable. However, a good speech should not suffer because you are too proud to use a manuscript early in the season or early in the development of the speech. Check with your coach for advice with this decision.

3. *Mastery of material:*
   Competitors should have done complete analysis and have all background knowledge needed to convey the message.

4. *Adequate coaching:*
   One coaching session of each event before each tournament is an absolute minimum, but each squad will have their own guidelines. People on the road to winning usually do the maximum rather than the minimum.

5. *Quality of performance:*
   Competitors should have done sufficient independent rehearsal to achieve "polish".

6. *Number of events:*
   You may be required to have a minimum number of events competition ready in order to be considered for the squad.

7. *Good class attendance:*
   This usually applies to all classes.

8. *Student status:*
   Some tournaments and many schools only allow those who are enrolled in a minimum number of hours attend tournaments.

9. *Passing grades:*
   "C" or above average for your overall semester average is the usual minimum, although your school may have different standards.

10. *A co-operative "team player" attitude:*
    This usually means such things has having exhibited a willingness to work and improve; having shown support for other teammates; having a record of promptness for classes and coaching sessions.

11. **_If the budget allows:_**
    Sometimes squads are limited in participation because of limited funds.

12. **_Play production schedule_**:
    If your forensic squad is connected to the theatre department in any way, the play production dates and requirements will be a factor. There is hope for those who do both forensics and theatre, but planning is required.

    Some play directors will let you miss rehearsal to go to contests <u>if</u>:

    * The tourney is early in the rehearsal schedule
    * You are as prepared OR more prepared than the rest of the cast.
    * Your missing won't seriously delay the rest of the rehearsal schedule. Some directors will tell you, before you audition, if they will be able to let you miss any rehearsals for competition.

COUNT DOWN TO TOURNAMENT:

Once again, this selection process is different for every team. But generally, the following things are to be seriously considered if you want to be on the forensics team.

1. **Scheduling of tournaments**-- Before you commit, find out when tournaments are to be held (even tentative dates will help). Then check dates against your exam, work, and play schedules. At this point, consider if you have time to work on competition -- don't forget to consider the current readiness or lack of readiness of your events. If there is time available, inform your coach which tournaments you can and wish to attend.

2. **2 or 3 weeks before a tournament**-- Make sure you are getting plenty of coaching. Coaches need to know and see your work. How else can they decide that you are one that should go? How else can you become your personal best?

3. **1 to 2 weeks before the tournament**-- During this time, your coach will probably make a final decision about who can go and in what events. They may have to limit your events due to tournament restrictions, your lack of preparation, lack of finances, etc.
   WHATEVER THE DECISION, KEEP WORKING -- There is more than one tournament during the year. Be so ready for the next one that you <u>have</u> to be included .

4. **1 week or less before you leave**-- Inform all of your teachers of your upcoming absence. Remember--it is your responsibility to make arrangements to take exams or makeup work, early or late. Arrange with a <u>good</u> student from your class to get any missed work/notes when you return. Be certain to get their phone number.

5. Find out and write down information about where the team will stay; how much food money you will receive (if any); when you will leave, and when you will return.[1]

---

[1] This is for parents and other concerned parties.

WORKING FORENSICS: A Competitor's Guide

SOME ODDS AND ENDS ABOUT CRITERIA
THAT YOU NEED TO KNOW

Generally speaking:

Before your first tournament, beginning competitors should be competition ready in at least 2 events.

Before the first tournament, experienced and second semester competitors should be prepared in at least 3 events.

As the year progresses, so do the number of events.

> Some schools require that you compete in one speech/one interp event. This is because those who consider themselves just "speakers" will profit from the skills learned in interp and that those who consider themselves just "interpers" will profit from the skills learned in speaking events.

> Some schools require other specific event participation.

> Some teams require more participation of scholarship folks. Find out as soon as possible what your team expects. You may want to begin work in the summer!

> Some teams have auditions for competitors. Some do not. Find out what your team does.

* In most cases, faculty members will determine entrants from their personal knowledge of your readiness.

* **In most cases, the faculty decision will be final.**

FALL 7 TIMES, STAND UP 8.

JAPANESE PROVERB

ADVICE: If your team does not have a Forensics Bulletin Board, see if you can find a central place to post information. Tournament information can be posted or updated almost daily. Check these postings at least twice weekly. Winners usually check them daily.

EVENT RULES

BASED ON 1993-94 AMERICAN FORENSICS ASSOCIATION RULES

We have chosen AFA as a bases because they are the rules used most often for the basic events. We are well aware that any tournament can construct its own rules. You will find that these rules apply for these events in the vast majority of cases.

Unless otherwise noted the time limits are 10 minutes total.

IMPROMPTU: An impromptu speech, serious in nature, with topic selections varied by round, section by section. Topics will be of a proverb nature. Speakers will have a total of 7 minutes for both preparation and speaking. Timing commences with the acceptance of the topics sheet. Limited notes are permitted. Each speaker in a given section will choose to speak from one of the same two topics offered.

EXTEMPORANEOUS: Contestants will be given 3 topics in the general area of current events, choose one, and have 30 minutes to prepare a speech that is the original work of the student. Maximum time limit for the speech is 7 minutes. Limited notes are permitted. Students will speak in listed order. Posting of topics will be staggered.

INFORMATIVE: An original, factual speech by the student on a realistic subject to fulfill the general aim to inform the audience. Audio-visuals may or may not be used to supplement and reinforce the message. Multiple sources should be used and cited in the development of the speech. Minimal notes are permitted.

PERSUASIVE: An original speech by the student designed to inspire, reinforce or change the beliefs, attitudes, values or actions of the audience. Audio-visual aids may or may not be used to supplement and reinforce the message. Multiple sources should be used and cited in the development of the speech. Minimal notes are permitted.

SPEAKING TO ENTERTAIN: An original humorous speech by the student, designed to exhibit sound speech composition, thematic coherence, direct communicative public speaking skills, and good taste. The speech should not resemble a night club act, an impersonation, or comic dialogue. Audio-visual aids may or may not be used to supplement and reinforce the message. Minimal notes are permitted.

COMMUNICATION ANALYSIS: An original speech by the student designed to offer an explanation and/or evaluation of a communication event such as a speech, speaker, movement, poem, poster, film, campaign, etc., through the use of rhetorical principles. Audio-visual aids may or may not be used to supplement and reinforce the message. Manuscripts are permitted.

POETRY: A selection or selections of poetry of literary merit, which may be drawn from more than one source. Play cuttings are prohibited[2]. Use of manuscript is required.

---

[2] There are plays written in poetic form.

PROSE: A selection or selections of prose material of literary merit, which may be drawn from more than one source. Play cuttings are prohibited. Use of manuscript is required.

DRAMATIC DUO: A cutting from a play, humorous or serious, involving the portrayal of 2 or more characters presented by 2 individuals. This material may be drawn from stage, screen, or radio. This is not an acting event. Thus, no costumes, props, lighting, etc., are to be used. Presentation is from the manuscript and the focus is off stage.

DRAMATIC INTERPRETATION: A cutting which represents one or more characters from a play or plays of literary merit. This material may be drawn from stage, screen or radio. Use of manuscript is required.

PROGRAM ORAL INTERPRETATION: A program of thematically linked selections of literary merit chosen from two or three recognized genres of competitive interpretation (prose, poetry, drama). A substantial portion of the total time must be devoted to each of the genres used in the program. Different genre means that material must appear in separate pieces of literature (e.g. A poem included in a short story that appears only in that short story does not constitute a poetry genre.) Use of manuscript is required. Maximum time limit is 10 minutes including original introduction and/or transitions.

HOW DO I CHOOSE EVENTS ?

1. *First, get familiar with what the events are all about.* They are listed in this manual (Refer to EVENT RULES). **They are different from high school events**, so don't assume you know. Read the descriptions. Your team may have video tapes of former teammates "doing" their events -- check it out. Ask to watch seasoned competitors perform their events. Even after you go to competition, you can investigate possible new events for yourself by watching them during your off-rounds. Explore all those events which interest you. If you continue to investigate, you may be surprised to find other events that appeal to you.

2. *Look at your own interests and abilities.* If you think of yourself as an actor, you may at first be drawn to interpretation. However, we have found that **many** events are interp events. Interpers (and actors) make wonderful speakers...and speakers frequently make excellent interpreters. But, **choose a first event that makes you feel happy and comfortable.**

3. *Make sure you understand conflict patterns and how they effect your choices.* Conflict patterns are groups of events which compete at the same time at a tournament.

    [Example: Between 10 - 11:30 Prose, Extemporaneous Speaking and Persuasive are scheduled. If you are entered in both Prose and Persuasive, you will have to compete in both events during one time period (cross-entering).

    While cross-entering is frequently done, it is physically and psychologically tiring. You need to be , at least, aware of the demands that come from such choices. Talk to your coach and/or teammates about usual conflict patterns at the tournaments your team normally attends. If you are a beginner, you probably need to try to plan events in different patterns every time you choose, so that you will have the fullest slate of non-conflicting events as possible by the final tournament. Be smart about this. But, DO NOT make it your only criteria for what is next for you.

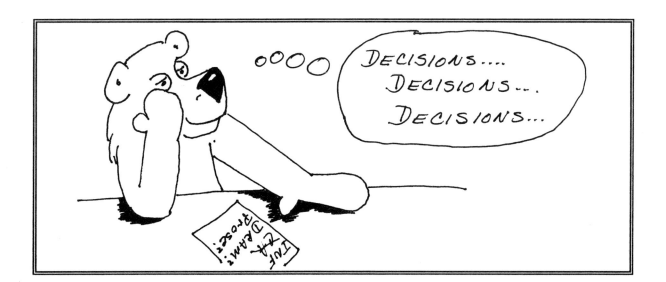

WORKING FORENSICS: A Competitor's Guide

4. ***Choose only 1 or 2 events in the beginning.*** While you may **want** to do 7 or 8, if you are working on too many events in the beginning, you don't make as much progress on them and that sometimes causes competitors to stop work altogether. In other words, when you bog down and can't move, you leave. This system seems to work better if you build a base of one or two polished events. Get them ready to shine. Then add another event...and then another. But again--check with your coach. Each school has different requirements for number of events per student. Frankly, we recommend that most of our students do a maximum of 4 or 5 events--more than this is rarely successful unless you are a true workaholic.

5. ***Consider that some events are more popular than others.*** Currently prose, informative and impromptu are frequently the most popular; Communication Analysis, the least. That means that you should, at least, keep an eye on how the events are stacking up on your squad. Obviously, if your team can only take 6 competitors in Prose to some tournaments, and 12 of you have Prose, then you are "competing" with 11 interpers on your own team for those 6 places. Your odds aren't as good as if you were one of two "competing" to get those 6 places.

    While you aren't really "competing" with the other members of your team, the situation that occurs in these instances is very apparent. The coaches must decide who will go, and someone will be disappointed. It is also true that tournaments provide more competition in more popular events. So, as we said, consider these things as you decide on your events.

6. ***Check with your coach*** after you have selected an event(s) that appeals to you. Then begin to find material.

HOW DO I CHOOSE EVENTS ?

1. *First, get familiar with what the events are all about.* They are listed in this manual (Refer to EVENT RULES). **They are different from high school events**, so don't assume you know. Read the descriptions. Your team may have video tapes of former teammates "doing" their events -- check it out. Ask to watch seasoned competitors perform their events. Even after you go to competition, you can investigate possible new events for yourself by watching them during your off-rounds. Explore all those events which interest you. If you continue to investigate, you may be surprised to find other events that appeal to you.

2. *Look at your own interests and abilities.* If you think of yourself as an actor, you may at first be drawn to interpretation. However, we have found that **many** events are interp events. Interpers (and actors) make wonderful speakers...and speakers frequently make excellent interpreters. But, **choose a first event that makes you feel happy and comfortable.**

3. *Make sure you understand conflict patterns and how they effect your choices.* Conflict patterns are groups of events which compete at the same time at a tournament.

   [Example: Between 10 - 11:30 Prose, Extemporaneous Speaking and Persuasive are scheduled. If you are entered in both Prose and Persuasive, you will have to compete in both events during one time period (cross-entering).

   While cross-entering is frequently done, it is physically and psychologically tiring. You need to be , at least, aware of the demands that come from such choices. Talk to your coach and/or teammates about usual conflict patterns at the tournaments your team normally attends. If you are a beginner, you probably need to try to plan events in different patterns every time you choose, so that you will have the fullest slate of non-conflicting events as possible by the final tournament. Be smart about this. But, DO NOT make it your only criteria for what is next for you.

WORKING FORENSICS: A Competitor's Guide

4. ***Choose only 1 or 2 events in the beginning.*** While you may **want** to do 7 or 8, if you are working on too many events in the beginning, you don't make as much progress on them and that sometimes causes competitors to stop work altogether. In other words, when you bog down and can't move, you leave. This system seems to work better if you build a base of one or two polished events. Get them ready to shine. Then add another event...and then another. But again--check with your coach. Each school has different requirements for number of events per student. Frankly, we recommend that most of our students do a maximum of 4 or 5 events--more than this is rarely successful unless you are a true workaholic.

5. ***Consider that some events are more popular than others.*** Currently prose, informative and impromptu are frequently the most popular; Communication Analysis, the least. That means that you should, at least, keep an eye on how the events are stacking up on your squad. Obviously, if your team can only take 6 competitors in Prose to some tournaments, and 12 of you have Prose, then you are "competing" with 11 interpers on your own team for those 6 places. Your odds aren't as good as if you were one of two "competing" to get those 6 places.

    While you aren't really "competing" with the other members of your team, the situation that occurs in these instances is very apparent. The coaches must decide who will go, and someone will be disappointed. It is also true that tournaments provide more competition in more popular events. So, as we said, consider these things as you decide on your events.

6. ***Check with your coach*** after you have selected an event(s) that appeals to you. Then begin to find material.

HOW DO I CHOOSE EVENTS ?

1. ***First, get familiar with what the events are all about.*** They are listed in this manual (Refer to EVENT RULES). **They are different from high school events**, so don't assume you know. Read the descriptions. Your team may have video tapes of former teammates "doing" their events -- check it out. Ask to watch seasoned competitors perform their events. Even after you go to competition, you can investigate possible new events for yourself by watching them during your off-rounds. Explore all those events which interest you. If you continue to investigate, you may be surprised to find other events that appeal to you.

2. ***Look at your own interests and abilities.*** If you think of yourself as an actor, you may at first be drawn to interpretation. However, we have found that **many** events are interp events. Interpers (and actors) make wonderful speakers...and speakers frequently make excellent interpreters. But, **choose a first event that makes you feel happy and comfortable.**

3. ***Make sure you understand conflict patterns and how they effect your choices.*** Conflict patterns are groups of events which compete at the same time at a tournament.

    [Example: Between 10 - 11:30 Prose, Extemporaneous Speaking and Persuasive are scheduled. If you are entered in both Prose and Persuasive, you will have to compete in both events during one time period (cross-entering).

    While cross-entering is frequently done, it is physically and psychologically tiring. You need to be , at least, aware of the demands that come from such choices. Talk to your coach and/or teammates about usual conflict patterns at the tournaments your team normally attends. If you are a beginner, you probably need to try to plan events in different patterns every time you choose, so that you will have the fullest slate of non-conflicting events as possible by the final tournament. Be smart about this. But, DO NOT make it your only criteria for what is next for you.

WORKING FORENSICS: A Competitor's Guide

4. ***Choose only 1 or 2 events in the beginning.*** While you may **want** to do 7 or 8, if you are working on too many events in the beginning, you don't make as much progress on them and that sometimes causes competitors to stop work altogether. In other words, when you bog down and can't move, you leave. This system seems to work better if you build a base of one or two polished events. Get them ready to shine. Then add another event...and then another. But again--check with your coach. Each school has different requirements for number of events per student. Frankly, we recommend that most of our students do a maximum of 4 or 5 events--more than this is rarely successful unless you are a true workaholic.

5. ***Consider that some events are more popular than others.*** Currently prose, informative and impromptu are frequently the most popular; Communication Analysis, the least. That means that you should, at least, keep an eye on how the events are stacking up on your squad. Obviously, if your team can only take 6 competitors in Prose to some tournaments, and 12 of you have Prose, then you are "competing" with 11 interpers on your own team for those 6 places. Your odds aren't as good as if you were one of two "competing" to get those 6 places.

   While you aren't really "competing" with the other members of your team, the situation that occurs in these instances is very apparent. The coaches must decide who will go, and someone will be disappointed. It is also true that tournaments provide more competition in more popular events. So, as we said, consider these things as you decide on your events.

6. ***Check with your coach*** after you have selected an event(s) that appeals to you. Then begin to find material.

A BRIEF OVERVIEW

OF WHAT'S INVOLVED

(AND OTHER USEFUL STUFF)

A BRIEF OVERVIEW OF WHAT'S INVOLVED
... and other useful stuff

Basically, in grouping events, they fall into three groups: prepared speaking events, low preparation events and interpretation events. Each has its own peculiarities and styles. So that you can get a little glimpse of how these work, let's look at each one briefly.

PREPARED SPEAKING EVENTS INCLUDE: informative, persuasive, speaking to entertain and communication analysis.

It may be that after reading event descriptions, checking with your coach about conflict patterns, looking at your own areas of strength and weakness and figuring out what you want to learn this year, you chose a prepared speaking event as one of your competition choices. If so, this will also be an important junction in which you look _realistically_ at your time and energy commitments so that you can decide if you have time to prepare a successful speech. If so, use the guidelines we will provide later in this book, to help you choose a topic.

Prepared speeches are built on the foundation of good research, followed by cleverly organized writing. They are first written in manuscript form so that they can be analyzed, criticized and revitalized[3] to the detail level. This is a somewhat tedious and time consuming process that pays off big time later. After the speech is finally temporarily "finalized". It will be memorized and work on the delivery will begin. Ultimately, the speech will be performed for anyone you can find, video taped, critiqued and re-critiqued. You will be able to perform it in your sleep, but don't stop working.

LOW PREPARATION EVENTS INCLUDE: extemporaneous speaking and impromptu speaking.

These events are only "called" low preparation events. In reality, they demand an equal amount of preparation, it is just in slightly different forms. These events require a steady amount of work all year, rather than one grand push at the beginning. Really there are two kinds of activity involved - first is the preparation, the second part is the actual speaking.

Preparation for low prep events requires that the speaker is current in world affairs, well read, literate. If the event is extemp, you must be willing to dedicate a regular block of time to the care and feeding of an extemp file. If you do extemp, you have a real, as well as a moral, obligation to maintain that file . Both kinds of low prep speeches share the requirement of a speaker who is able to analyze and organize material quickly and effectively.

In order to achieve perfection, you will be steadily working on and performing practice speeches. Games, devices, and coaching sessions are used to hone the skill and wit of low prep speakers. Unfortunately, none of them is as effective as regular practicing by giving the speeches to critical listeners. It requires discipline and steady, unrelenting effort but it is uniquely able to develop poise and critical thinking skills in the novice competitor.

---

[3] ... and on occasion circumcised [oops!... well meant cut]

INTERPRETATION EVENTS INCLUDE: prose, poetry, dramatic interpretation, duo interpretation, program oral interpretation.

If you love literature and are excited about sharing it, you may have chosen an interpretation event or two. They will give you an opportunity to analyze in depth, and to develop strong performance skills.

The most frustrating and time consuming part of interpretation events is locating the right material. The perfect selection is one that is perfect for you -- You love it, it suits your style and abilities, it is stimulating to you. It's a little like dating in order to find a perfect mate. You may look at a lot of wrong choices but its worth it when you find the right one. So don't give up. Keep looking. No shortcut is worth it.

Once you have a perfect selection, you will want to know everything there is to know about it. Where it came from. What it means. All those little allusions and illusions that make it so special. What its zodiac sign is. We call it analyzing. And we believe you can't ever do enough of it. There is always a nuance you will want to unravel.

Just as you will want to understand it completely you will, of course, want to introduce your beloved selection to the audience properly. And you will want to understand it completely. That quest for understanding will lead you to new ways to express how you feel. you may choose such creative means of expression as physicalization, characterization, internalization and imaging to communicate how your selection makes you feel.

This continuous analysis will keep the romance alive and boredom from setting in. Technical things about delivery will also be worked out as you continue to work and work... and work -- out loud, to perfect your performance of this perfect piece.

IF YOU WAIT,
ALL THAT HAPPENS IS THAT YOU GET OLDER.

Larry McMurtry

TRADITIONS

It is rather easy for us to talk about tradition, because we have a squad that has been in existence for more than sixty years. What we have learned from that experience is that traditions have a way of binding a group of individuals together into a team. *The establishment of a team spirit is crucial to the functioning of a team member.* For that reason - if for no other - we have added this section to a book that is primarily addressed to the competitor.

The pride that a team has in themselves carries over into performance. The team that has a recognized identity and unity has an advantage over the individual that is basically performing on his/her own. The same idea of esprit de corps that builds Marines, builds speech teams as well. While boot camp is not recommended for forensic students, it is helpful if your team establishes traditions that reflect their team personality.

Our team has a number of simple and sometimes silly rituals.[4] The passing on of these rituals builds a sense of continuity in the program. They help each team feel involved with teams and teammates that have gone before and will come after when they see such things as a trophy case filled with the trophies of the past and present. As trophies frequently belong to the individual and will eventually go home with them, our team has adopted the policy of public display of the year's winnings. Every trophy won during a school year is placed in a public display to be admired by the general population. As a part of the year's end celebration, each competitor who has won hardware is permitted to take his or her "loot" home. The team retains any team trophies and "summary plaques" engraved with the winnings from each tournament during the year are put in a permanent display case. In this way, a record can be displayed for the future. This is a tradition that builds the sense of Team Continuity. *You become a part of something greater than yourself.*

---

[4] For instance, we have a statue of our late college president in front of our building. For luck, each contestant rubs the head of the statue before loading the van.

BE A PART INSTEAD OF APART

This being a part instead of apart should be reinforced as often as possible. This can be done in many ways.

~It has been our practice to eat as a team as often as possible. In this way, each member is able to stay in touch with their teammates' progress during the course of a tournament. This builds a sense of genuine caring and concern.

~We have team meetings often during the tournament that are brief, but supportive.

~We aren't dogmatic. But, we have worked to build into the team tradition the standards of dress and conduct that we want to represent our school. The students want to live up to the expectations of that team reputation and in this way, other precepts can be taught. Behavior, attitude, dress, responsibility are all areas that can become a part of the tradition.

~Our team has a mascot (a name that is different from any other organization on campus). This separate identity[5] helps us feel special and a part of something special. It is not unusual to see team members wearing some subtle item of jewelry or clothing that reinforces this identity.

~Songs, "secret" energy tricks, traveling together, forensics folk lore -- all lend themselves to the kind of behavior that can be reinforced through tradition building activities.

YOU can start your team's traditions. You can be the one that writes the songs, creates the lore, establishes team pride. Try it.

---

[5] We are called Polar Bears. Don't ask. Or, if you do, be prepared for a loooong story.

THE CARE OF COACHES

Coaches are very special people who sometimes need a little extra care and attention. They are often overworked and stressed out. The following comments may make your life together run more smoothly.

1. **THE COACH'S OFFICE** - The coach's office is the primary work space of a very busy person. Offices are frequently not tidy because too many demands are made on the owners too often. Do not judge their ability by the neatness of their space. Remember that creativity is not a pretty sight.

    Things are further complicated by students who feel free to use the space, the supplies, the equipment. These things are not the property of students. Common sense and common courtesy require that the faculty deserves better.

    A. **DO NOT** enter any office without permission.

    B. **DO** knock before entering.

    C. **DO NOT** enter any unoccupied office unless expressly asked to do so or given permission to do so.

    D. **DO** ask permission to use office phones.

    E. **DO** ask permission before borrowing .....ANYTHING.

    F. **DO** return things borrowed promptly and to the correct spot. You got it off the shelf, return it to the shelf.

    G. **DO** return everything immediately after use.

    H. **DO** remember: Many items (pencils, pads, etc.) have to be replaced out of your coach's own pocket.

    I. **DO** be courteous to other students. You don't like to wait as other students chit-chat and gossip with the coach during your advisory or coaching time, so.....don't use up time that way. When time is at a premium, respect it.

    J. **DO** feel free to stop by on a regular basis. Just not during someone else's scheduled time. We can work together better that way.

> ASK NOT
> WHAT YOUR FORENSIC COACH CAN DO FOR YOU
> BUT WHAT YOU CAN DO FOR YOURSELF

WORKING FORENSICS: A Competitor's Guide

2. **REMEMBER that coaches are real people.** They often have families that occasionally need them to be at home.

3. **Try a little kindness, old fashioned politeness, humane treatment.** Try thinking, if not actually saying, a term of respect when you address them. "Oh, Wise One...," might be nice, Grasshopper[6].

4. **Treats are nice,** but since nearly everyone in the world is on a diet, we suggest a more practical gift: Do what you say you are going to do. If you can't, then don't say it. Call to cancel appointments - don't leave your coach waiting.

5. **Remember the coach's books.** Coaches love their books. Coaches are often generous with their books. Coaches should not lose books to inconsiderate students.

6. **Show gestures of caring.** Consider that if the coach has stayed up until 2 a.m. coaching you, or re-cutting for you, researching for you or doing laundry for you, maybe a tangible gesture would be nice. It could be a cup of tea at the right moment, an <u>offer</u> to run errands (school or domestic), a card, or lunch. This is what friends do for one another.

7. **Remember that coaches are humans.** We need hugs, we need help, we are right, we are wrong, we succeed, we fail, we have good days, we have bad days, we get angry, we forgive, we need to be forgiven.

---

[6]This reference is to an old TV show -- If you don't get, you don't get it.

We found this somewhere and adapted it. We don't know the originator but it is too good to leave out.

HOUSE RULES

If you open it, close it
Especially if it is file drawers.

If you turn it on, turn it off.
This includes copiers and computers.

If you unlock it, lock it
And return the key...

If you break it, repair it
Or have it repaired.

If you borrow it, return it
Promptly and with a thank you, please.

If you use it, don't abuse it.
This goes for people as well as things.

If you move it, put it back
Exactly where you found it...

If you don't know how to operate it,
Leave it alone.

If it doesn't concern you, don't mess with it.
This applies to gossip and gadgets.

BEFORE YOU TURN THE PAGE
A Bridge Before Section II

Now, if you started at the first of the book, you should have some solid understanding of what forensics is, what the basic rules are, how you choose your events and why you should take care of your coach(es).

Assuming that you have your events chosen, it may be time to begin the actual preparation process. The next three sections of this text divide the eleven events into their categories: prepared speeches, low-preparation speeches and interpretation.

After reading the generic information preceding the specific stuff concering each event, locate your specific event choices and begin there.

Example: Under "Prepared Speaking Events" you might choose to peruse Informative, Persuasive, Speaking to Entertain or Communication Analysis.

Use the worksheets for every chosen event. Write out your answers as you follow the path to a completed event.

On your mark...
        Get set...
                Find your events!!!

**HE CAN WHO THINKS HE CAN,
AND HE CAN'T WHO THINKS HE CAN'T.
THIS IS AN INEXORABLE, INDISPUTABLE LAW.**

Orison Sweet Marden

II.

PREPARED SPEAKING EVENTS

GENERAL INFORMATION

HOW TO WRITE A SPEECH

A BRIEF OVERVIEW... One of Many

It should be noted that there is no "one" approach to writing a speech. Feel free to adapt this suggested way to your coach's personal method, if it differs.

The following "8 Steps" will guide you in preparing your competitive speech. At any step of speech preparation, you should feel free to ask your coach or a seasoned teammate if you have any questions. You will follow these steps in completing the worksheets for each chosen speaking event.

After the "8 Step Process" you will find different sub-headings about various aspects of speeches (from topic selection to preparing visual aids to delivery). Our approach may seem a bit fragmented, but we wanted you to be able to quickly turn to whatever information you needed at any given moment.

If you are truly a novice speaker, you might ask your coach to recommend a good speech textbook to fill in any gaps we were unable to cover here -- OR, consider taking a beginning speech class! In today's society, knowing public speaking skills is almost essential.

**THE REWARDS FOR THOSE WHO PERSEVERE
FAR EXCEED THE PAIN THAT MUST PRECEDE
THE VICTORY.**

Ted Engstrom & R. Alec MacKenzie

THE 8 STEP PROCESS

1. **SELECT TOPIC**: When choosing a topic for competition, start by thinking of topics that are of interest to you. Then consider whether the topic will be one of interest to the audience. Is the topic narrow enough to cover in ten minutes? For topic ideas, you may check with your coach (he/she might have a list of possible topics), current magazines, your team file drawer of topics, the vertical files in the library, etc. Or just brainstorm for ideas--list your hobbies, pastimes, curiosities, etc. Please see "CRITERIA FOR SELECTING TOPICS" , "THE SPEAKER'S FIRST SOJOURN INTO THE LIBRARY" and "IF YOU WERE A SPEECH TOPIC, WHERE WOULD YOU HIDE?" for further important information on selecting your topic.

2. **SELECT PURPOSE**: Every worthwhile and winning speech has a specific purpose. The general purpose of a speech is dictated by the event (either Informative, Persuasive, Entertaining or, as in the case of CA, either informative or persuasive.) To decide on the specific purpose for the speech, you first need to do some analysis of the audience, the occasion, and yourself.

   A. **ANALYSIS OF THE AUDIENCE**: Forensic audiences are composed of fellow competitors (college students with some knowledge and awareness of communication, like yourself) and a judge. The judge is usually a forensic coach, a former competitor or a "lay" judge, such as a lawyer, a college professor from a different discipline or a business person from the community[7].

   Therefore, you can **assume that your forensic audience is fairly well read and "up" on current events**. Because of this, many topics are unsuitable for competition because your judges have already heard too much about them. But of course, that does not always mean that the topic is not usable, it might be that you can come up with a very different angle or approach. After you have considered your audience, you are ready for the second part of analysis.

   B. **ANALYSIS FOR THE OCCASION**: You must realize that **competition occasions are a bit artificial.** Your audience, being composed of a judge and fellow competitors and maybe a few occasional well wishers is neither hostile nor friendly--but the air of comparison is prevalent. At this point of your speech preparation, it is best not to worry about that. Just realize that you will be giving the same speech to at least two (hopefully three or four) audiences per tournament, which will be composed of some of the same audience members. Therefore, **your speech must have "staying power"**. In addition, it is imperative that it fit the time limit and requirements.

THE WORK PRAISES THE MAN – Irish Proverb

---

[7] Which ever kind of judge, your job is to appeal to them.

WORKING FORENSICS: A Competitor's Guide

C. **ANALYSIS OF SELF**: At this point, you may be feeling some nervous apprehension. That is both natural and good for you. You are only reading Step 2 of preparation, so of course you are nervous. Some nervousness at this stage means you care enough to want to do well. Use those nerves to propel you through the remaining steps of preparation. As to analysis of self, consider whether the topic appeals to you and is something you really feel is of interest and is significant enough to spend time on. (Frequently, analyzing your interests or special areas of expertise will help you find topics.)

After you have done your brief analysis of your audience, your occasion, and yourself--you will need to determine your purpose. In other words, what is the main thesis or thrust of your speech? **Why should the audience be interested in your topic?** Does it fulfill the stated purpose? (i.e. Is it informative? Does it persuade?) What is the impact of your topic on your audience? Identifying it helps you to mentally focus upon your goal. (Besides, your coaches are going to ask you what your purpose is!!!) Write it down as succinctly and clearly as you can.

3. **RESEARCHING YOUR TOPIC**: Now that you clearly know where you want to go with the speech, proceed with the research. You probably did some preliminary research on the topic while you were choosing it. At this step, you will need to go into depth. The more you know about your topic, the better off you will be. Research magazine articles, newspapers, knowledgeable people in the community, state, county, and federal agencies, etc. Look in the periodical guide, the vertical file, index file, etc., in the libraries. Try to find some very current material that makes this subject appealing--at this point in time. Photocopy the stuff you may use. (Write all bibliographical info on the photocopy.) You should have enough time to write for information from some agency or business or, you may interview "in person" or by phone some key people. Check with your coaches to see if they have any additional advice on special sources for your topic. Keep all this info in a safe place. Facts will go in and facts will come out as you change the speech.[8]

4. **ORGANIZING THE BODY OF YOUR SPEECH**: Your speech is organized into 3 main sections: the introduction, the body, and the conclusion. Each of these sections is organized separately and then fused together with good transitions. It is common sense to begin organizing the body of your speech first, then work on the introduction and finally the conclusion. The best way to organize your body[9] is with an outline (the same one English teachers have asked for all these years). See the appropriate worksheets for more detail. After your organization is approved, you will probably write word for word what you intend to say--this is called your manuscript. The manuscript will include the introduction and conclusion.

5. **INTRODUCTION (HOW DO I BEGIN?)**: After you complete the body of your speech, you will then prepare the introduction. The introduction should fulfill **four main purposes**:
    --gain the audience's attention
    --state your thesis or purpose
    --relate the importance or significance of your topic
    --preview your main ideas (sign-posting/mapping)

But first and foremost, the introduction **must** make people want to hear the rest of your speech.

---

[8]Check out "TAKING STEPS TO WRITE A TERM PAPER" for some research techniques.

[9]... the body of your speech, that is.

6. **CONCLUSION (HOW DO I END MY SPEECH?)**: After you have organized the body and written the introduction, you are ready to conclude your speech. Rounds can be won or lost by an effective conclusion. A successful conclusion must fulfill **three purposes**:
   --summarize your main ideas
   --reinforce your thesis
   --unify your speech

   All this while wrapping up the speech in a memorable way that reminds us of the introduction.

   Example: If you began your speech with a story about a lost child, you might end the speech by telling how that child was found, etc.

7. **CHECKING YOUR CONTENT**: This is the "catch all" step where you stop and evaluate your progress. Are you satisfied with your organization? Have you written out all 3 sections of your speech? Do you have smooth transitions from each section to section and from point to point? Do you need any visual aid support? Do you need any type of additional support for any of your ideas? Do you have the bibliography prepared? Is your language appropriate for you and your audience? (No personal pronouns; no overly formal words) Is your language vivid? Do the words conjure up pictures? Have you emphasized what you needed to emphasize? (Hint: Use repetition or restatement) Did you involve the audience? (You can do this with an allusion or a reference to a common experience, placing the audience in a hypothetical situation, asking the audience rhetorical questions.) Did you define words that needed defining?

   After you are satisfied with your manuscript, read it aloud at an easy conversational speed and time it. Then trim the speech as much as it may need. Please check with your coaches and let them read your manuscript before you begin to memorize. It is painful to memorize, <u>then</u> have to make major changes. It is much better to be approved first. Except for rare exceptions at the early part of the year, all prepared speeches should be memorized. Check it out.

For more complete details, see the appropriate Worksheets.

YOU MAY HAVE TO FIGHT A BATTLE MORE THAN ONCE TO WIN IT.

Margaret Thatcher

WORKING FORENSICS: A Competitor's Guide

8. **PRACTICE**: Remember, nothing makes you feel more comfortable in front of a judge during competition than a good solid backlog of practice. You must practice your speech OUT LOUD and in front of various audiences to discover what changes need to be made and to become relaxed and natural in your delivery.

   Refer to "PRACTICE PRACTICES" and **"EFFECTIVE SPEECH DELIVERY"** for more detailed help. You may also consider:

   * Concentrating on your subject, not yourself
   * Showing enthusiasm for what you have to say
   * Making your speech sound like a conversation
   * Looking directly at the audience while you talk (practice this!)
   * Sounding spontaneous
   * Making doubly sure that your articulation and pronunciation are correct
   * Being aware of your movement (no nervous gesturing)
   * Practicing your speech as it is written. Trust what you have done... OR change it.
   * Controlling volume so that it is appropriate for the size of the room — Not too soft in a large room or too loud in a small room
   * Trusting that your coach will help you develop good techniques for variety in pitch, volume, speed, etc.
   * Preparing and/or gathering VA's while you are memorizing — Then working with them every time.
   * Videotaping, especially after the VA's are inserted, is a super idea. But **better** when you watch the tape with learning on your mind.

THE SPEAKER'S FIRST SOJOURN INTO THE LIBRARY

A Few Hints for Speech Writers

* If the topic seems as if it might fly, gather up a few dimes, and go to the library and do research.

* Look in the periodical guide, the vertical files, and the index files.

* Look under different listings.
  Example: for "Chocolate as a Drug", look under chocolate, addiction, drugs, and candy. Then cross reference the things you find in the first stuff (words, titles, names). It may be that under candy you find the Hershey company as one of the largest manufacturers. When you look up (cross reference) Hershey you might get more specific information about your topic.

* If you don't know how to use these guide/file things, get someone to teach you. The librarians will help if you act humble.

* Photocopy the good stuff (usually, 10 cents per) and write all bibliographic info on the photocopy. Yes, you **MUST** have a bibliography written for some tourneys. Besides, you may need to refer back to the source later.

* Keep a record of where you found all the info you didn't photocopy, just in case you need to find it again.

* **KEEP ALL INFO.** What might not be used now, may be used in a re-write. This is why you have spent all those years learning to make note cards.

IF YOU WERE A SPEECH TOPIC, WHERE WOULD YOU HIDE?
or
HOW TO FIND A SPEECH TOPIC

* Read widely always "keeping an eye out" for **good** topics. Learn to think "topic!".

* Constantly scan such magazines as **READER'S DIGEST**, **OMNI**, **U.S. NEWS & WORLD REPORT**, **TIME**, **DISCOVERY**.

* Or you might form the habit of listening to the **early morning talk shows or evening magazine shows** for an idea of what is new or hot just now.

* Listen <u>regularly</u> to some **news shows** like CNN or Nightline.

* Don't neglect sources in the library (including the **FACTS ON FILE**, vertical file) for possible topics.

* Keep a file of any interesting articles you read or notes of interesting broadcasts you hear. This can be a little spiral notebook or a small card file. Keep this in one location only–not one note here and another in your history folder. Don't trust your memory.

* Examine *ideas that you, personally, are passionate about.* Ask yourself what makes you mad? Frightens you? Puzzles you? Amazes you? What makes you righteously indignant? This could be the seed of a persuasive <u>or</u> an informative.

* **Make a list** of all of your beliefs; things that concern you; things you wish more people would do; things you wish people would care about. Persuasive material should be something you care about.

* **Make a list** of all of your hobbies; the things you do well; things about which you are an expert. An informative topic may be hiding in your everyday life.

* Be curious about objects and ideas around you. **Make yet another list.**

* **Think about the lists you make.**

* Brainstorm using the lists you make. You can do it alone or, better yet, with a group that just happens to be over for the *weekly brainstorm-and-popcorn therapy session*.

* Keep notes on the things that come about when you brainstorm because even if they don't seem relevant at this time, these same ideas might work for another speech later on.

* Check with your coaches for lists of topic ideas that they may have. Nearly every coach has a few topics about which they wish someone would write a speech. Maybe one of these will appeal to you.

CRITERIA FOR SPEECH TOPICS

In General:

* The topic should be **appropriate to the type of speech** [info., pers., etc.].

* The topic should **fit your own personality and style.**

* The topic should be of **"universal"** interest, yet still be unique and creative. You should be able to demonstrate the topic's importance or significance in the world at large.

* Be sure that your topic has not been "overdone" in the media. Has there been too much written about the topic recently? Has it been on every talk show in the world? Remember that in such cases, your audience could be bored with a topic **unless**, you have a **unique** "angle". You would have to be able to make the audience look at the topic from some new prospective.

* This often means making us see the importance of the topic to ourselves...and possibly to future generations. It is that old WIIFM[10] bit. *Give audience a reason that they, personally, should listen to what you have to say.*

* The topic should be interesting or be made **interesting to both sexes**.

* The topic should be of interest to a broad range of age levels -- yet primarily aimed toward college students and well educated adults.

* Be sure your topic will be of interest to not only your geographical region, but also to audiences throughout the state and nation.

* The topic must have the potential for **sound documentation and worthwhile development.** In other words, is there enough stuff written about the topic to support your speech (i.e. magazine articles, books, newspaper articles, knowledgeable people).

YOU SHOULD LOVE YOUR TOPIC
YOU WILL BE TOGETHER A LONG TIME.

---

[10] WIIFM (pronounced wiffem) means What's In It For Me.

WORKING FORENSICS: A Competitor's Guide

EFFECTIVE SPEECH DELIVERY
Use of Body and Voice

The importance of a speaker's delivery can not be over-emphasized. While it may seem that content should be more important than delivery, often in competition the content is equal and so the delivery may be more of a deciding factor. Too, no matter how excellent the speech content, it will not be apparent if the delivery is poor.

The term delivery includes what one does with both his/her body and voice -- it is the non-verbal aspect of public communication. Researchers have for years documented that the non-verbal part of a message carries more weight than the verbal (words).

Dictating or prescribing what makes up good delivery is almost an impossible task. Why? Because delivery first of all, is a personal thing. What is effective, or what works, for one person may not work for another. Also, there are regional differences in delivery style. So, we heartily recommend that when you are ready to begin work on your speech's delivery, you get coaching. In the meantime, especially for your novice speakers, here are some of the most common mistakes in delivery that you should avoid.

MISTAKES IN VOCAL DELIVERY

monotone
sing-song pattern
any recognizable pattern
too soft
too loud
no variety in pitch
nasality
gravel-throated
breathiness
mispronunciations
inarticulation
   -omitting sound ("somethin" instead of "something")
   -substituting sounds ("thang" for "thing")
   -adding sound ("athuhlete" for "athlete")
   -stress errors (mis **chee** vious instead of **mis** cha vus)
Non-conversational
Pausing at inappropriate times
Not pausing at all
Fluency

MISTAKES IN BODILY DELIVERY [Face, gestures, movement]:

FACE --
    artificial (obviously pre-planned facial expression)
    head moving from side to side like an oscillating fan
    little or no eye contact
    eye contact that is too quick - eye skating
    no REAL eye contact
    smile at inappropriate times
    grimaces when a trivial mistake is made

bobbing head
constant starring at floor, or ceiling, or some person or object to avoid communication
"fig leafing" - holding hands over your vulnerable area
shifting from side to side or front to back
rocking front to back on the balls of your feet
keeping elbows locked to sides
have "dead fish" arm - it just hangs there
cross-legged stance
cross-legged crossing - this awkward move can be cured by always leading off with the foot away from the audience and/or nearest your distination
slapping your body for emphasis
standing too close to your audience - your should not invade their personal space
wringing your hands
playing with your hair or constantly pushing it aside
playing with clothes and/or jewelry

A PERSON'S DREAMS

ARE AN INDEX TO HIS GREATNESS.

Zadok Rabinowitz

VISUAL AIDS
or
SHOW AND TELL

AKA:[11] VAs, visuals

Definition: Anything that is used to appeal to the visual sense is a visual aid. At times this definition is stretched to include sound as well. Among other things, VAs can include: the object being discussed, models, pictures, drawings, sketches, charts, films, slides, projections, demonstrations. VAs should look professional, be used effortlessly, and must be able to be carried everywhere you go while at tournament. An effective visual aid should be integrated into the speech as a vital part, not added as a post script.

Using Visual Aids: As with any other speech skill, you must practice using visual aids to get the most from them. The following are some useful guidelines for you to consider in your practice.

1. **Set them up properly.**
   Be sure that before you stand to begin your speech, you inconspicuously put your VAs in order (including cover sheets) and check that order. Ideally, part of this can be done in the hall before you enter the competition room. A smooth set-up of your VAs is one of the first impressions that you make. If you are using an easel, be certain that you know the easiest way to set it up and can do it in the fewest motions possible.

2. **Show visual aids only when you are talking about them.**
   If your VA is still in view when you are talking about something else, the audience will still be inclined to give attention to the VA. So, when the VA does not contribute to the point you are making, keep it out of sight. Cover it with a blank sheet/poster or remove it from sight. Perhaps you could stand in front of it.

3. **Talk about the VA while you are showing it.**
   Although a picture may be worth a thousand words, you need to point out what in particular you wish them to see. You should tell the audience what to look for; you should explain the various parts; or explain the significance of figures, symbols, and percentages.

4. **Make sure that everyone in the audience can see them.**
   If you hold the VA, hold it out away from your body[12] and directed toward the audience. If you place your visual aid on an easel, stand to one side and point with the arm nearest the VA. Do not cover up your own VA as you exhibit it.

5. **Talk to your audience and not to your VA.**
   You may need to look at the VA occasionally, but you want to maintain eye contact with the audience as much as possible. When a person is too engrossed in their own VA, they tend to lose audience contact entirely.

---

[11]"AKA" commonly stands for "Also known as"

[12]Not at arm's length, but certainly not hugged so close that you appear self-conscious.

6. **Don't overdo the use of VAs.**
   VAs are a form of emphasis; but emphasizing too many things results in no emphasis at all.
   A VA is an aid and not a substitute for a good speech.

Producing Visual Aids:

1. If your VA is paper (poster, chart, etc.), **it should be well rendered.** If you aren't an artist, get someone else to do them for you. Many schools now have the art work done by the campus graphics department. This is not currently against any rule.

    Another option is to use an opaque projector to "trace" a drawing.

    Press-on lettering is good if your own is not.

    Originality and neatness both count....a lot.

2. **Poster board** or **sketching pads** work well for charts, illustrations, lists, etc.

3. Poster board works much better if it is **heavy** (art store quality, if you can afford it). Make sure it is a size that will not "flop" when placed on stand (1/2 regular poster board size is usually the minimum).

4. If using spiral sketch pads instead of loose poster boards, leave blank pages for **cover sheets**. Also remember to leave <u>extra</u> "blank" pages between VAs in case you decide to add new VAs at a later date.

5. VAs should be easy to read, easy to see, and easy to understand. **Don't clutter.** The simpler, the better.

6. **Use humor when it applies**.

7. Most forensic departments have some easels. You may be able to check these out. If not, buy your own. Most departments have some **VA cases**. You may be able to check these out. If not, buy your own. Whatever the case, **you must find something professional looking in which to carry your VAs and display them.**

8. The **cost** of the VAs is usually yours. But your department may have a way to get, borrow, or procure the materials without cost to you. Check it out.

9. When writing the rough draft of your speech, mark where you think a VA would help. **Discuss your VAs with your coaches before you spend too much time or money.**

10. **Don't forget cover sheets** (see rule # 2 - on prior page).

11. **Make your VAs durable.** They get a lot of wear in a year of travel and rounds. It is usually a good idea to laminate them. If not, find some way to protect them. They need to look as good at the end of the year as at the beginning.

WHAT JUDGES LOOK FOR IN SPEAKING EVENTS

It is true that there are as many styles of judging as there are judges and each one looks for different things in performance. This list is an attempt to identify some of the criteria for you. The list is taken from ballots and our own preferences. There are, undoubtedly, more criteria. However, this list will give you a good start in understanding where the judges' minds are set before you enter the room.

An introduction that
- .....catches the attention
- .....is original
- .....shows a need to know this information - the significance of the topic
- .....makes each audience member want to listen (both by your delivery & the message)
- .....previews coming attractions (points, main ideas, etc.)

During the body of the speech judges look for these basics:
- .....Continued reference to the significance of the topic -- OR why the topic is important to your listeners
- .....Has levels of intensity, rather than being on one level of information giving
- .....Analysis that is clear, clean, and amazing
- .....Conversationality--talk _to_ us, not _at_ us
- .....Dress that is appropriate and professional
- .....Examples and illustrations that illuminate your ideas and give life to your information
- .....Fresh material and ideas that are well researched and yet original
- .....Gestures that _do not_ illustrate nervousness; that _do_ work as extensions of the thought
- .....Humor--yes, even speeches other than STE need humor
- .....Articulation, diction, and pronunciation that are correct and done without stumbles
- .....Logical organization without rambling on or being sidetracked
- .....Energetic (not zombie-like nor robotic)
- .....Natural movements that underline main points but do not appear planned
- .....Within the time limit
- .....Pacing of delivery that is not too slow, or too fast, or uneven
- .....Effective source citations (no more than 20% of a speech should ever be direct quotations)
- .....Smooth, polished and confident in your presentation
- .....Use of words and ideas that you truly understand -- don't fake it!
- .....VAs that are professional in appearance and that are used smoothly in the speech
- ....."Well" is not a good way to start a sentence. Neither is "yeah" or "Oh" or "OK" or "Ummm".
- .....Smooth transitions (avoid "well", "yeah", "oh", or "ok, or "ummmm")
- .....Plenty of attention maintaining material.
- .....Sincere enthusiasm for your topic

Conclusions should
- ....include a brief summary
- ....have impact
- ....tie into the introduction, if possible
- ....make each audience member feel a response of some kind
- ....unify the speech (be final without having to say, "That's all.")

PREPARED SPEAKING EVENTS

DESCRIPTIONS
&
WORKSHEETS

SPEAKING EVENTS
How to Begin - Phase 1: The Commitment

In this sub-section of you will find general information for each event including: other names that events are known by (AKA), generic rules, and a few additional notes that explain aspects of the event that are worthy of note, and then there will be a set of worksheets (divided into 6 phases).

Before you can truly begin to work on ANY type of speech however, you must first complete PHASE ONE[13].

PHASE ONE: COMMITMENT

If you have not decided which events in which you wish to compete, NOW IS THE TIME. Quit procrastinating. If you skipped it before, now is the time to turn back and read (or re-read) "HOW TO CHOOSE EVENTS".

.... Now!... We'll wait for you.

wait wait wait wait wait wait wait wait wait....[14]

Now, armed with that information, you need to remember that college speaking competition comes in two flavors: prepared speeches and low-preparation speeches. [These do not necessarily parallel the high school events with which some of you might be familiar -- so be alerted!] Prepared speaking events include: Informative, Persuasive, Communication Analysis and Speech to Entertain. These events are usually written as manuscript, committed to memory and delivered naturally. The skills involved are the desire to research a topic thoroughly, to organize and write a manuscript, the willingness to rewrite that manuscript often, to memorize, and to develop a natural seeming speaking style.

If you have read the rules, etc. and talked to your coach, you now have enough knowledge concerning the general procedures for each type of speech. Which one or ones interest you most? You are ready to go to the page that has the event name in bold print and begin. However, ... before you do, let us forewarn you. This Phase One was the easiest phase to read (although, we are well aware that true commitment may be the most difficult to achieve). Phase Two through Phase Six of the worksheets are at times laborious lists. May we gently remind you that the title of this text has the word "working" in it. Did we promise you a rose garden? You're not backing out are you? Naah! You have made a commitment. You want to learn and grow and become an effective public speaker. Go to your first speech choice. [By the way, work the phases IN ORDER and don't forget the coaching that accompanies.]

---

[13] This phase 1 is the phase one for each set of worksheets. So, each set of worksheets begins with phase 2.

[14] Waiting got boring so we decided to go over to Pooh's howse and have some tea. We'll see you later.

INFORMATIVE SPEAKING
or
LET ME EXPLAIN

AKA: Info.; Informative; Expository; Expos

Generic Rules:

An original, factual speech by the student on a realistic subject to fulfill the general aim to inform the audience. Audio-visuals may or may not be used to supplement and reinforce the message. Multiple sources should be used and cited in the development of the speech. Minimal notes are permitted. 10 minute time limit.

A FEW EXTRA NOTES:

<u>An informative speech</u> must:

1. present new facts or ideas or

2. provide new interpretations or insights about already known information. In other words tell the audience something they don't know or tell them something new about something they already know about. All the strategies used in an informative speech are aimed toward clarity of expression and ease of retention---keep it simple and interesting so they will remember it.

The speech may be either concrete or abstract[15]. And it doesn't hurt if you use a little humor to do that.

If you have never written a speech, you might need a nudge for ideas. Between the Companion Reading and your coaches, you can do it.

An informative speaker is interested in his topic; willing to do research; feels a commitment to the subject; will write and rewrite information; can organize thoughts; is original and creative; is able to memorize and re-memorize; can deliver a speech in a natural, conversational way.

Or an informative speaker is someone willing to learn and become the informative speaker described above.

---

[15] See Lexicon for definitions.

INFORMATIVE WORKSHEET PHASE 2.1

INFORMATIVE SPEAKING WORKSHEET
Phase 2: SELECTING A TOPIC

COMPANION READING:

IF YOU WERE A SPEECH TOPIC, WHERE WOULD YOU HIDE?
CRITERIA FOR SPEECH TOPICS
HOW TO WRITE A SPEECH: STEP 1

Locating materials:

With IF YOU WERE A SPEECH TOPIC, WHERE WOULD YOU HIDE? in front of you, do the following and/or write the answers to the following questions (on a separate sheet of paper).

____ 1. Using the guidelines in "IF YOU WERE A SPEECH TOPIC, WHERE WOULD YOU HIDE?", generate a list. Write down at least 5 [usually it is more than 20].
REMEMBER, you can generate this list by:
   a. Brainstorming
   b. Talking to your coach(es)
   c. Talking to your teammates
   d. Watching network shows [like 20/20, 60 minutes, Primetime]
   e. Reading or scanning magazines

____ 2. Which of the topics on your list are appropriate for a informative speech?

____ 3. Which of these topics best suits your personality?

____ 4. Which of the topics has broad (universal) appeal?

____ 5. Which of the topics do you think you'll be able to find current information about?

____ 6. Are any of your topics currently "overdone" in the media? While you might find a perfect topic in the media, be wary of anything that appears on everything [for example, if Phil, Oprah, Sally and Maury have ALL discussed it, you don't need it.[16]

____ 7. Have you narrowed your topic list to five or less hopeful topics? You probably have. So, arrange them in order from most appealing to least appealing to you.

____ 8. Arrange them in the same kind of order for audience appeal.

____ 9. Which topics appear near the top of both lists? These are your topic choices.

---

[16]Don't even think about touching anything on Geraldo!

INFORMATIVE WORKSHEET PHASE 2.2

____ 10. Now, check with the coach for topic guidance. Some really good topics, such as AIDS, are done so often that you are defeated by the topic. Your coach can help prevent that disaster. After this, you should have a your topic.

____ 11. If you still have a choice, chose the topic that has the most appeal to you because you will be working with it for a long time.

CONGRATULATIONS!
YOU ARE A PROUD OWNER OF AN INFORMATIVE SPEECH TOPIC!

ONCE YOU HAVE RECEIVED APPROVAL FOR THE TOPIC, GO TO PHASE 3.

SUCCESS HAS ALWAYS BEEN EASY TO MEASURE.
IT IS THE DISTANCE BETWEEN
ONE'S ORIGINS AND ONE'S FINAL ACHIEVEMENT.

Michael Korda

INFORMATIVE WORKSHEET PHASE 3.1

INFORMATIVE SPEAKING WORKSHEET
Phase 3: RESEARCH AND NARROWING TOPIC

WHY DO THIS PHASE?

Before you can write a speech, you must do both preliminary and in-depth research. You can't begin to narrow the topic until you know what material is available. The best information may be something you don't know yet... or the newest research something you have yet to discover. This research will be the foundation of your speech, so the time you spend now, really examining this subject, will forge the future of this event for you.

COMPANION READING:

THE SPEAKER'S FIRST SOJOURN INTO THE LIBRARY
HOW TO WRITE A SPEECH: STEPS 2 AND 3

RESEARCH:

_____ 1. Do you have your library card? If not, get one. You are going to need it. Don't forget that there is more than one library.

_____ 2. Have you collected change for the photocopying machine?

_____ 3. Once in the library, check the obvious sources in the library: vertical file, card catalogue, periodical guide, microfilm, index, Facts on File for everything you can find on your topic.

_____ 4. Follow up the leads that you found in those sources?

_____ 5. Keep note cards or photocopies of the material you found?

_____ 6. Write the source on the photocopies?

_____ 7. Do these sources have credibility? For instance, The National Inquirer is not the most credible source. Don't write a speech with it as one of your sources.

_____ 8. Do you have **at least** 3 viable sources for the speech? You probably have many more than that at this stage but some will get weeded out.

_____ 9. Have you investigated possible sources outside the library such as knowledgeable persons; agencies, organizations, etc.?

INFORMATIVE WORKSHEET PHASE 3.2

NARROWING THE TOPIC:

_____ 1. The key to a strong organization is a tightly written statement of purpose. State your specific purpose, by completing the following statement: "At the end of my speech, I want my audience to _____."

Some key words might be: know, understand, be aware of, identify...

_____ 2. Are you keeping in mind what there is about this topic that will appeal to your audience?

_____ 3. Does your topic need to be more specific or more narrowed?

IT'S PROBABLY A GOOD IDEA TO CHECK NOW WITH YOUR COACH.

INFORMATIVE WORKSHEET PHASE 4.1

INFORMATIVE SPEAKING WORKSHEET
Phase 4: OUTLINING AND ROUGH DRAFTS

WHY DO THIS PHASE?

Contrary to what you may have always done, the outline actually should be written first. It will save time, frustration and problems only if you do it first. Otherwise, it creates them. Rough drafts are done because your speech is always considered in progress until it is finally settled in -- late in the season.

COMPANION READING:

HOW TO WRITE A SPEECH: PARTS 4-7 (The Sequel)
VISUAL AIDS[17]

THE ROUGH DRAFT: On a separate piece of paper (not in this book), complete the following:

_____ 1. List all of the things you want your audience to remember (your major points). Most speeches have 2-3 major ideas but you should never have more than 5.

_____ 2. Arrange those major points in the best sequence for your informative purpose. For instance, if you were giving a speech on aluminum, the points might be composition, uses, and strength. The order would depend on your purpose and your audience.

_____ 3. Look at **each** major point independently. Outline your research material for that specific point.

After you complete matching the research material into each of your points of your outline, you are ready to continue by working on the introduction and conclusion.

> ### NO ONE EVER EXCUSED HIS WAY TO SUCCESS.
>
> Dave Del Dotto

---

[17]We know it didn't say anything about visual aids in the title but you will have to consider them in the rough draft.

INFORMATIVE WORKSHEET PHASE 4.2

THE INTRODUCTION:

Write a rough draft of the beginning of your speech. Then answer the following questions.

_____ 1. Does your introduction gain the attention of your audience?

_____ 2. Does your introduction give your audience a reason to listen?

_____ 3. Does your introduction state the purpose of your speech?

_____ 4. Does your introduction preview your main ideas with a smooth transition to the body?

If you answer "no" to any of the preceding questions, rewrite your introduction so that you can answer "yes".

CONCLUSION:

All good informative speeches have a conclusion that leaves the audience feeling enlightened. Write a rough draft of how you plan to end your speech.

Does your conclusion:

_____ 1. Have a smooth transition from the body of your speech?

_____ 2. Summarize your main ideas?

_____ 3. Refer to the audience (how the topic was of interest and/or benefit to them).

_____ 4. Have a final unifying statement so that the audience will know you are through without you having to resort to a tag line like "Thank you."?

_____ 5. Relate to the beginning of your speech?

_____ 6. Leave the audience with an impact statement or question (of a stay-on-your-mind quality)?

If you answered "no" to any of the preceding questions, rewrite your conclusion.

WORKING FORENSICS: A Competitor's Guide

INFORMATIVE WORKSHEET PHASE 4.3

FIRST ROUGH DRAFT:

Since all successful competition speeches will eventually be memorized, you should now write a complete manuscript of your speech. As you are writing your first draft, remember:

1. It is helpful to skip every other line in your manuscript so that editing is easier.

2. Write in oral style (speeches are written to be heard, not read).

3. Realize you will be doing additional drafts, because good speeches are always in revision and they get better with every change. Be positive about rewrites.

READ YOUR SPEECH ALOUD AND THEN:

____ 1. Make any changes necessary to help your speech "sound" better.

____ 2. Consider whether a visual aid would enhance or clarify the information in any part of your speech.

____ 3. Note the current time of your speech? _____

If the draft is overtime:

Refer to the general tips in HOW TO CUT and consider: How much do you need to cut?
Make a photocopy and make your 'cuts' on the photocopy. Consider cutting: side issues (sub-points); "flowery sentences" [make them simple]; number of examples [if you use three, can you get by with one?].
Now, re-time your speech. If it is still too long, you may need to narrow your topic farther. Get help from your coach. By the way, expect this whole process of cutting to take **at least** 2-3 days.

If it is seriously undertime [less than 8 minutes]:

Rethink your development and consider adding more material. More research may uncover a new direction.
If you need additional help in writing a speech, any good basic speech book or course will be of help to you. Ask your coach to help you find what you need.
Remember we told you this was a first draft? After your coaching session, expect to do many more drafts. It is not uncommon for the writing stage to last several weeks. Neither is it uncommon for a speech to go through several drafts--even throughout the entire forensic season. (Remember that patience and perseverance are virtues.)

SCHEDULE A COACHING SESSION.

INFORMATIVE WORKSHEET PHASE 5.1

INFORMATIVE SPEAKING WORKSHEET
Phase 5: VISUAL AID PREPARATION AND FINAL DRAFT

COMPANION READING:

VISUAL AIDS

PRELIMINARY DESIGN of VAs:

This is the time to make quick sketches of possible layouts of posters: drawings, rough ideas of how words would look on a poster or sketches of models or lists of things needed for demonstration, etc. Now that your drafts are becoming more finalized, you need to give serious consideration to your use of visual aids.

_____ 1. Are you going to use any?

_____ 2. If so, how many? what type?

_____ 3. At **exactly** what point in your speech?

_____ 4. Have you done a preliminary design on scratch paper or a model (if appropriate)?

_____ 5. Who will produce the actual VA? Will you, a friend, a professional? Think about it. Let your coach approve your ideas.

HOW YOU DO YOUR WORK

IS A PORTRAIT OF YOURSELF.

H. J. Brown, Jr.

WORKING FORENSICS: A Competitor's Guide

INFORMATIVE WORKSHEET PHASE 5.2

FINAL DRAFT:

The word "final" is probably a misnomer because you may <u>never</u> be finished revising your speech. Dedicated speakers will frequently revise their speech after every tournament, if they received valid criticisms on their ballots or revise it as new material becomes available. We are referring in this instance to the final draft you are planning to take to its first competition.

So, rewrite your speech <u>again... and ask yourself</u>:

_____ 1. Do you have good sentence structure?

_____ 2. Do you have correct grammar?

_____ 3. Do you have variety in word choice?

_____ 4. Can the audience can visualize what you are talking about?

_____ 5. Whether your examples are clear?

_____ 6. All of the dozens of things you normally check when you are trying to write an impressive English paper.[18]

Then:

_____ 7. Do you use occasional humor when appropriate?

_____ 8. Does your language choice sound like you are talking to them not reading to them (oral style vs. written style)?

_____ 9. What is the current time of speech [Read slowly enough and with all the appropriate pauses]? Ideally, it should be between 8 - 9.5 minutes. If it is not...fix it, now!

Check back with your coach so that she/he can enjoy the glory of a project well done!

---

[18] Check out "Taking Steps to Write a Term Paper".

WORKING FORENSICS: A Competitor's Guide

INFORMATIVE WORKSHEET PHASE 6.1

INFORMATIVE SPEAKING WORKSHEET
Phase 6: POLISH AND TAPE

WHY DO THIS PHASE?

Now that your speech is researched and written, the fun work of getting it ready to "stand" on its own begins. Your commitment here has to be perfecting your oral style and overall delivery.

COMPANION READING:

SOME NOTES ON MEMORIZING
PRACTICE PRACTICES
WHAT JUDGES LOOK FOR IN SPEAKING EVENTS

POLISH:

Answer, of course, on a separate piece of paper.

_____ 1. Have you had your final draft approved by your coach?

_____ 2. Have you made the suggested revisions?

_____ 3. Have you read SOME NOTES ON MEMORIZING? Put all those pointers to use as you commit this draft to memory. [You don't have you speech memorized before you begin performing for audiences.] Allow some time and don't get impatient with yourself.

_____ 4. Have you performed for some live audiences? Your roommate, teammates, classes, your mom? As many reasonably willing people as you can corner? As often as you can? Listen to the information you hear from them about your speech and your performance.

_____ 5. Does it sound more conversational?

_____ 6. What is the current time of the speech? _____

_____ 7. Have you put it on tape?
[While audio tapes are helpful -- video tapes are far more beneficial. Video taping and watching yourself is a short cut to "perfection".]

WORKING FORENSICS: A Competitor's Guide

INFORMATIVE WORKSHEET PHASE 6.2

TAPE:

We strongly suggest that when video taping, you tape your entire performance, from walking into the room to your exit at the end of the speech. It may be helpful to have a small audience at the taping [maybe other "tapees"]. Now watch the tape critically. (Is there any other way?)

_____ 1. Was the performance lively enough to hold audience interest?

_____ 2. Did you seem sincere and honest?

_____ 3. Did the visual seem helpful or awkward?

_____ 4. Watch the video with the sound turned off. Was the body natural and smooth in motion, or did it call attention to your discomfort?

_____ 5. Do you show distracting mannerisms? You will discover that both speech and body improve as you continue to rehearse. You may want to tape again after a few more rehearsals and see the improvement for yourself.

_____ 6. Do your hands call attention to themselves?

_____ 7. Do you walk during the delivery--at times that emphasize ideas? At times that detract from ideas?

_____ 8. Are you looking directly at audience members?

_____ 9. Do you appear to be "enjoying" the performance of the speech or does it look like it is hard work?

_____ 10. Do you believe this speech is ready and will do well? If not, find out why not and fix it. You should feel that your speech is a contender.

Continue to get coaching. Perform as often as possible to develop a fluent speaking style that is fresh and natural sounding. Keep looking for new audiences. Ask your teachers in other disciplines if you can use 10 minutes of class time. They may love it and you'll get goodwill bonus points .

PERSUASIVE SPEAKING
or
JOIN ME ON THE RIGHT SIDE!

AKA: Persuasive; Pers.; Convince; Speech of Proof; Oratory

GENERIC RULES:

An original speech by the student designed to inspire, reinforce or change the beliefs, attitudes, values or actions of the audience. Audio-visual aids may or may not be used to supplement and reinforce the message. Multiple sources should be used and cited in the development of the speech. Minimal notes are permitted. Time limit 10 minutes.

A FEW NOTES ON PERSUASIVE SPEAKING:

In this event the speaker's primary purpose is to influence the beliefs, attitudes, or the behavior of the listeners.

THE SOLUTION:

A persuasive speech must always tell the audience <u>specifically</u> what action each individual should take. The more specific, the better. Convince each listener to **do** something (boycott a product; vote a certain way); or to **believe** something (the earth <u>is</u> the center of the universe). Aim at individual responses not a general "Something must be done..."

The difference in a persuasive speech and an informative speech is that you expect a response from the audience in persuasive. This is critical in topic selection and in formatting the speech.

To be convincing, it helps to speak on a topic for which you have strong feelings. One must care enough to do considerable research, because documentation needs to be flawless for this event.

Also, in a persuasive speech it is essential that you have analyzed your audience because they are an essential element in this speech.

Persuasion is very audience-response oriented. Keep your audience in mind at all times. Think about built-in biases and prejudices that you might have to overcome.

PERSUASIVE WORKSHEET PHASE 2.1

PERSUASIVE SPEAKING WORKSHEET
Phase 2: DECIDING YOUR TOPIC

COMPANION READING:

IF YOU WERE A SPEECH TOPIC, WHERE WOULD YOU HIDE?
CRITERIA FOR SPEECH TOPICS
HOW TO WRITE A SPEECH: PART 1

Locating materials:

With IF YOU WERE A SPEECH TOPIC, WHERE WOULD YOU HIDE? in front of you, do the following and/or write the answers to the following questions (on a separate sheet of paper).

____ 1. Using the guidelines in "IF YOU WERE A SPEECH TOPIC, WHERE WOULD YOU HIDE?", generate a list. Write down at least 5 [usually it is more than 20].
REMEMBER, you can generate this list by:
a. Brainstorming
b. Talking to your coach(es)
c. Talking to your teammates
d. Watching network shows [like 20/20, 60 minutes, Primetime]
e. Reading or scanning magazines

____ 2. Which of the topics on your list are appropriate for a persuasive speech?

____ 3. Which of these topics best suits your personality?

____ 4. Which of these topics are the most significant? Persuasive?

____ 5. Which of the topics has broad (universal) appeal?

____ 6. Which of the topics do you think you'll be able to find current information about?

____ 7. Are any of your topics currently "overdone" in the media? While you might find a perfect topic in the media, be wary of anything that appears on everything [for example, if Phil, Oprah, Sally and Maury have ALL discussed it, you don't need it.[19]] Are they likely to be solved very soon?

____ 8. Have you narrowed your topic list to five or less hopeful topics? You probably have. So, arrange them in order from most appealing to least appealing to you.

____ 9. Arrange them in the same kind of order for audience appeal.

---

[19]Don't even think about touching anything on Geraldo!

PERSUASIVE WORKSHEET PHASE 2.2

____ 10. Which topics appear near the top of both lists? These are your topic choices.

____ 11. Now, check with the coach for topic guidance. Some really good topics, such as abortion, are done so often that you are defeated by the topic. Your coach can help prevent that disaster. After this, you should have a your topic.

____ 12. If you still have a choice, chose the topic that has the most appeal to you because you will be working with it for a long time.

CONGRATULATIONS!
YOU ARE A PROUD OWNER OF A PERSUASIVE SPEECH TOPIC!

ONCE YOU HAVE RECEIVED APPROVAL FOR THE TOPIC, GO TO PHASE 3.

IGNORE WHAT A MAN DESIRES AND YOU IGNORE THE VERY SOURCE OF HIS POWER.

Walter Lippman

WORKING FORENSICS: A Competitor's Guide

PERSUASIVE WORKSHEET PHASE 3.1

PERSUASIVE SPEAKING WORKSHEET
Phase 3: RESEARCHING AND NARROWING TOPIC

WHY DO THIS PHASE?

Before you can write a speech, you must do both preliminary and in-depth research. You can't begin to narrow the topic until you know what material is available. The best information may be something you don't know yet... or the newest research something you have yet to discover. This research will be the foundation of your speech, so the time you spend now, really examining this subject, will forge the future of this event for you.

COMPANION READING:

THE SPEAKER'S FIRST SOJOURN INTO THE LIBRARY
HOW TO WRITE A SPEECH: STEPS 2 AND 3

RESEARCH:

_____ 1. Do you have your library card? If not, get one. You are going to need it. Don't forget that there is more than one library.

_____ 2. Have you collected change for photocopying machine?

_____ 3. Once in the library, check the obvious sources in the library: vertical file, card catalogue, periodical guide, microfilm, index, Facts on File for current information on your topic.

_____ 4. Follow up the leads that you found in those sources?

_____ 5. Keep note cards or photocopies of the material you found?

_____ 6. Write the source on the photocopies?

_____ 7. Do these sources have credibility? For instance, The National Inquirer is not the most credible source. Don't write a speech with it as one of your sources.

_____ 8. Do you have **at least** 3 viable sources for the speech? You probably have many more than that at this stage but some will get weeded out.

_____ 9. Have you investigated possible sources outside the library such as knowledgeable persons; agencies, organizations, etc.?

PERSUASIVE WORKSHEET PHASE 3.2

NARROWING THE TOPIC:

_____ 1. The key to a strong organization is a tightly written statement of purpose. State your specific purpose, by completing the following statement: "At the end of my speech, I want my audience to _____."

Some key words might be: know, understand, be aware of, identify...

_____ 2. Are you keeping in mind what there is about this topic that will appeal to your audience? Make it important to them as individuals?

_____ 3. Does your topic need to be more specific or more narrowed?

IT'S PROBABLY A GOOD IDEA TO CHECK NOW WITH YOUR COACH.

PERSUASIVE WORKSHEET PHASE 4.1

PERSUASIVE SPEAKING WORKSHEET
Phase 4: OUTLINING AND ROUGH DRAFTS

WHY DO THIS PHASE?

Contrary to what you may have always done, the outline actually should be written first. It will save time, frustration and problems only if you do it first. Trust us on this one. Otherwise, it creates them. Rough drafts are done because your speech is always considered in progress until it is finally settled in -- late in the season.

COMPANION READING:

HOW TO WRITE A SPEECH: STEPS 4-7 (The Sequel)
VISUAL AIDS[20]

THE ROUGH DRAFT: On a separate piece of paper, complete the following:

_____ 1. A list all of the things you want your audience to remember (your major points). Most speeches have 2-3 major ideas but you should never have more than 5.

_____ 2. Relating those ideas directly to your specific purpose, arrange those major points in the best sequence for your persuasive speech. For instance, if you were giving a speech on aluminum, the points might be in this order: the ill health effects of drinking from aluminum cans, the economic and ecological effects of aluminum compared to that of glass containers, then a solution in which aluminum cans are phased out and replaced by returnable glass bottles.

_____ 3. Look at **each** major point independently. Outline your research material for that specific point.

After you complete the fitting of research material to outline for each of your points, you are ready to continue by working on the introduction and conclusion.

> ONLY THE MEDIOCRE ARE ALWAYS AT THEIR BEST.
>
> Jean Giraudoux

---

[20] We know it didn't say anything about visual aids in the title but you will have to consider them in the rough draft.

PERSUASIVE WORKSHEET PHASE 4.2

THE INTRODUCTION:

Write a rough draft of the beginning of your speech. Then answer the following questions.

_____ 1. Does your introduction make the audience **need** to listen? Remember that just because they are sitting in the room does not qualify as a reason to listen.

_____ 2. Does your introduction state the purpose of your speech?

_____ 3. Does your introduction preview your main ideas with a smooth transition to the body?

If you answer "no" to any of the preceding questions, rewrite your introduction so that you can answer "yes".

CONCLUSION:

All good persuasive speeches have a conclusion that leaves the audience feeling enlightened. Write a rough draft of how you plan to end your speech.

Does your conclusion:

_____ 1. Have a smooth transition from the body of your speech?

_____ 2. Summarize your main ideas?

_____ 3. Refer to the audience (How the topic was of interest and/or benefit to them?)

_____ 4. Have a final unifying statement so that the audience will know you are through without you having to resort to a tag line like "Thank you."?

_____ 5. Tie back into the beginning of your speech?

_____ 6. Leave the audience with an impact statement or question (of a stay-on-your-mind quality)?

If you answered "no" to any of the preceding questions, rewrite your conclusion.

PERSUASIVE WORKSHEET PHASE 4.3

FIRST ROUGH DRAFT:

Since all successful competition speeches will eventually be memorized, you should now write a complete manuscript of your speech. As you are writing your first draft, remember:

1. It is helpful to skip every other line in your manuscript so that editing is easier.

2. Write in oral style (speeches are written to be heard, not read).

3. Realize you will be doing additional drafts, because good speeches are always in revision and they get better with every change. Be positive about rewrites.

READ YOUR SPEECH ALOUD AND THEN:

____ 1. Make any changes necessary to help your speech "sound" better.

____ 2. Consider whether a visual aid would enhance or clarify the information in any part of your speech. Visual aids are rarely used in persuasion but it is not -- so far as we know -- against any rules. If you **need** them, use them.

____ 3. Read your speech aloud at an effective rate with pauses -- as you would perform it. Note the current time of your speech? _____

If the draft is overtime:

Refer to the general tips in HOW TO CUT and consider: How much do you need to cut? Make a photocopy and make your 'cuts' on the photocopy. Consider cutting: side issues (sub-points); "flowery sentences" [make them simple]; number of examples [if you use three, can you get by with one?].
Now, re-time your speech. If it is still too long, you may need to narrow your topic farther. Get help from your coach. By the way, expect this whole process of cutting to take **at least** 2-3 days.

If it is seriously undertime [less than 8 minutes]:

Rethink your development and consider adding more material. More research may uncover a new direction.
If you need additional help in writing a speech, any good basic speech book or course will be of help to you. Ask your coach to help you find what you need.
Remember we told you this was a first draft? After your coaching session, expect to do many more drafts. It is not uncommon for the writing stage to last several weeks. Neither is it uncommon for a speech to go through several drafts--even throughout the entire forensic season. (Remember that patience and perseverance are virtues.)
Perseverance pays!

SCHEDULE A COACHING SESSION.

PERSUASIVE WORKSHEET PHASE 5.1

PERSUASIVE SPEAKING WORKSHEET
Phase 5: VISUAL AID PREPARATION AND FINAL DRAFT

COMPANION READING:

VISUAL AIDS

PRELIMINARY DESIGN of VAs:

This is the time to make quick sketches of possible layouts of posters: drawings, rough ideas of how words would look on a poster or sketches of models or lists of things needed for demonstration, etc. Now that your drafts are becoming more finalized, you need to give serious consideration to your use of visual aids.

_____ 1. Are you going to use any?

_____ 2. If so, how many? what type?

_____ 3. At **exactly** what point in your speech?

_____ 4. Have you done a preliminary design on scratch paper or a model (if appropriate)?

_____ 5. Who will produce the actual VA? Will you, a friend, a professional? Think about it. Let your coach approve your ideas.

HE WHO IS AFRAID OF ASKING IS ASHAMED OF LEARNING

Danish Proverb

PERSUASIVE WORKSHEET PHASE 5.2

FINAL DRAFT:

The word "final" is probably a misnomer because you may <u>never</u> be finished revising your speech. Dedicated speakers will frequently revise their speech after every tournament, if they received valid criticisms on their ballots or revise it as new material becomes available. We are referring in this instance to the final draft you are going to memorize and are planning to take to its first competition.

So, rewrite your speech <u>again... and ask yourself</u>:

____ 1. Do you have good sentence structure?

____ 2. Do you have correct grammar?

____ 3. Do you have variety in word choice?

____ 4. Whether the audience can visualize what you are talking about?

____ 5. Whether your examples are clear?

____ 6. All of the dozens of things you normally check when you are trying to write an impressive English paper.[21]

Then:

____ 7. Do you use occasional humor when appropriate?

____ 8. Does your language choice sound like you are talking to them, not reading to them (oral style vs. written style)?

____ 9. Does it accomplish your stated purpose?

____ 10. What is the current time of speech [Read slowly enough and with all the appropriate pauses]? Ideally, it should be between 8 - 9.5 minutes. If it is not...fix it, now!

Check back with your coach so that she/he can enjoy the glory of a project well done!

---

[21] Check page 34.

PERSUASIVE WORKSHEET PHASE 6.1

PERSUASIVE SPEAKING WORKSHEET
Phase 6: POLISH AND TAPE

WHY DO THIS PHASE?

Now that your speech is researched and written, the fun work of getting it ready to "stand" on its own begins. Your commitment here has to be perfecting your oral style and overall delivery.

COMPANION READING:

SOME NOTES ON MEMORIZING
PRACTICE PRACTICES
WHAT JUDGES LOOK FOR IN SPEAKING EVENTS

POLISH:

Answer, of course, on a separate piece of paper.

_____ 1. Have you had your final draft approved by your coach?

_____ 2. Have you made the suggested revisions? Has anything happened lately that will make your speech more timely or current? Or more dated? Can it be revised in your speech?

Example: Some years ago a student of ours was running a persuasive speech on the use of chewing tobacco. As luck would have it, his solution just happened to become a bill which then became a law before the end of the year. Adjustments had to continually be made.

_____ 3. Have you read SOME NOTES ON MEMORIZING? Put all those pointers to use as you commit this draft to memory. [You don't have your speech memorized before you begin performing for audiences.] Allow some time and don't get impatient with yourself.

_____ 4. Have you performed for some live audiences? Your roommate, teammates, classes, your mom? As many reasonably willing people as you can corner? As often as you can? Listen to the information you hear from them about your speech and your performance.

_____ 5. Does it sound more conversational?

_____ 6. What is the current time of the speech? _____

_____ 7. Have you put it on tape? Have you watched it?
[While audio tapes are helpful -- video tapes are far more beneficial. Video taping and watching yourself is a short cut to "perfection".]

WORKING FORENSICS: A Competitor's Guide

PERSUASIVE WORKSHEET PHASE 6.2

TAPE:

We strongly suggest that when video taping, you tape your entire performance, from walking into the room to your exit at the end of the speech. It may be helpful to have a small audience at the taping [maybe other "tapees"]. Now watch the tape critically. (Is there any other way?) If something bothers you rewind and re-watch until you isolate the problem.

After viewing answer these questions:

____ 1. Was the performance lively enough to hold audience interest?

____ 2. Did you seem sincere and honest?

____ 3. Did the visual seem helpful or awkward?

____ 4. Watch the video with the sound turned off. Was your body natural and smooth in motion, or did it call attention to your discomfort?

____ 5. Do you show distracting mannerisms? You will discover that both speech and body language improve as you continue to rehearse. You may want to tape again after a few more rehearsals and see the improvement for yourself.

____ 6. Do your hands call attention to themselves?

____ 7. Do you walk during the delivery--at times that emphasize ideas? At times that detract from ideas?

____ 8. Are you looking directly at audience members?

____ 9. Do you appear to be "enjoying" the performance of the speech or does it look like it is hard work?

____ 10. Do you believe this speech is ready and will do well? If not, find out why not and fix it. You should feel that your speech is a contender.

Continue to get coaching. Perform as often as possible to develop a fluent speaking style that is fresh and natural sounding. Keep looking for new audiences. Ask your teachers in other disciplines if you can use 10 minutes of class time. They may love it and you'll get goodwill bonus points .

Too, it will help you feel confident when you finally "take it out".

SPEAKING TO ENTERTAIN
or
COMEDY WITH A PURPOSE

AKA: STE; After Dinner Speaking; ADS; Ha-Ha Speech

GENERIC RULES:

An original humorous speech by the student, designed to exhibit sound speech composition, thematic coherence, direct communicative public speaking skills, and good taste. The speech should not resemble a night club act, an impersonation, or comic dialogue. Audio-visual aids may or may not be used to supplement and reinforce the message. Minimal notes are permitted. Time limit 10 minutes.

SOME MORE "FEW NOTES" :

Starting a Ha-ha speech is a little different. A Speech to Entertain is designed to give information and/or persuasive appeals, while depending heavily on humor. The humor of the approach does not mean that the purpose of the speech is a light-hearted one. The speaker should have a specific serious purpose or goal just as if he/she were going to give an informative or persuasive speech.

This speech is designed to give the audience pleasure and enjoyment without making heavy demands on their serious nature. But, this is definitely not a comedy monologue spot. The speaker does want to provoke laughter and/or pleasurable emotions and usually avoids such disturbing responses as anger, fear, and grief. Generally the speaker will deal with simple, easy-to-grasp concepts and will depend heavily on humor. But never forget that the speech has a "significant purpose" and a "reason for being", and like any speech must be carefully organized and bridged by transitions.

In recent years, visual aids have become a "thing" for ADS. You may wish to consider them ONLY if they will help. We have noted no apparent consistent correlation between winning and VA gimmicks.

Remember, at all times, that this is a speech. Therefore, it is approached like any other speech. There must be a purpose, citing of references (although it is permissible to make some of these up for humor), logical sequence of ideas, and finally, a comic approach.

A serious speech may be turned into an ADS. Practically everything is life <u>can</u> be made funny.

Two of the hardest things about this speech are learning not to "push" for humor, and to trust your speech. You must **not** improvise. You do it as written. Many a brilliant speech has failed because the speaker panicked when one joke did not get the reaction expected. Then the speaker "pushed" for response and/or started to make up new things. **This DOES NOT work.** Audiences are different, but your speech must stay basically the same. Trust your coach and learn to trust yourself and your speech.

WORKING FORENSICS: A Competitor's Guide

STE WORKSHEET PHASE 2.1

SPEAKING TO ENTERTAIN WORKSHEET
Phase 2: DECIDING YOUR TOPIC

COMPANION READING:

IF YOU WERE A SPEECH TOPIC, WHERE WOULD YOU HIDE?
CRITERIA FOR SPEECH TOPICS
HOW TO WRITE A SPEECH: STEP 1

Locating materials:

With IF YOU WERE A SPEECH TOPIC, WHERE WOULD YOU HIDE? in front of you, do the following on a separate sheet of paper.

____ 1. Using the guidelines in "IF YOU WERE A SPEECH TOPIC, WHERE WOULD YOU HIDE?", generate a list. Write down at least 5 [usually it is more than 20].
REMEMBER, you can generate this list by:

    a. Brainstorming
    b. Talking to your coach(es)
    c. Talking to your teammates
    d. Watching network shows [like 20/20, 60 minutes, Primetime]
    e. Reading or scanning magazines

____ 2. Which of the topics on your list has the better potential for humor?

____ 3. Which of these topics best suits your personality?

____ 4. Which of the topics has broad (universal) appeal?

____ 5. Which of the topics do you think you'll be able to find current enough information about?

____ 6. Are any of your topics in poor taste or offensive?

____ 7. Have you narrowed your topic list to five or less hopeful topics? You probably have. So, arrange them in order from most appealing to least appealing to you.

____ 8. Arrange them in the same kind of order for audience appeal.

____ 9. Which topics appear near the top of both lists? These are your topic choices.

PERSUASIVE WORKSHEET PHASE 2.2

____ 10. Some really good topics, such as family relationships (brothers and sisters), are done so often that your are defeated by the topic. Your coach can prevent that disappointment by guiding your topic selection.

____ 11. If you still have a choice, chose the topic that has the most appeal to you because you will be working with it for a long time.

CONGRATULATIONS!
YOU ARE A PROUD OWNER OF A S.T.E. SPEECH TOPIC!

ONCE YOU HAVE RECEIVE APPROVAL FOR THE TOPIC, GO TO PHASE 3.

SUCCESS SEEMS TO BE

LARGELY A MATTER OF HANGING ON

AFTER OTHERS HAVE LET GO.

William Feather

STE WORKSHEET PHASE 3.1

SPEAKING TO ENTERTAIN WORKSHEET
Phase 3: RESEARCH AND NARROWING TOPIC

WHY DO THIS PHASE?

Before you can write a speech, you must do both preliminary and in-depth research. You can't begin to narrow the topic until you know what material is available. The best information may be something you don't know yet... or the newest research something you have yet to discover. This research will be the foundation of your speech, so the time you spend now, really examining this subject, will forge the future of this event for you.

COMPANION READING:

THE SPEAKER'S FIRST SOJOURN INTO THE LIBRARY
HOW TO WRITE A SPEECH: STEPS 2 AND 3

RESEARCH:

YES! Even STE's are researched. At heart, every good humorous speech is a serious and well research document. Some of the funniest bits are facts discovered in encyclopedias or other seriously written research sources. Therefore:

_____ 1. Do you have your library card? If not, get one. You are going to need it. Too, don't forget that there is more than one library.

_____ 2. Have you collected change for photocopying machine?

_____ 3. Once in the library, check the obvious sources in the library: vertical file, card catalogue, periodical guide, microfilm, index, Facts on File for the needed information?

_____ 4. Follow up the leads that you found in those sources?

_____ 5. Keep note cards or photocopies of the material you found?

_____ 6. Write the source on the photocopies?

_____ 7. Do these sources have credibility? For instance, The National Inquirer is not the most credible source. Well... maybe, sometimes -- with STE -- but, don't write a speech with that as your only source.

_____ 8. Do you have **at least** 3 viable sources for the speech? You probably have many more than that at this stage but some will get weeded out.

STE WORKSHEET PHASE 3.1

_____ 9. Have you investigated possible sources outside the library such as knowledgeable persons; agencies, organizations, etc.?

SLIMMING THE TOPIC DOWN:

_____ 1. The key to a strong organization is a tightly written statement of purpose. State your specific purpose, by completing the following statement: "At the end of my speech, I want my audience to _____." STE purposes can be either persuasive or informative, but they should **always** be serious under the humor.

Some key words might be: know, understand, be aware of, identify...

_____ 2. Are you keeping in mind what there is about this topic that will appeal to your audience?

_____ 3. Does your topic need to be more specific or more narrowed?

_____ 4. Is there a unique angle that gives this topic an unexpected twist or turn?

What you have is research and a purpose for a serious speech, OK? Don't worry. That's what you're supposed to have at this stage.

**HOWEVER, IT'S PROBABLY A GOOD IDEA TO
REPORT NOW TO YOUR COACH TO BE SURE YOUR ARE ON THE RIGHT TRACK.**

STE WORKSHEET PHASE 4.1

SPEAKING TO ENTERTAIN WORKSHEET
Phase 4: OUTLINING AND ROUGH DRAFTS

WHY DO THIS PHASE?

Contrary to what you may have always done, the outline actually should be written first. It will save time, frustration and problems only if you do it first. Otherwise, it creates them. Rough drafts are done because your speech is always considered in progress until it is finally settled in -- late in the season.

COMPANION READING:

HOW TO WRITE A SPEECH: STEPS 4-7 (The Sequel)
VISUAL AIDS[22]

THE ROUGH DRAFT:

Go ahead as if this were a serious speech. Remember to keep this draft short so that you will still be within the time constrictions after you add the humor.

On a separate piece of paper, complete the following:

_____ 1. List all of the things you want your audience to remember (your major points). Most speeches have 2-3 major ideas but you should never have more than 5.

_____ 2. Arrange those major points in the best sequence for your purpose. For instance, if you were giving a speech on Aluminum -- The Conversation Topic of the Century, your points might be discussing the origin of pronunciations as an ice breaker at parties, discussing creative uses of aluminum as a way to entice someone up see your personal collection of alum-sculpture and (as the ever present serious point) discussing recycling of aluminum as a way to disengage yourself from a aluminum groupie. See where this is headed?

_____ 3. Look at **each** major point independently. Outline your research material for that specific point.

After you complete outlining and arranging facts for each of your points, you are ready to continue by working on the introduction and conclusion.

---

[22]We know it didn't say anything about visual aids in the title but you will have to consider them in the rough draft.

STE WORKSHEET PHASE 4.2

THE INTRODUCTION:

Write a rough draft of the beginning of your speech. Then answer the following questions.

_____ 1. Does your introduction grab the attention of your audience?

_____ 2. Does your introduction give your audience a reason to listen?

_____ 3. Does your introduction state the purpose of your speech?

_____ 4. Does your introduction preview your main ideas with a smooth transition to the body?

If you answer "no" to any of the preceding questions, rewrite your introduction so that you can answer "yes".

CONCLUSION:

All good speeches have a sound conclusion. The STE is no exception. Write a rough draft of how you plan to end your speech. This is usually the "obligatory" serious part of the speech. But it doesn't "have" to be.

Does your conclusion:

_____ 1. Have a smooth transition from the body of your speech?

_____ 2. Summarize your main ideas?

_____ 3. Refer to the audience (how the topic was of interest and/or benefit to them).

_____ 4. Have a final unifying statement so that the audience will know you are through without you having to resort to a final line like "Thank you."?

_____ 5. Have a funny "tag" line?

_____ 6. Relate to the beginning of your speech?

If you answered "no" to any of the preceding questions, rewrite your conclusion.

WORKING FORENSICS: A Competitor's Guide

STE WORKSHEET PHASE 4.3

FIRST ROUGH DRAFT:

Since all successful competition speeches will eventually be memorized, you should now write a complete manuscript of your speech. As you are writing your first draft, remember:

1. It is helpful to skip every other line in your manuscript so that editing is easier.

2. Write in oral style (speeches are written to be heard, not read).

3. Realize you will be doing additional drafts, because good speeches are always in revision and they get better with every change. Be positive about rewrites.

READ YOUR SPEECH ALOUD AND THEN:

____ 1. Make any changes necessary to help your speech "sound" better.

____ 2. Consider whether a visual aid would enhance or clarify the information in any part of your speech.

____ 3. Note the current time of your speech? _____
It should be no more than 5-6 minutes (no laughs yet).

If the draft is overtime:

Refer to the general tips in HOW TO CUT and consider: How much do you need to cut?
Make a photocopy and make your 'cuts' on the photocopy. Consider cutting: side issues (sub-points); "flowery sentences" [make them simple]; number of examples [if you use three, can you get by with one?].
Now, re-time your speech. If it is still too long, you may need to narrow your topic farther. Get help from your coach. By the way, expect this whole process of cutting to take **at least** 2-3 days.

If it is seriously undertime:

Rethink your development and consider adding more material. More research may uncover a new direction.
If you need additional help in writing a speech, any good basic speech book or course will be of help to you. Ask your coach to help you find what you need.
Remember we told you this was a first draft? After your coaching session, expect to do many more drafts. It is not uncommon for the writing stage to last several weeks. Neither is it uncommon for a speech to go through several drafts--even throughout the entire forensic season. (Remember that patience and perseverance are virtues.)

SCHEDULE A COACHING SESSION.

STE WORKSHEET PHASE 5.1

SPEAKING TO ENTERTAIN WORKSHEET
Phase 5: HUMOR, VISUAL AIDS, THE FINAL DRAFT AND YOU

COMPANION READING:

VISUAL AIDS

HUMOR:

Now that you have a basically good speech, you are ready to add the humor. Probably a little humor has already crept into your early draft, leave it. Don't be afraid to try humor that "might" work, or to change words in your existing draft to accommodate humor. As you humorously revise your speech you might consider using one or more of the following techniques.

_____ 1. Have you examined the possibility for pun (the use of double meaning for words)?

_____ 2. Have you looked at malapropism or the ludicrous misuse of a word? (Samuel Goldwyn is a much quoted author of such misuse of the language.)

_____ 3. Have you used exaggeration or overstatement of a circumstance until it becomes ridiculous?

_____ 4. Have you used understatement or describing things in terms ridiculously inadequate?

_____ 5. Are you using satire which involves poking fun at social custom, manners and behavior? It can be cutting as criticism. Be careful, too, about humor which belittles any group. Alienated audiences are hard to amuse.

_____ 6. Now may be a good time to invite a few of your funniest friends or teammates over for the weekly "STE-in". This truly can be a regular meeting of the folk fortunate enough to be entered in this event. Read your speech aloud. Allow plenty of time for your friends to add their comments. Some of them will work! Write them down on scratch paper. Tomorrow some of them won't make sense. Cut them out.

_____ 7. Now, time the speech. If it is overtime (and they usually are) cut out what needs to be out, in order to stay legal in this event. **Allow some time for laughing.** Even the most generous tourney only allows a 30 second laugh extension.

_____ 8. Did you remember that the humor is to enhance or underline your serious purpose? Men and women tend to have different styles of humor. Does your humor appeal to both sexes? Will either find it offensive?

WORKING FORENSICS: A Competitor's Guide

STE WORKSHEET PHASE 5.2

PRELIMINARY DESIGN of VAs:

Now that your drafts are becoming more finalized, you need to give serious consideration to the use of visual aids. This is the time to make quick sketches of drawings, rough ideas of how words would look on a poster. What props would work, etc. VA's for STE's tend to be one of the major sources of humor. Don't be afraid to go for the laugh here.

____ 1. Are you going to use any?

____ 2. If so, how many? What type?

____ 3. At exactly what point in your speech?

____ 4. Have you done a preliminary design on scratch paper or a model (if appropriate)?

____ 5. Who will produce the actual VA? Will you, a friend, a professional? Think about it.

____ 6. Is there any other humor that can be enhanced visually. Think wildly -- brainstorm. Then try it. Let your coach approve your ideas.

WIT HAS TRUTH IN IT;

WISECRACKING IS SIMPLY CALISTHENISCS WITH WORDS.

Dorothy Parker

STE WORKSHEET PHASE 5.3

FINAL DRAFT:

"Final" is never final because you may never be finished revising your speech. Dedicated speakers frequently revise their speech after every tournament if they received valid criticisms on their ballots or think of a funnier way to do it. We are referring here to the final draft you are planning to memorize and take to the first competition.

So, rewrite your speech again and check:

____ 1. For good sentence structure?

____ 2. For correct grammar?

____ 3. For variety in word choice?

____ 4. If the audience, can visualizes what your are talking about?

____ 5. If your examples are clear?

____ 6. Check all of the dozens of things you normally check when you are trying to write an impressive English paper.

Then:

____ 7. Does your language choice sound like you are talking to them not reading to them (oral style versus written style)?

____ 8. Do you use humor when appropriate and as often as possible?

____ 9. Have you included a variety of forms of humor?

____ 10. Current time of speech? ideally, it should be between 7-9 minutes. If it is not... fix it, now! Allow for laughs...

Check back with your coach so that he/she can:

(a) worry
(b) enjoy
(c) destroy your efforts up until now!
(d) praise your efforts up until now!

WORKING FORENSICS: A Competitor's Guide

STE WORKSHEET PHASE 6.1

SPEAKING TO ENTERTAIN WORKSHEET
Phase 6: POLISH AND TAPE

COMPANION READING:

SOME NOTES ON MEMORIZING
WHAT JUDGES LOOK FOR IN PREPARED SPEECHES
PRACTICE PRACTICES

POLISH:

Answer, of course, on a separate piece of paper.

____ 1. Have you had your final draft approved by your coach?

____ 2. Have you made the suggested revisions?

____ 3. Have you read "SOME NOTES ON MEMORIZING"? Put all those pointers to use as you commit this draft to memory. Allow some time and don't get impatient with yourself.

____ 4. Have you performed for some live audiences? Your roommate, teammates, classes, your mom? As many reasonably willing people as you can number? As often as you can? This is especially important in STE. Fortunately, it is also easier to get an audience for STE rehearsal. Listen to the information you hear from them.

____ 5. What is the current time of the speech? _____

____ 6. Have you put it on tape?

____ 7. Have you performed for your funniest friend and asked them to help you add humor?

STE WORKSHEET PHASE 6.2

TAPING:

We strongly suggest video taping your entire performance, from walking into the room to your exit at the end of the speech. It may be helpful to have a small audience at the taping. Now watch the tape critically.

_____ 1. Was the performance lively enough to hold audience interest? Without pushing for laughs?

_____ 2. Do you use humorous gestures and facial expressions when necessary or appropriate? Don't allow them to become "mugging" -- exaggerated facial expressions.

_____ 3. Did you seem real, rather than plastic?

_____ 4. Does the visuals seem helpful or awkward?

_____ 5. Watch the video with the sound turned off. Was your body natural and smooth in motion, or did it call attention to your discomfort?

_____ 6. Do you show distracting mannerisms? You will discover that both speech and body language improve as you continue to rehearse. You may want to tape again after a few more rehearsals and see the improvement for yourself.

_____ 7. Do your hands call attention to themselves?

_____ 8. Do you walk during the delivery--at times that emphasize ideas? at times that detract from ideas?

_____ 9. Are you looking directly at audience members? Talking to them?

_____ 10. Do you appear to be "enjoying" the performance of the speech or does it look like it is hard work?

_____ 11. Do you believe this speech is ready and will do well? If not, find out why not and fix it. You should feel that your speech is a contender.

Continue to get coaching. Perform as often as possible in order to develop a fluent speaking style that is fresh and natural sounding. Continue to find new audiences.

COMMUNICATION ANALYSIS

or
ADVENTURE IN RHETORIC

AKA: CA; Rhetorical Criticism; RC

GENERIC RULES:

An original speech by the student designed to offer an explanation and/or evaluation of a communication event such as a speech, speaker, movement, poem, poster, film, campaign, etcetera, through the use of rhetorical principles. Audio visual aids may or may not be used to supplement and reinforce the message. Manuscripts are permitted. Maximum time limit is 10 minutes[20].

A FEW NOTES ABOUT COMMUNICATION ANALYSIS:

Don't believe what anyone tells you about C.A.[1] It is a simple speech to write, and it's been a long time since anyone found it dull or boring. The real problem is that it really should be a 20 minute event, but it isn't! It is a 10 minute limit, so it demands that you clarify your ideas, use clear penetrating examples and be time-economical. It also requires much more time to put together, so begin early. Basically, you will be comparing a communication event to a communication model. Now, it is immediately apparent that this is a much narrower range than the other prepared speaking events. It is complex, in that your have tw o sets of information to handle in the same time frame. Sooooo lets look at those tw o areas.

THE COMMUNICATION ACT

AKA: The artifact, rhetorical acts, communication event

NOTES ON THE COMMUNICATION ACT --

Until recently, these artifacts were usually historical and frequently rhetorical acts such as speeches (i.e. The Emancipation Proclamation). They were also frequently used as entertainment at insomniac conventions [guaranteed to put you to sleep]

Then someone discovered that if you chose a bright interesting rhetorical act (i.e. swatch watch design) people actually enjoyed CA and a new day dawned. In the "Golden Age of CA", the communication act is frequently based on audience appeal. Year audience, not to mention you and your judge, well enjoy the CA much more if they can relate to the topics. Half the battle is keeping the judge awake. Therefore, artifacts relating to communication is its broadest interpretation is frequently used. Advertising, packaging, public relations, politics, speeches, cartoons, media, publications, philosophy, -- in fact, any act of communication can be used for this event. But it must be specific. Time insists.

---

[20]Authors' comment: This is probably not an event choice for an inexperienced speaker.

WORKING FORENSICS: A Competitor's Guide

THE COMMUNICATION MODEL

AKA: The rhetorical standard, the tool, criteria, rhetorical principal

NOTES ON THE COMMUNICATION MODEL --

This is the criterion that will be used for comparison. These models are usually found hiding in serious communication publications, but on occasion have been spotted in less scholarly places. Any place that an expert explains the elements of or the criteria needed to understand or qualify a communication act - to put it succinctly -- an expert tells what it takes to accomplish a certain effect. [i.e. Stephen King (model) in Danse Macabre telling what horror is. You might use this as the standard to prove that the Movie Braum Stoker's Dracula (act) did or did not accomplish the goal of being a "horror" film]. It doesn't matter where you find them as much as just finding them. The only way to find these little gems is to

(a) sit down in the library with a depressingly large stack of magazines and look for them... or
(b) make friends with the rhetoric coach and pick their brain or
(c) accidentally run across one in something (maybe even Playboy) and find an artifact to fit it. [This is a real possibility, believe it or not!]

ENCOURAGING WORD: If your library is linked to Library of Congress, the journals are listed under P, PN or PQ.

ENCOURAGING WORD II: There is a wonderful index by topic of most of the Communication journals called Index to Journals in Communication Studies[21]. If your library doesn't have one, talk someone into getting one. This finding of models is nothing but work. Do it and get it over with.

Ok! You have it! CA is an easy comparison of event and model. You prove or disprove the validity of the "Act" by comparing it to the Model...."Might Mouse is a hero because Aristotle said a hero was _____." It isn't that tough, but we'll help you anyway. Lighten up. This is going to be fun. I know you committed yourself in Phase I. Recommit now to one challenging, exhilarating Rhetorical Adventure.

---

[21] Available through SCA.

CA WORKSHEET PHASE 2.1

COMMUNICATION ANALYSIS WORKSHEET
PHASE 2: SELECTING ACT & COMMUNICATION MODEL

COMPANION READING:

COMMUNICATION ANALYSIS
HOW TO WRITE A SPEECH: STEP 1
COMMUNICATION ANALYSIS: AN OVERVIEW

LOCATING A COMMUNICATION ACT:

As we have discussed, you are looking for any attempt (successful or not) at communication. It should be interesting to you and appealing to your audience. You should have some idea what you want to prove about it. A few categories and examples might be:

Speeches: Clinton's inauguration, Attorney General Reno's defense of Koresh incident, Malcolm X
Images: Madonna or Clinton
Movements: Apartheid--recent changes, volunteer army
Posters: Uncle Sam Wants You or Sado Masochism in Rock Posters
Film: Non-verbal language in *Body Heat*
Campaigns: "Milk-- It does a body Good"
Cartoons: Pogo and the Nixon Disaster

.... just to name a few. You get the picture. The field is wide open. A few avoids:
Avoid acts that are too complicated. They take too much time to set up. Avoid acts that are too foreign or obscure for the same reason. You have enough to do without explaining the legal system in Botswana. Avoid acts that are difficult to group or identify.

A few criteria for helping select the communication act.

____ 1. Are you interested enough to spend lots of time in research, analysis and performance?

____ 2. Does it have any significance for your audience?

____ 3. It is, possible to prove or disprove it by a rhetorical standard or communication model?

____ 4. Will your audience be interested? Or can you make them interested?

If you answered "no" to any of the above questions -- keep looking. If you answered "yes" to all of them make a photocopy of the act (or any researched data you found about it) and be sure to write bibliographical data on it.

WORKING FORENSICS: A Competitor's Guide

CA WORKSHEET PHASE 2.2

Now, go check with your coach to be sure you are on the right track. Some really good topics, such as Martin Luther King, Jr or JFK speeches have been done so often that your are defeated by the topic choice. Your coach can prevent that disaster.

SELECTING A COMMUNICATION MODEL (or tool or standard, whatever...)

This is the yucky part, but we have already talked about some shortcuts. The current trend seems to be toward very complex models, but this is very difficult with the 10 minutes time constraint. Simpler models will give you a little more flexibility.

Look for these models in communication journals[22] or rhetorical theory books[23]. Some suggestions are:

The Quarterly Journal of Speech
Communication Monographs
Communication Education
Critical Studies in Mass Communication
Southern Speech Communication Journal
Western Journal of Speech Communication
Central States Speech Journal
Communication Quarterly
Association for Communication Administration Bulletin
Philosophy and Rhetoric
Journal of Communication
Human Communication Research
Journalism Quarterly
Journal of Broadcasting and Electronic Media
Journal of the American Forensic Association

If your have selected an act, you have some idea what aspect of your communication act you need the model to address, so cross referencing in the journals and books is easier. It is just a matter of perseverance and hard work. You are looking for a model that will

    1.) Address the communication act directly
    2.) Be concise enough to be useful
    3.) Will make it possible to prove/disprove your analysis

Now is a good time to consult with the resident expert, your coach.

After your consultation, you will be ready for Phase 3.

---

[22] Such as *The Quarterly Journal of Speech*

[23] Such as *The Rhetorical Act* by Karolyn Kohrs Campbell

WORKING FORENSICS: A Competitor's Guide

CA WORKSHEET PHASE 3.1

COMMUNICATION ANALYSIS WORKSHEET
Phase 3: RESEARCH AND DEFINING THE TOPIC

WHY DO THIS PHASE?

The CA is a speech dependent on good solid research and analysis. You will be finding background and corollary information, as well as the facts you need to form the analysis. Using your best library technique, and armed with change, a library card, your computer codes (if needed) march to the library.

COMPANION READING:

THE SPEAKER'S FIRST SOJOURN INTO THE LIBRARY
HOW TO WRITE A SPEECH: PARTS 2 AND 3

RESEARCH:

You will be looking primarily for information pertaining to your communication act. You will want to find:

_____ 1.   Everything you can surrounding the act itself.

_____ 2.   Any sort of background information concerning it.

_____ 3.   Critical comments by others concerning it.

_____ 4.   If any related visual representation exists and is available for your use.

Ready... Get set... research!!

Back so soon? (It actually may take more than one trip to do this!!)

Did you...

_____ 1.   Write down the references so that you can document them?

_____ 2.   Check the obvious sources? [vertical files, card catalogue, microfilm, periodical guide, <u>Facts on File</u>]

_____ 3.   Follow up the cross reference leads you found?

CA WORKSHEET PHASE 3.2

PURPOSE:

By now, you should have a pretty good idea where your CA is going; what your analysis will pursue, what the act and model will show. In an effort to clarify your organization it seems to be a good time to clearly state your objective. Be as specific as possible.

An example might be:

"I want my audience to understand that the movie Star Wars was a mythological quest based on the criterion of Joseph Campbell."

Key words might be : prove, disprove, believe, understand, agree, appreciate, disagree.

Back to basics -- see your coach for approval.

A PROFESSIONAL IS SOMEONE WHO CAN DO HIS BEST WORK WHEN HE DOESN'T FEEL LIKE IT.

Alistair Cooke

CA WORKSHEET PHASE 4.1

COMMUNICATION ANALYSIS WORKSHEET
Phase 4: OUTLINING AND ROUGH DRAFTS

WHY DO THIS PHASE?

Because...

COMPANION READING:

HOW TO WRITE A SPEECH: STEPS 4-7
VISUAL AIDS

A NOTE ABOUT OUTLINES:

CA is complex to put together. Therefore outlining becomes supremely important. Several organizational formats will work.

In the simplest, arrange the main points of your model leaving space between them and simply arrange (or plug in) the proof. We'll give you a sample. ....Hang on.

Introduction

In a CA, the introduction may be longer than in other forms of speeches. Here you begin to introduce the threads you will weave into the CA. Like any other introduction, however, it should do certain things like:

1.) Get the attention of the audience. Make them excited about listening.
2.) Show the relevance of this communication act and its analysis to them as individuals
3.) Usually the criteria is introduced early in the speech.
4.) Preview the structure with smooth transitions into the body.

Conclusion:

All good CAs have good conclusions that help the audience feel enlightened. It has certain obligations that must be met:

1.) It should smoothly lead from the body of the speech
2.) It should summarize the main ideas by reinforcing how they developed your analysis.
3.) It should remind them of the significance of the communication act.
4.) It should have a unifying statement that will leave the audience with a strong impression

CA WORKSHEET PHASE 4.2

SAMPLE OUTLINE:

This is one example of a Communication Analysis Outline. Obviously, you won't be able to do everything on this outline in one speech. But be careful about omitting from the introduction and conclusion parts. You **do need** all of that. Tailor the rest to your specific needs dictated by your style and your communication act.

I. Introduction
    A. Attention getter
    B. Identify the communication act and its significance (at this point, really just a mention)
    C. Identify the Communication model with a brief overview
    D. A "Why this applies" statement
    E. Preview of the whole statement

II. Body
    A. Setting up the comparison
        1. describe the model
            a. identify it: source, name, authors, qualifications
            b. briefly explain what it proposes and why it is appropriate for this communication act
        2. Use the number of elements in the model to establish the number of areas to be discussed.
           (If it says XYZ; you apply X to act; then Y to act, etc.)
        3. Within each area
            a. set up that element and its purpose
            b. compare the element of the model with the act
            c. Use information to support those claims
            d. Set up the connection with the next element.
           (repeat for each element -- XYZ)
    B. Conclusions (what was learned by doing this analysis)
        1. What did you learn
        2. What is the significance of it
        3. What is your support for it
        4. Any generalizations that can be made

III. Conclusion
    A. Review
    B. Some thought provoking statement about "what we learned"
    C. Return to attention getter

Okay, go get your coach's approval of your outline. Once it's approved, you're ready to write the 1st rough draft. Congratulations -- you are well on the way to being ready to compete. Keep at it!

CA WORKSHEET PHASE 4.3

FIRST ROUGH DRAFT:

Since most winning speeches will eventually be memorized, you should now write a complete manuscript of your speech. As you are writing your first draft, **remember** that:

1. It is helpful to skip every other line in your manuscript so that editing is easier.

2. You should write in an oral style (speeches are written to be heard, not read).

3. You will be doing additional drafts, because good speeches keep being revised and they get better with every change.

READ YOUR SPEECH ALOUD AND THEN:

____ 1.   Make any changes necessary to help your speech "sound" more conversational.

____ 2.   Revise any points that are unclear.

____ 3.   Decide if a visual aid would enhance or clarify any parts of your speech?

____ 4.   Note the current time of your speech? _____

If it is overtime: Refer to general tips in HOW TO CUT and consider: How much material do you need to cut?

Make a photocopy of the CA and make your 'cuts' on the photocopy. Consider cutting: side issues (sub-points); "flowery sentences" [make them simple]; number of examples [if you use three, can you get by with one?].

Now, re-time your speech. If it is still too long, go get help from your coach or a seasoned teammate. By the way, expect this whole process of cutting to take <u>at least</u> 2-3 days.

If it is significantly undertime: Rethink your analysis and add to it, or do further research.

NOTE: If you need additional help in writing a speech, any good basic speech book or course will be of help to you[26]. Ask your coach to help you find what you need. Remember we told you this was a first draft? After your coaching session, expect to do many more drafts. It is not uncommon for the writing stage to last several weeks. Neither is it uncommon for a speech to go through several drafts--even throughout the entire forensic season.

SCHEDULE A COACHING SESSION.

---

[26]Of course, CA is not really a good first speech event choice, so you may need to be redirected.

82   *WORKING FORENSICS: A Competitor's Guide*

CA WORKSHEET PHASE 5.1

COMMUNICATION ANALYSIS WORKSHEET
Phase 5: VISUAL AID PREPARATION AND FINAL DRAFT

Visuals are definitely "in" in CA.
Now that your drafts are becoming more finalized, you need to give serious consideration to your use of visual aids.

PRELIMINARY DESIGN of VAs:

You may already have made quick sketches of drawings, or rough designs of how words would look on a poster, or have gathered working props, etc.. If not, do so. It might help to answer the following questions.

_____ 1. Are you going to use any VAs?

_____ 2. If so, how many? What type?

_____ 3. At exactly what point in your speech?

_____ 4. Have you done a preliminary design on scratch paper or a model (if appropriate)?

_____ 5. Who will produce the actual VA? You? A friend? A professional? Think about it.

Let your coach check your ideas.

REMEMBER

WINNERS DO
WHAT LOSERS DON'T WANT TO DO.

My Mother

WORKING FORENSICS: A Competitor's Guide

CA WORKSHEET PHASE 5.2

FINAL DRAFT:

The word <u>final</u> is probably a misnomer because you may <u>never</u> be finished revising your speech[27]. Dedicated speakers will frequently revise their CA after every tournament if they received valid criticisms on their ballots. We are referring in this instance to the final draft that you are planning to take to the first competition.

So, rewrite your speech <u>again</u>, if you need to, and check:

____ 1. Have you used good sentence structure?

____ 2. Have you used correct grammar?

____ 3. Have you used variety in word choice?

____ 4. Can the audience visualize what you are talking about?

____ 5. Are your examples clear? Is your analysis clear?

____ 6. Check all of the dozens of things you normally check when you are trying to write an impressive English paper.

Then:

____ 7. Do you use occasional humor when appropriate?

____ 8. Does your language choice sound like you are talking to the audience and not reading to them (oral style vs written style)?

____ 9. Current time of speech? Ideally, it should be between 8 - 9.5 minutes. If it is not...fix it, now!

Check back with your coach so that she/he can enjoy the glory of a project well done!

---

[27] We once heard a wise coach make an analogy between birthing a child and communication analysis: During the 9 months a lot of growing and changing must occur so hopefully by the end of the forensic season you can birth a truly beautifully complete CA! And if you are lucky, your pregnancy may be much shorter than nine months!

CA WORKSHEET PHASE 6.1

COMMUNICATION ANALYSIS WORKSHEET
Phase 6: POLISH AND TAPE

WHY DO THIS PHASE?

You've come too far in the process to quit now! Don't get discouraged if you have to make major changes in your speech as the forensic season progresses.

Some changes might include:

1. Continuing to update the examples, illustrations, etc.
2. Research concerns that judges mention on their ballots
3. Finding a better criteria, or
4. Deciding a different approach or angle would be more effective

So long as you are growing and learning, you're fine. Hang in there and keep polishing!

COMPANION READING:

SOME NOTES ON MEMORIZING
WHAT JUDGES LOOK FOR IN PREPARED SPEECHES
PRACTICE PRACTICES

POLISH:

Answer, of course, on a separate piece of paper.

____ 1. Have you had your final draft approved by your coach?

____ 2. Have you made the suggested revisions?

____ 3. Have you read SOME NOTES ON MEMORIZING? Put all those pointers to use as you commit this draft to memory. Allow some time and don't get impatient with yourself.

____ 4. Have you performed for some live audiences? Your roommate, teammates, classes, your mom? As many reasonably willing people as you can number? As often as you can? Listened to the information you hear from these people.

____ 5. What is the current time of the speech?_____

____ 6. Have you put it on tape?

CA WORKSHEET PHASE 6.2

TAPING:

We strongly suggest video taping your entire performance, from walking into the room to your exit at the end of the speech. It may be helpful to have a small audience at the taping. Now watch the tape critically.

____ 1. Was the performance lively enough to hold audience interest?

____ 2. Did you seem sincere and honest?

____ 3. Did the visual seem helpful or awkward?

____ 4. Watch the video with the sound turned off. Was your body natural and smooth in motion, or did it call attention to your discomfort?

____ 5. Do you show distracting mannerisms? You will discover that both speech and body language improve as you continue to rehearse. You may want to tape again after a few more rehearsals and see the improvement for yourself.

____ 6. Do your hands call attention to themselves?

____ 7. Do you walk during the delivery--at times that emphasize ideas or at times that detract from ideas?

____ 8. Are you looking directly at audience members? Talking <u>to</u> them?

____ 9. Do you appear to be "enjoying" the performance of the speech or does it look like it is hard work?

____ 10. Do you believe this speech is ready and will do well? If not, find out why not and fix it. You should feel that your speech is a contender.

Continue to get coaching. Perform as often as possible. Develop a fluent speaking style that is fresh and natural sounding.

III.

LOW-PREPARATION SPEAKING EVENTS

DESCRIPTIONS
&
WORKSHEETS

&
A BUNCH OF OTHER STUFF

LOW-PREPARATION SPEAKING EVENTS
HOW TO BEGIN -- PHASE ONE: THE COMMITMENT

In this sub-section of "Low-Preparation Speaking Events: you will find general information for both Extemporaneous and Impromptu speaking. The information will include: other names that the events are know as (AKA), generic rules, a few additional notes that explain aspects of the event, and then a set of worksheets (divided into phases). We have also included some additional help by giving you advice concerning how to set up extemp files, organizational help, and games that you and your teammates may play to increase your knowledge and fluency.

Before you can truly begin to work on either of these types of speeches however, you must first complete PHASE ONE.

PHASE ONE: COMMITMENT

If you have not decided in which event you wish to compete, NOW IS THE TIME. Procrastinating time is over. If you skipped it before, now is the time to turn back and read (or re-read) "HOW TO CHOOSE EVENTS".

Go ahead. Read it now!... We'll hum a little tune while you're gone...

HUM HUM HUM HUM HUMMM HUMMM HUM...[28]

Now, loaded with that information, you need to remember that college competition speeches come in two assortments: prepared speeches and low-preparation speeches. [These do not necessarily parallel the high school events with which some of you might be familiar -- so be forewarned!] As mentioned before, low-preparation events include extemporaneous speaking and impromptu speaking. These events may be performed with or without notes, with prep times which range from 30 minutes to less than 2 minutes. The basic skills involve staying abreast of current events, the ability to organize ideas quickly and well, the gift of fluency and a natural conversational style.

Having read the rules and talked to your coach, you should now have enough knowledge concerning the general procedures for each type of speech. Which one interests you most? Or, do you want to do both? You are ready to go to the page that has the event name in big print and begin. However, before you go, once again we want to warn you. This Phase One was the easiest phase to read (although, true commitment may be the most difficult to achieve. All phases of the worksheets are at times laborious list. May we once again remind you that the title of this text has the word "working" in it.....You're not backing out just because of work are you?....
No, of course not! You have made a commitment to yourself. You want to learn and grow and increase your fluency and ease in public speaking.

Go to your first speech choice... But remember...
work the phases IN ORDER and get coaching on a regular basis!

---

[28] A catchy tune, don't you think? You don't like it? Well, read faster!

EXTEMPORANEOUS SPEAKING

or
NEWS HOUND SPEAKS

AKA: Extemp, Ext.

GENERIC RULES:

Contestants will be given 3 topics in the general area of current events, choose one, and have 30 minutes to prepare a speech that is the original work of the student. Maximum time limit for the speech is 7 minutes. Limited notes are permitted. Students will speak in listed order.

MORE THAN A FEW NOTES:

WHAT IT TAKES FOR EXTEMP --

The ability to "**think clearly** on one's feet" is a requirement for a student desiring to compete in Extemp. To this add a sincere interest in current events. Even though the technical description of the event is "a student delivering a 5-7 minute speech on a current event topic that he/she receives 30 minutes prior to the speech"-- much more preparation than "30 minutes" goes into successful extemp speeches.

Actually, Extemp can almost be a team event, because several students may research and work together to maintain the team file. This team effort is a time saving device, **but only** if: (1) all information is placed into the file in the same manner, (2) care is taken to avoid duplication of information/articles since 2 or more students are putting the same info into the file, (3) and if each student accepts responsibility to be familiar with what everyone has placed in the filed. [A general rule of thumb is that one file can service up to 3 or 4 students. If you have more than 4 students you may need to have multiple files.]

Normally, the only info that is 'filed' is published info, such as articles found in **TIME**, **NEWSWEEK**, **U.S. NEWS AND WORLD REPORT**, **U.S.A. TODAY**, **CHRISTIAN SCIENCE MONITOR**, newspapers, or any other pertinent articles. A serious competitor should also regularly listen to network news and such programs as 20/20, Nightline, and CNN on a regular basis. The more well versed you are in current events, the better chance you have of preparing a truly super speech.

YOU MIGHT BE INTERESTED TO KNOW:

1. Contrary to rumors that you might hear, extemp speakers who consistently do well **DO NOT MAKE UP** information. Not only is it unethical, but most judges are well read and topical enough to spot it.

2. Extempers do frequently quote from literary sources or make a literary point in their speech.

3. Debaters frequently are extempers, however, it is not the same kind of on-your-feet thinking. Different skills are required and generally a different style of speaking is used [We don't like it, but that is real-world forensics].

4. Topics are more often than not in a persuasive format. Most often you will have a choice of 3.

5. Judges dislike (and can usually spot) generic introductions.

A WEEK OR TWO BEFORE YOU GO TO CONTEST:

It has been a practice of ours to sit down a make a list of the 5 "biggies" - currently the most dominant news events or the ones that are beginning to rise into that category. These then become the focus of most of our time immediately prior to contest. It is true that not all of the topics will be the 5 biggies but, the odds are that at least one of them will be on your plate. **It is a gamble.** But when your team is small it helps ease the pressure.

AT THE CONTEST:

One of the first things you will do at the contest is to find out where the "prep/extemp draw" room is and put your files there. You are allowed to be in the prep room at almost any time during the contest. At the designated time for draw, extemp competitors gather there. You must know your speaker position and **be on time** for the "draw". Draw will be in order and timed. Respect that demand.

A person in charge will call out "Speakers one." Then all competitors in the first speaker position will go to the front of the room and receive 3 topics. These three "topics" are generally stated as questions and usually come from at least 2 of these 3 areas: international politics; domestic issues; economic issues. These topics are frequently typed on a small single slip of paper referred to as a "topic slip".

The first speakers' prep time begins when he/she draws. Then 7-10 minutes later the person in charge will call out "Speaker 2." This keeps the speakers a few minutes apart, which allows the judges time to write more complete ballots and assures that everyone's prep time is equal. That means that punctuality is a big thing in Extemp.

HINT: If your are cross-entered, you normally always do your extemp speech first. One exception might be if you were listed as 1st speaker in your other event, and 6th speaker in extemp. Under normal conditions you would have more than enough time to do your other event and still get back to extemp draw in plenty of time. However, you have **little or no** flexibility about speaker order in extemp; therefore, arrange your cross-entries around that commitment, not vice-versa.

During prep:

Remember, you have a total of 30 minutes. Here are some guidelines about how you should spend that time.

Decide on your topic choice: This should be done in 1-2 minutes. When deciding, consider throwing out any topic that you know absolute nothing about. Consider whether you have any or enough information in the files to use (hopefully, the information will have come from several sources so that you can make various citations - impressive to judges). Consider which topic you can make into a stronger persuasive or analytical case.

Decide on the purpose of the speech: This should be done in 1-3 minutes. Usually you can either agree or disagree and give "evidence" to support your decision. Or you may have to predict the future. In which case, you make your prediction and then give evidence to support your prediction.

Find pertinent info in your file[29]: This should not take long if your files are well organized (ideally, less than 2 minutes). It might help to create a cross-reference system that list names and topics and then tells in what files information on such can be found.

Review the information: If you know what your purpose is, scan only for such information as needed. If your margin notations and highlighting are done well, this should take a minimum of time.

Outline the speech on an acceptable size card or paper[30] : The form can come in any of several patterns, but will probably include:

> **INTRODUCTION** -should be an attention getter, should state the topic clearly, should give a preview of the speech
>
> **BODY** - Usually has 3 points or 2 points with 2 sub-headings each. It should begin with any definitions or background information needed to fully understand the topic. At the end of each point or division the speaker should tell us how that relates back to the main topic (never assume that the audience will figure it out - that is your job, not theirs). Remember to cite the sources of your information.
>
> **CONCLUSION** - The conclusion should re-state the topic and the major points and then link back to the "catchy" introduction.

Practice: Most speakers leave the prep room to practice. They find a hall close to the competition room or they practice outside - keeping an eye on the time.

Arrive at the competition room, early if possible. The speaker prior to you will let you know when they are finished. If no one is in the room you can just sign-in to let the judge know you are there. Remember that you do not have to speak until your 30 minutes are up. Take your practice time.

---

[29] We have written about how to set up a file. It is after the worksheets.

[30] This varies with the contest--anything from a 3X5 card to a legal pad has been used. But the size is frequently legislated by specific tournament rules.

At the competition room:

Wait quietly outside the door of your competition room until time for your speech (30 minutes after draw). Most of the time it is just you and the judge(s) in the room, but a competitor is usually allowed to stay and listen after their own speech is done[31]. Evenso, ask for permission.

Like we said, usually the competitor speaking before you will tell you that he/she is finished as they leave. If it is still early, and you wish to practice some more, look in on your judge and let the judge know you are there and you have "____" minutes left. Or you and the judge may be ready early. If you and the judge agree, you are allowed to speak early as long as the order remains the same. You MUST begin at 30 minutes from your draw [EXCEPTION: the previous speaker is still speaking!]. If the draw has started late, the judge will probably know[32]. If not, you may inform the judge.

Before you begin speaking you should give the judge the topic slip. After they have noted the topic, the judge will usually let you know how they are going to give time signals. If not, ask him/her, if you need to. It is always okay to ask the judge (before you begin) what his signals are. They vary greatly.

DO NOT hold the notes while you speak, if at all possible. Set them, if you need them, on a desk in front of you. Then you can easily pick them up to glance at them if needed.

CITING SOURCES: During your speech you must let the audience know the sources of your information. The less obtrusively YOU DO THIS, the better.

> Example: "In today's New York Times..." "According to the May 5th Newsweek..."
> "In an interview on CNN 2 weeks ago..."

Obviously, the more current citations are pretty impressive.

TIME:

There is no minimum length BUT realistically your speeches need to be at least 5 minutes long. Do not worry if, early in the season, they are not. With work, they will be.

The judge will usually give hand signals to let you know how much time you have left. When you have run out of time, finish your sentence and shut up. If you go over this line, you may be disqualified. As you practice and become more seasoned, you will develop an internal clock, so you don't have to rely totally on the judges' time signals. In tough competitions the better speakers usually speak 6:45 to 7:00 on the button.

---

[31] It is a very helpful learning tool to hear the remaining speakers.

[32] If you are the first speaker, you will probably be the one asked to tell the judge.

To give you some guidelines to how you may actually use your 7 minutes of allotted speaking time, here is a time-table/outline to follow:

FIRST 1 to 1 3/4 MINUTES:

INTRODUCTION - ATTENTION GETTER

Gain attention
Get audience interested
   Read topic - Reading it from the slip is not enough
   Startling facts or statistics
   Analogies
   Hypotheticals
"Canned intros" are no-nos
   Often have no relevance to current speech
   Judges know -- it sounds bad
   May have heard it before
   Points off for lack of original thinking...
       "Canned intro? Maybe canned speech?", thought the judge.

STATE TOPIC -- break it down to specific topic

RELEVANCE OF TOPIC -- Why is this important?
   Why should judge listen or care or be concerned?

ANSWER TOPIC (IF PERSUASIVE)
   Give purpose or direction

PREVIEW ORGANIZATION OF YOUR SPEECH
   Should have at least 2 main ideas, no more than 4
   It is possible to have break downs of main ideas into sub-points, but it is a judgement call on your part if you should preview these sub-points now or wait until you get to the points within the speech

NEXT 4 - 5 MINUTES:

Body [timed to be on last point when you have one minute left]
   Develop ideas
   Between main ideas -
   use internal summaries when possible
   Keep linking ideas to your stated purpose

LAST MINUTE:

Summarize body
Re-answer topic (if persuasive)
Concluding statements
   Tie intro into conclusion, if at all possible -
   link to attention getter

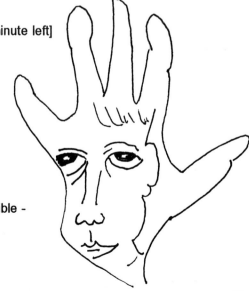

WORKING FORENSICS: A Competitor's Guide

EXTEMP WORKSHEET PHASE 2.1

EXTEMPORANEOUS SPEAKING WORKSHEET
Phase 2: SETTING UP FOR RESEARCH

COMPANION READING:

EXTEMPORANEOUS SPEAKING
SETTING UP AND MAINTAINING AN EXTEMP FILE
THE SPEAKER'S FIRST SOJOURN INTO THE LIBRARY

MATERIALS: Have you gathered the following items?

_____ 1. A portable filing case which is identified (labeled) with the school name on the inside.

_____ 2. Plenty (at least 50 at the start) of manila file folders.

_____ 3. Highlighters in at least 2 easy-to-read-through colors.

_____ 4. A stapler

_____ 5. Assorted office supplies such as pens, pencils, scissors.

_____ 6. Ideally, access to a photocopy machine.

_____ 7. Regularly accessible magazines and newspapers. [Check with your coach to see what is available for your use. You must be able to cut up or at least photocopy from the magazines. Some suggested magazines for your perusal are listed late in the text. See "HELPFUL PUBLICATIONS FOR EXTEMPORANEOUS SPEAKING".

_____ 8. Have you checked the library for <u>Facts on File</u> or any current issues of such publications as the <u>Social Issue Resource Series</u>.

_____ 9. World Almanac, a quote book and a small dictionary and any other small, condensed general information book that you might use quickly..

SCHEDULE:

_____ 1. Have you and your extemp-mates found a mutual weekly time to work on the file? At least an hour to an hour and a half?

_____ 2. If not, have you identified separate weekly times to work? (This really demands more discipline from extemp-mates as you must keep up on the reading of everyone's filings.)

_____ 3. What is that time? Is it posted? Does your coach know the schedule? On your mark... get set... go to Phase 3. .... The work is about to begin!

EXTEMP WORKSHEETS PHASE 3.1

EXTEMPORANEOUS SPEAKING
Phase 3: RESEARCH AND FILE

COMPANION READING:

SETTING UP AND MAINTAINING AND EXTEMP FILE

Now that you and your group are scheduled and have assembled the right equipment, you are ready to get to nitty-gritty extemp research.

RESEARCH:

_____ 1. Have you formed the habit of a daily news show? (This can be radio and/or tv) Daily is best, three times a week is a minimum.

_____ 2. Have you formed the habit of watching informative in depth television programming such as Prime Time, McNeil/Lahr Report, CNN, Washington Week in Review, Nightline?

_____ 3. Do you read a newspaper? Want to try something special--like <u>Christian Science Monitor</u> or <u>Wall Street Journal</u> or <u>Washington Post</u> or even <u>USA Today</u>?

_____ 4. Have you struck up a "drop-by-for-a-chat" relationship with an economics person (such as a professor or professional), a history person, a political science person, or any knowledgeable person who keeps up with what's going on in the world today?

_____ 5. Do you have access to magazines that can be cut up? You need every issue of at least 2 of the big news magazines such as:

   __ <u>NEWSWEEK</u>   __ <u>TIME</u>   __ <u>U.S. NEWS AND WORLD REPORT</u>

If your squad doesn't subscribe to these, investigate friends, family, or businesses that will let you have their week-old issues.

WORKING FORENSICS: A Competitor's Guide

EXTEMP WORKSHEET PHASE 3.2

FILING:

A. Yet another check list. Have you formed good filing habits such as:

    _____ 1. Locating magazine articles of value by scanning the index and/or the entire articles?

    _____ 2. Double checking to see if the back side of the article has an item of interest? If so, copy it immediately. [Be sure the name of publication and date of the article are on the copy and the page you want for the file.]

    _____ 3. Neatly clipping the article from the magazine or newspaper article.

    _____ 4. <u>Stapling</u> (not paper clipping) the article pages together.

    _____ 5. Read the articles with highlighter in hand. Highlight the <u>most important facts</u> that you will need later in a speech as you read the article.

    _____ 6. Indicating the <u>key</u> phrase or two by marking with an asterisk or star.

B. Have you set up your filing system with:

    _____ 1. Clearly labeled file folders on major current issues (such as Tax Reform, Candidates, Middle East, etc.)

    _____ 2. Alphabetized the order of files.

    _____ 3. Separate the groups of files into categories such as: International, Domestic, Economics.

Your files should be taking shape by now. You may even be able to use them at a tournament. Perhaps you are ready for PHASE FOUR.

EXTEMP WORKSHEET PHASE 4.1

EXTEMPORANEOUS WORKSHEET
Phase 4: PUTTING IT ALL TOGETHER AND TALKING ABOUT IT

COMPANION READING:

HOW TO WRITE A SPEECH
WHAT JUDGES LOOK FOR IN SPEAKING EVENTS

Lets pretend you've never given an extemp speech:

The topics will usually be stated as questions in areas of national, international or economic interest. For practice rounds get 3 topic choices from:

    ____ A. Your coach
    ____ B. A fellow extemper (maybe at your weekly meeting)
    ____ C. Make up topics yourself
            (you might find them on covers, or indexes of the Big 3 magazines)

Begin your prep time: 30 minutes till blast off[33]...

<u>1st 5 minutes</u>[34] Select a topic based on:

_____ 1. Your interest

_____ 2. Information in flies -- Remember, you may simplify your topic selection by omitting the topic(s) about which you know you <u>have no information</u>.

_____ 3. Possibilities of topic -- i.e. possible angles, analysis.

---

[33] For the most part, this is a repeat. We left it because many of our readers will skip around in the text.

[34] The times given for each section are arbitrary. They are to give you a guideline. Remember that we are pretending that you have never done this before.

WORKING FORENSICS: A Competitor's Guide

EXTEMP WORKSHEET PHASE 4.2

The next 10 minutes

_____ 1. Find the appropriate folders. Pull them.

_____ 2. Skim the information highlighted in them.

_____ 3. Jot down main ideas as you skim.

The next 5 minutes

_____ 1. Organize main points. Do all these points directly relate to your selected topic or answer the question?

_____ 2. Flesh-out those ideas

_____ 3. Think of how you plan to introduce your speech.

_____ 4. Does your introduction include the extemp topic/question exactly as written and the answer to that question?

_____ 5. Does your introduction include a quick preview of your main points?

_____ 6. How do you plan to conclude your speech?

_____ 7. Have you restated your question and answer together with a summary?

_____ 8. Do you have a tie-in (link) with your introduction?

_____ 9. Does the speech have a "clincher"--a final strong statement?

The last 10 minutes

_____ 1. Find a quiet corner somewhere between the draw room and your competition room to rehearse--a hallway, a stairwell, an outdoor location. Set your stopwatch so that you are aware of the time to get to your round.

_____ 2. Be certain to arrive at your final destination for speaking with a little time to spare.

_____ 3. What was the time of your first speech?_____

This first effort will seem a little awkward, but it will get smoother and easier the more you practice...so, do it often, as often as possible. For now, read PHASE 5.

EXTEMP WORKSHEET PHASE 5.1

EXTEMPORANEOUS WORKSHEET
Phase 5: FURTHER PREPARATION

WHY DO THIS PHASE?

It seems all too easy to become lazy in preparing for this event. We have seen many fine speakers never reach their potential because they either quit researching and filing or they quit regularly practicing. It takes commitment on your part to do well in this event.....

COMPANION READING:

SETTING UP AND <u>MAINTAINING</u> AN EXTEMP FILE
EXTEMP GAMES

CHECK THE FOLLOWING:

____ 1. Have you now formed good filing habits?

____ 2. Do you up-date the file at least once a week?

____ 3. Do you regularly check for duplications of items or to consolidate files?

____ 4. Are you still in a good media mode?

____ 5. Are you giving at least 3 practice speeches a week? You may not always have an audience, but your weekly extemp meeting is a good available slot. Periodically coaches need to hear you, and remember, video tape is one of the best learning tools. And don't forget friends, family and classes as audience possibilities.

____ 6. Are you and/or your extemp-mates playing the Extemp Games at your meetings -- of course, maybe we should ask if you are having meetings?

KEEP WORKING AND PROCEED TO PHASE 6

WORKING FORENSICS: A Competitor's Guide

EXTEMP WORKSHEET PHASE 6.1

EXTEMPORANEOUS WORKSHEET
Phase 6: POLISH AND TAPE

WHY DO THIS PHASE?

Just as in Phase 5, it is still too easy to slack off - to assume you are 'ready enough' for competition. Don't settle for mediocrity. Challenge yourself to do this event as it should be done -- with full commitment to becoming well versed in all areas of current events and dedicated to improving your organization and fluency skills.

COMPANION READING:

PRACTICE PRACTICES

Polish:

_____ 1. Are you continuing to up-date your files?

_____ 2. Do you still stay "news aware"?

_____ 3. Have you performed for some live audiences? Your roommate, teammates, classes, your mom? As many reasonably willing people as you can number? As often as you can? [Ideally -- still practicing out loud 2 -3 times per week.] Listen to the information you hear from them.

_____ 4. Is your analysis in each speech becoming clearer and more in depth?

_____ 5. Do you always relate your analysis and development of ideas to answering the specific question of your chosen topic?

_____ 6. Are your speeches consistently hitting lengths of more than 5 minutes? Can they become consistently 7 minutes in length?

_____ 7. Are you continuing to chat with knowledgeable people [like history and economic professors] about current events?

EXTEMP WORKSHEET PHASE 6.2

Video Tape:

We strongly suggest video taping your entire performance, from walking into the room to your exit at the end of the speech. It may be helpful to have a small audience at the taping. Now watch the tape critically. (Is there any other way?)

____ 1. Was the performance lively enough to hold audience interest?

____ 2. Did you seem sincere and honest?

____ 3. Watch the video with the sound turned off. Was your body natural and smooth in motion, or did it call attention to your discomfort?

____ 4. Do you show distracting mannerisms? You will discover that both speech and body language improve as you continue to rehearse. You may want to tape again after a few more rehearsals and see the improvement for yourself.

____ 5. Do your hands call attention to themselves?

____ 6. Do you walk during the delivery--at times that emphasize ideas or at times that detract from ideas?

____ 7. Are you looking directly at audience members?

____ 8. Do you appear to be "enjoying" the performance of the speech or does it look like it is hard work? [You need to look like you are in control.]

____ 9. Do you feel confident in your ability to research, organize, and deliver a good extemp speech? If not, find out why not and fix it. You should feel that your abilities make you a contender.

Continue to get coaching. Perform as often as possible to keep your speech sounding fluent, and fresh and natural sounding and the ideas flowing.

SETTING UP AND MAINTAINING AN EXTEMP FILE

The real secrets of a winning extemper:

1. A current, effective extemp file

2. Plenty of practice-speaking time

Here are some guidelines in helping you to prepare and/or maintain "a good, effective extemp file":

1. **You must be organized.** Organization is often a very personal thing. But unless your team has a system that is already working, we recommend the following filing system. It is simple and works with great success. This method involves having a "cat case" (or a plastic portable file case) filled with alphabetically filed folders labeled with dozens of different national, international, and economic topic areas. (For example: Abortion, NATO, Supreme Court, Presidential Candidates, Tax Reform).

   Once a sufficient number of folders have been prepared and filled, extempers frequently split the files into 2 'cat cases'—one being for U.S. topics and the second one being for International topics. It is possible to split the files even further, but it presents a logistical problem if the files get too unwieldy. Check with your coach to see if your team has its own unique style of filing.

   The point is to have a workable system.

2. **Your material must have "substance".** Once you have the file folders, what do you put into them? Frequently, topics for tournaments are taken from the past 3 months issues of **TIME**, **NEWSWEEK**, and **U.S. NEWS AND WORLD REPORT**.

   WARNING: This does <u>not</u> mean that your research or files should be limited to only these three sources!

YOU CAN NOT BUILD A REPUTATION ON WHAT YOU ARE GOING TO DO.

HENRY FORD

Ideally, on a weekly basis, you should:

A. Scan-read the magazines and newspapers you have available for your squad's use.

B. Highlight while you scan-read[35]. Highlight only the most important facts, quotations, or other pertinent data. Do **NOT** over highlight...too much is as bad as none.

C. Star (*) the "have-to-use" info in the articles -- dynamite quotes; fantastic stats; stupendous support sections. It is also useful if you label the info in the margin.

D. Carefully tear out/cut the articles that are worth saving, making sure the source and date are on each page, and...

E. File the articles in the correct folder.

F. A great extemper also reads newspapers for articles to clip and put into the file.[36] They may even make notes on TV news specials.

Before long, the files will be growing in size and number, and so will your wisdom.

3. **You must be familiar with the material.** Unless you frequently update and look through the extemp file, you are not using it properly. You usually are working as a team (2-4 people preparing the file) so make sure you know what others have contributed to the file. You need to be familiar with <u>all</u> the information in the file <u>before</u> you get to the tournament. This takes time.

By the way, if you have more than 4 extempers, you might consider preparing additional sets of files. Why? Because, just as we noted before, it is difficult for 5 or more to work out of the same set of files at a tournament. It simply gets too crowded.

---

[35]Putting an unhighlighted article in the file is as helpful as a case of mumps.

[36]Wonderful papers: Christian Science Monitor; USA Today; The Wall Street Journal; Washington Post.

WORKING FORENSICS: A Competitor's Guide

4. **The major topics need outlines.** Another real plus is for you to prepare "skeleton outlines" for all major topic areas. You may use these outlines in rehearsals, keep them in the extemp files, and then have them handy for reference while preparing to speak at a competition. It takes less of your prep time if you are adapting an outline that you have previously prepared. This is not plagiarism or cheating. It is hard-earned advanced preparation for a difficult event.
NOTE: THIS IS **NOT** A CANNED SPEECH BUT AN OUTLINE.

5. **You must practice using the file.** An extemp file, no matter how organized and complete, is worthless unless you have had sufficient practice in using it. Make it a habit to give a minimum of 3 extemp speeches per week to classes, coaches, other extempers, friends, or yourself.

    NOTE: If you are given the privilege of being responsible for the file, take it seriously. It is harder to do extemp with the file in another town.

    Remember.... discipline and hard work are the keys to success in any event.

GOOD LUCK

HELPFUL PUBLICATIONS FOR EXTEMPORANEOUS SPEAKING

EXTEMPORANEOUS SPEAKING: THE CREATIVE SPEAKING SERIES
A booklet that covers the entire process of extemporaneous speaking. While at times, the booklet is a bit wordy, it gives a lot of good information that both novices and advanced speakers could appreciate.

   Address: Extemporaneous Speaking, The Creative Speaking Series, National Textbook Co., 8259 Niles Center Rd., Skokie, Ill. 60077

STEPS: An English textbook written by David Yount and Paul Dekock, this book has an excellent chapter on "Basic Essays." The steps they discuss are identical to those a good extemporaneous speech should include.

   Address: Steps, Published by INTERACT, P.O. Box 262, Lakeside, CA 920040

Specialized magazines and newspapers which are definitely helpful for extempers (whether you subscribe OR investigate in the local or school library or get a doctor's or lawyer's office to donate):

Brookings Review
Business Week
Challenge
Christian Science Monitor
Commentary
Commonweal
Congressional Digest
Contemporary Review
Current
Current History
Economist
European Affairs
Far Eastern Economic Review
Fletcher Forum of World Policy
Foreign Affairs
Foreign Policy
Gallup Report
Harvard Internal Business Review
International Affairs
Nation
National Journal
New Republic
New Statesman
New York Times
Orbis
USA Today
Washington Post Weekly
Washington Times Insight
World Press Review
World Policy Journal

WORKING FORENSICS: A Competitor's Guide

EXTEMP GAMES

At your weekly extemp work sessions you can make double use of your time if you have activities to do while filing. If you happen to be the only extemper on your squad, you can adapt some of these games to play by yourself or you can play them with your coach or any other interested person. These are only ideas for games...jumping off places. You will create rules and variations as you play.

1. **COUNTRY HOPPING**

   One person calls out the name of a country (other than the U.S.) and any other person quickly identifies it on a world map or globe or if none is available, verbally identifies its location.

2. **COUNTRY BIO**

   This is an extended version of COUNTRY HOPPING. After the location you also include such items as the leader's name, the type of government, main product, world status, main problem, current war, etc.

3. **NAME THAT WAR**

   Name a war or a country that is in a state of war, who the opponents are, and then list the cause or reasons (for both sides). Trace the origins if possible. This can be played in teams.

4. **NAME THAT ACRONYM**

   One person lists an acronym--the other states what the letters stand for <u>and</u> something about that organization or movement.

   (For instance, there is a significance difference between the IRA and the IRS!)

5. **I'LL EXPLAIN MINE, IF YOU'LL EXPLAIN YOURS**

   All of these games require background knowledge or some pre-assigned research. In this game, each person has a concept or idea that they teach the others. Examples: stock trading, deficit spending, or Palestine Liberation Organization.

   Hint: We assign topics the week before the meeting and then play this at the next gathering or on the van trip.

6. **BOTH SIDES OF THE FENCE**

   Take a generic broad issue (like drug testing or nuclear disarmament). Then take 30 seconds to list 3 "good" points and then 3 "negative" points about the topic.

7. BRAINSTORM TOPICS

All the extemp-mates discuss and decide what are the "big" topics are for the next tournament. You might then assign these topic areas and report back during the next session (Like playing "I'LL EXPLAIN MINE, IF YOU'LL EXPLAIN YOURS"). Knowing general background information always helps.

8. THE ORGANIZATION GAME

A topic is announced and each extemp-mate has to organize it into a 2-4 point format. Then everyone shares their organization and a discussion can be held considering which patterns would work better.

Obviously there are many versions of these games that you can devise. You can even make up a point system to keep score if you like (Loser buys the pizza!). The point of all of these games is to familiarize yourself with as much about the world and what is happening in it as possible!

These games are wonderful for long forensics trips. Not only are they good training tools, they are fun.

THE GREAT PLEASURE IN LIFE

IS DOING WHAT PEOPLE SAY

YOU CANNOT DO.

Walter Bagehot

IMPROMPTU SPEAKING
or
I CAN SPEAK ON ANYTHING

AKA: IMPROMPTU; IMP.

GENERIC RULES:

An impromptu speech, serious in nature, with topic selections varied by round, section by section. Topics will be of a proverb-like nature. Speakers will have a total of 7 minutes for both preparation and speaking. Timing commences with the acceptance of the topics sheet. Limited notes are permitted. Each speaker in a given section will choose to speak from one of the same two topics offered.

WHAT IT TAKES:

This is a very popular event because many perceive it as a non-preparation event. However, to do impromptu well, a competitor must have the ability to analyze the topic and apply it in an original, creative manner and also possess the ability to articulate instantly and effortlessly. It also helps to have a broad knowledge base (general and varied) coupled with a very lively interest in literature. Dedicated impromptu speakers practice regularly to increase their fluency and overall naturalness. A thirst for general knowledge (being a trivia collector) helps, since topics vary so widely and the broader your base of knowledge the better. It also helps if you have a broad base of information concerning both literature and philosophy (these aren't essential, but they certainly help!)

AT THE CONTEST:

You will arrive at your assigned competition room to discover that you will probably get to wait in the hallway with your fellow competitors until it is your turn to speak. Most tournaments do not allow competitors to stay in the room until they have spoken, since all contestants frequently use the same choices of topics. At some tournaments you will be allowed to remain in the room and listen to the competitors that speak after you--at some you will not. It is always a good learning experience to hear other people perform your event, if you can. Before your speech, give the topic slip to the judge.

HOW TO DIVIDE UP YOUR 7 MINUTES:

Remember, you only have a total of 7 minutes -- that's for both preparation and speaking. It takes considerable practice to perfect the use of this time. While how much prep time is used varies greatly, [not only with the experience of the speaker, but also the region] the vast majority use between 30 second and 2 minutes. If you use less, judges may become suspicious that you are using a "canned" or prepared speech. If you use more than 2 minutes, your are seriously jeopardizing your chances of having enough time left to develop a worthwhile speech.

USE OF PREP TIME:

When you receive the topic slip it will normally have 2 or 3 choices on it. Most tournaments use topics with a proverb nature (like biblical, classical and/or modern) but some may use single words (like Fate, Love, Hope), quotations, famous movie line, political cartoons or, in some cases, even objects (fans, motorcycle, cupie dolls). Check with your coach to see what type is most often run in your region.

Regardless of the type of topics you have to choose from, you should make your decision quickly (5 - 30 seconds). It's normally best to go with your first instinct and stick with it. The clock is ticking!!

Technically, there is no maximum amount of time that one should use for preparation. More than 2 minutes is frowned upon. But, ideally, you want to use between 30 seconds and 2 minutes. This will leave you 5 to 6 1/2 minutes of speaking time. Use as much time as possible in speaking. Ideally, use all of it, certainly use no less than 4 minutes.

The judge will give you verbal signals of the time you have used in preparation ("30 seconds"..."1 minute") and hand signals of the time remaining from 5 minutes down. Judges may vary on this way of notifying about time. So it is a good idea to ask before you begin. Remember, judges sometime get busy with your ballot and their time signals become a little inaccurate. So, stay flexible. As time goes on, you will develop an 'internal clock' that will help you judge your time more accurately.

You must decide what your thesis or purpose is. Are you in agreement or disagreement with the sentiment stated in the topic? Be sure you say that.

DURING SPEAKING TIME:

Even though this is a spontaneous speech, you are still expected to have clear organization and full speech development.

INTRODUCTION -- should be an attention getter (story, example, analogy, etc.), should state the topic clearly, should indicate analysis choice and should preview main ideas.

BODY -- usually as 2-4 points that clarify or illustrate your line of analysis on the topic (through literature, movies, history, current events, personal examples, hypothetical examples, etc.) . At the end of each main point or idea, the speaker should tell how it relates back to the main topic -- never assume that the judge will make the same connection that you do.

CONCLUSION -- This should re-state the topic, summarize the main ideas/points and then unify the speech by linking back to how you began (i.e. story, analogy, etc.).

When you finish speaking, leave the room OR ask to stay and watch the other speakers. If you stay, be quiet, attentive, polite. If you leave, don't make a big deal out of it.

To a novice, this probably seems like an overwhelming amount of things to do within 7 minutes. It is. BUT, with practice and coaching, no other event can give you quite the same amount of pride in development of thinking-on-your-feet fluency and poise. This is a challenge worth taking. Remember, you have already committed to this event in PHASE ONE. Go to the next page -- you are ready for Phase 2.

IMPROMPTU WORKSHEET PHASE 2.1

IMPROMPTU SPEAKING WORKSHEET
Phase 2: GATHERING RESEARCH

WHY DO THIS PHASE?

Even though Impromptu is labeled, "Low-prep", it is not. To become proficient at doing impromptu speeches, you have to do a whale of a lot of background reading and topic gathering before you begin to practice.

COMPANION READING:

IMPROMPTU SPEAKING or I CAN SPEAK ON ANYTHING
THE SPEAKER'S FIRST SOJOURN INTO THE LIBRARY

MATERIALS:

_____ 1. You need to get a list of at least 20 possible topics. If there are others on your team -- each team member should have his/her own list to contribute to the practice topics.

Possible topics come in the following forms:

_____ Proverbs: you can find proverbs in quote books, fortune cookies, the Bible, old wives tales, Aesop's fables

_____ Quotes: you can find quotes in a large variety of quote books, the year end issue of <u>Life Magazine</u>, or take them from famous movies or song lyrics.

_____ Cartoons: you can find these just where you would expect. Political cartoons are the favorite choices, but don't be surprised to find Garfield or Peanuts.

_____ Objects: any object might be used or any combination of same. Example: sandpaper; banana; comb

_____ 2. Have these topics typed or written neatly in a way that they can be cut apart in sets of 2.

_____ 3. Now get your coach's approval of these topics. Then cut them apart and put them in a box (or hat or hermetically sealed mayonnaise jar) <u>labeled</u> Impromptu Topics.

IMPROMPTU WORKSHEET PHASE 2.2

YOU ALSO NEED TO OBTAIN:

_____ 4. A thumbnail book of philosophy. Brief summaries (no more than a page) of the major philosophies of the world.

_____ 5. A thumbnail book of literature. Brief (no more than a page) summaries of major literary works.

_____ 6. Some books on values such as <u>Value Clarification</u> or <u>American Values</u>. Knowing why you believe something is very helpful in analysis. You call it pre-thinking on basic human concerns.

_____ 7. Joseph Campbell's video tapes on religion, myths, etc. (These are available for rent at most large video stores. They were produced by Bill Moyer and believe it or not, are entertaining to watch!). Others might do as well, we still aren't aware of any at this printing.

_____ 8. Some blank note cards. Any size will work as long as its legal at the tournament, however, small looks better and is easier to handle.

SCHEDULE:

_____ 1. Have you and your impromptu-mates found a weekly time to work together? At least an hour to an hour and a half.

_____ 2. If not, have you identified separate weekly times to work? This really demands more discipline from impromptu-mates because it's harder to work by yourself.

_____ 3. What is that time? Is it posted? Does your coach know the schedule?

On your mark...get set...go to the library with Phase 3 worksheet. The work is about to begin!

IMPROMPTU WORKSHEET PHASE 3.1

IMPROMPTU WORKSHEET
Phase 3: RESEARCH AND MIND SETTING

COMPANION READING:

THE SPEAKER'S FIRST SOJOURN INTO THE LIBRARY
MENTAL TOUGHNESS
Thumbnail philosophy and literature books.

Now that you are scheduled and have assembled the right materials, you are ready to get to the nitty gritty of impromptu.

RESEARCH:

_____ 1. Have you read some of the philosophies of Plato, Socrates, Twain, Thoreau, Emerson, Disraeli, Gandhi, Lao Tsu, The Yellow Emperor?

_____ 2. Do you know who these people are? Why they get quoted? Something about their life[37]?

_____ 3. Are you a news follower? Have you formed the habit of watching some informative, in-depth television programming such as Prime Time, McNeil/Lahr News Hour, CNN, Washington Week in Review, Nightline? Do you regularly read a newspaper, keeping current on what is happening in the world?

_____ 4. Have you struck up a "drop-by-for-a-visit" relationship with a philosophy or logic teacher?

```
         EVERYTHING LOOKS IMPOSSIBLE
      FOR THE PEOPLE WHO NEVER TRY ANYTHING.

                 Jean-Louis Etienne
```

---

[37] THEY (the infamous "they") lied when they called this a low-prep event. To do it right takes WORK.

IMPROMPTU WORKSHEET PHASE 3.2

MIND SETTING:

It helps if you have an encyclopedic memory but if you don't you might try:

_____ 1. Highlighting the thumbnail books (if they belong to you.)

_____ 2. Keeping a notebook of the best of your findings, that you occasionally thumb through.

_____ 3. Keeping note cards filed in a small box. The act of writing tends to encourage memory.

_____ 4. Are you meeting regularly with your impromptu-mates[38]?

_____ 5. Are you positively preparing to be successful at this event?

If you answered "yes" to that last question, **GOOD!** You are ready to prepare an impromptu speech...Go on to Phase 4

ALL GREAT ACHIEVEMENTS REQUIRE TIME.

David Joseph Schwartz

---

[38] We don't mean casual sex!

IMPROMPTU WORKSHEET PHASE 4.1

IMPROMPTU WORKSHEET
PHASE 4: PUTTING IT ALL TOGETHER AND TALKING ABOUT IT

COMPANION READING:

HOW TO WRITE A SPEECH
SPEECH ORGANIZATION
WHAT JUDGES LOOK FOR IN SPEAKING EVENTS

Lets pretend you've never given an impromptu speech:

The topics will usually be quotes in the nature of a proverb, but can be cartoons, objects or anything that the tournament rules listed. For practice rounds get 3 topic choices from:

_____ your approved topics

_____ a fellow impromptu speaker (maybe at your weekly meeting)

Begin your prep time[39]: 2 minutes or less till blast off...

<u>1st 5 seconds</u> Select one of the topics - based on:

_____ A. your interest

_____ B. your grasp of the concept

_____ C. possibilities of topic: i.e. possible angles, analysis.

<u>The next 10 seconds</u>

_____ 1. Jot down main ideas

---

[39]The times given for each section are arbitrary. They are to give you a guideline. Remember that we are pretending that you have never done this before.

IMPROMPTU WORKSHEET PHASE 4.2

With whatever amount of time you wish to use of the remaining 1 minute, 45 seconds of a maximum 2 minute prep time:

____ 1. Organize main points. How do all of these points directly relate to your selected topic?

____ 2. Flesh-out ideas

____ 3. Think of how you plan to introduce your speech.

____ 4. Does your introduction include the impromptu topic exactly as written?

____ 5. Does your introduction include a quick preview of your main points?

____ 6. How do you plan to conclude your speech?

____ 7. How do you plan to restate your topic together with a summary?

____ 8. Do you have a tie-in (link) with your introduction?

____ 9. Does the speech have a "clincher"--a final strong statement?

Now stand up and speak!!!!!

What was the time of your first speech?_____

This first effort will seem a little awkward, but it will get smoother and easier the more you practice...so, do it often, as often as possible. For now, read Phase 5.

WORKING FORENSICS: A Competitor's Guide

IMPROMPTU WORKSHEET PHASE 5.1

IMPROMPTU WORKSHEET
Phase 5: FURTHER PREPARATION

COMPANION READING:

IMPROMPTU GAMES

CHECK THE FOLLOWING:

____ 1. Are you still in a good media mode? Watching/reading news?

____ 2. Are you giving at least 3 practice speeches a week? You may not always have an audience, but your weekly impromptu meeting is a good available slot. Periodically coaches need to hear you and remember video tape is one of the best learning tools. Don't forget friends, family and classes as audience possibilities.

____ 3. Are you and/or your impromptu-mates playing at least one of the Impromptu Games on a regular basis?

IT USUALLY TAKES MORE THAN TWO WEEKS

TO PREPARE

A GOOD IMPROMPTU SPEECH.

Mark Twain

IMPROMPTU WORKSHEET PHASE 5.2

Now that you are giving speeches regularly, you may want to check your speeches for some of the things judges look for when they review your work.

_____ 1. Do you clearly and correctly state the topic?

_____ 2. Do you explain what the topic means?

_____ 3. Do you preview the contents of your speech?

_____ 4. Is your introduction creative and original?

_____ 5. Do you use transitions that lead smoothly from idea to idea?

_____ 6. Do you use key phrases from the topic?

_____ 7. Are you stretching the topic to fit what you want to say? Or saying what the topic does?

_____ 8. Do you use clear examples that are specific to the topic?

_____ 9. Surely you don't announce that "this is an example"?

_____ 10. Is your analysis sound? Do you show it to the audience?

_____ 11. Is your vocabulary appropriate and **properly** used?

_____ 12. Do you adhere to the topic?

_____ 13. Do you use sufficient illustration?

_____ 14. (Perhaps the #1 voting issue) Is it organized?

_____ 15. Do you have personal touches?

_____ 16. Does your summary take less than 30 seconds and include summarizing and restating the quote?

_____ 17. Do you have a strong conclusion?

KEEP WORKING AND PROCEED TO PHASE 6

IMPROMPTU WORKSHEET
Phase 6: POLISH AND TAPE

COMPANION READING:

WHAT JUDGES LOOK FOR IN SPEAKING EVENTS
PRACTICE PRACTICES

POLISH:

_____ 1. Are you continuing to increase your knowledge of philosophy and literature/writers?

_____ 2. Do you still stay "value aware"?

_____ 3. Have you performed for some live audiences? Your roommate, teammates, classes, your mom? As many reasonably willing people as you can number? As often as you can? Listen to the information you hear from them.

_____ 4. Is your speaking style becoming more and more fluent and conversational?

_____ 5. Are your analyses of topics becoming clearer and focused on the topic?

_____ 6. Are your analyses of topics becoming deeper and richer in meaning?

_____ 7. Are your speeches consistently hitting lengths of more than 5 minutes? Are you consistently using less than 2 minutes in prep time?

THE TROUBLE WITH PEOPLE WHO TALK TOO FAST

IS THAT THEY OFTEN SAY SOMETHING

THEY HAVEN'T THOUGHT OF YET.

Anonymous

IMPROMPTU WORKSHEET PHASE 6.2

VIDEO TAPING:

We strongly suggest video taping your entire performance, from walking into the room to your exit at the end of the speech. It may be helpful to have a small audience at the taping. Now watch to the tape critically. (Is there any other way?)

____ 1. Was the performance lively enough to hold audience interest?

____ 2. Did you seem sincere and honest?

____ 3. Watch the video with the sound turned off. Was your body natural and smooth in motion, or did it call attention to your discomfort?

____ 4. Do you show distracting mannerisms? You will discover that both speech and body language improve as you continue to rehearse. You may want to tape again after a few more rehearsals and see the improvement for yourself.

____ 5. Do your hands call attention to themselves?

____ 6. Do you walk during the delivery--at times that emphasize ideas or at times that detract from ideas?

____ 7. Are you looking directly at audience members?

____ 8. Do you appear to be "enjoying" the performance of the speech or does it look like it is hard work?

____ 9. Do you feel confident in your ability to organize and deliver a good impromptu speech? If not, find out why not and fix it. You should feel that your abilities make you a contender.

Continue to get coaching. Perform as often as possible to develop a fluent speaking style that is fresh and natural.

Remember:
Commitment means continued work -- not just settling for "I know how and I can wing it."

IMPROMPTU GAMES

At your weekly meetings with your fellow impromptu speakers, you can add fun to the practice sessions by playing some of these games. If you are the only person doing impromptu speaking on your squad, you can adapt some of these games to play by yourself or you can play them with your coach or any other interested person. These are only skeleton ideas for games--you may flesh them out any way that suits your needs.

1. **WHAT'S MY ANALYSIS?**

   One person holds a list of topics and a stopwatch. He/she reads one topic aloud and starts the watch. All others write down on a piece of paper their thesis or purpose and their main ideas (2-4). The stopwatch holder calls out prep time as it progresses. At 2 minutes everyone stops.

   Everyone then takes turns <u>briefly</u> listing their purpose statement and main points, being sure to point out how their points add to the analysis of the topic. (Note: This is a favorite game and has proven to be especially successful in training novice impromptu speakers. It is easy to play on the way to tournament.)

2. **BOTH SIDES OF THE FENCE**

   Take a generic broad issue (like the welfare system, the education system, adoption) and in 30 seconds list 3 "good" points and 3 "bad" points about the issue.

3. **NAME THAT PHILOSOPHY**

   The first person calls out a famous philosopher. The next person must in less than 30 seconds briefly capsulize for what the philosopher was best known.

4. **PARAPHRASE**

   Take a list of topics (usually quotations) and read one out loud. Then quickly put it into your own words/paraphrase in one sentence. You can then ask a fellow team member if they agree or disagree with your paraphrase and why.

**I CAN GIVE A SIX-WORD FORMULA FOR SUCCESS:
THINK THINGS THROUGH --THEN FOLLOW THROUGH**

Eddie Richenbacher

---

5. **APPLIED BRAINSTORMING**

(This game is best played in pairs, even a coach-student one!)
The first impromptu speaker takes a sheet of paper and divides it into 3 or 4 columns. The second speaker gives the number one speaker headings for the columns (such as political figures, TV shows, movies, hobbies, children). The first speaker then has 1 minute to brainstorm and write down anything that comes to mind under the given headings. When the time is up, the second speaker gives the first a quotation and asks that he/she prepare an impromptu speech using at least one example from each of the headings (the speaker may choose to use or not use examples brainstormed).

6. **ROUND TABLE CRITIQUE**

In a group of impromptu speakers, everyone prepares to do a speech on the same topic (no more than 2-3 minutes preparation). Then, one speaker is chosen <u>at random</u> to give their speech. All others listen and jot down notes. At the end of the speech, all join in on **constructively** criticizing the speaker's speech. You may choose different aspects to criticize (delivery, organization, analysis) and focus only on that aspect. After the critique, a new topic is chosen. Everyone prepares again, a new speaker is chosen <u>at random</u> and the critique starts again.

EFFORT ONLY FULLY RELEASES ITS REWARD

AFTER A PERSON REFUSES TO QUIT.

SOME ORGANIZATIONAL HELP FOR SPEECHES

Creative, yet functional organization for a low-prep speech makes the speaker's job easier and the overall performance more memorable. The following lists of trios and pairs can give you some ideas about less common ways to organize material.

EXAMPLE:

In a preview a speaker could say "I will support this contention with 3 points. Point 1 will cover an example from history, point 2 will be an example from literature, and point 3 will be an example from my personal life."

Or the speaker could say "The truth can be divided into 3 categories -- the good, the bad and the ugly."

How much more creative to say "The Clinton plan can be divided into 3 kinds of savings: dime savings, nickel savings and penny savings. The dime savings are the big cuts in social programs..... In conclusion it could be said that the Clinton plan may nickel and dime us to death but it is the penny saved that is really the penny earned."

Obviously these lists are not appropriate for all types of speeches. They are intended for use primarily in impromptu and extemporaneous speaking. However, some of them could be adapted for use in the other speaking events.

Look over them and start expanding your own preconception about what organization should be. You can probably add to these lists with ideas of your own and/or create a new list of "quads for organization!"

Read over them...expand your brain...and enjoy!

GENERAL TRIOS FOR EXTEMP OR IMPROMPTU ORGANIZATION

go	caution	stop
green	yellow	red
black	white	grey
black	white	hispanic
dime	nickel	penny
large	medium	small
all	partial	none
steam	water	ice
hot	warm	cold
gas	liquid	solid
sociological	economical	political
radical	conservative	liberal
dictatorship	aristocracy	democracy
communistic	socialistic	democratic
congressional	presidential	judicial
local	state	national
state	country	world
government	business	private
home	church	family
scientific	religious	political
atheistic	religious	agnostic
moral	political	social
mental	physical	spiritual
honest	unethical	dishonest
truth	justice	the American way
good	bad	ugly, indifferent, mediocre
alike	combination	different

WORKING FORENSICS: A Competitor's Guide

you	them	me
child	adult	elder
birth	growth	death
past	present	future
yesterday	today	tomorrow
male	female	androgenous
solo	duo	group
single	married	family
love	honor	obey
love	like	hate
love	tolerate	hate
peace	compromise	war
fast	stand still	slow
idea	plan	action
hypothesis	theory	proof
dream	fantasy	illusion
unknown	theory	known
no	maybe	yes
possibility	plausibility	probability
fight	be neutral	run away
repair	live with it	eliminate
make it better	ignore it	make it worse
help	observe	hinder
auditory	visual	kinesthetic
watch it	ignore it	join it
lead it	go along	stay behind
work	retire	resign
up	stationary	down

PAIRS FOR IMPROMPTU OR EXTEMP ORGANIZATION

criminal -- honest	love -- war	male -- female
over/under achieve	macro - micro	private -- public
national -- international	status quo -- with change	child -- adult
plant -- animal	fantasy -- reality	black -- white
state -- nation	mind -- body	physical -- mental
verbal -- non-verbal	medical -- psychiatric	communistic -- democratic
personal -- state	big picture -- little picture	socialistic -- democratic
personal -- national	big -- little	socialistic -- communistic
mind -- matter	large -- small	laissez faire -- interfere
religious -- agnostic	hope -- reality	good -- bad
spiritual -- worldly	dream -- reality	hinder -- help
religious -- atheistic	wish -- reality	professional -- amateur
agnostic -- atheistic	want -- get	vocation -- avocation
judicial -- congressional	them -- us	job -- hobby
presidential -- judicial	then, past -- now, present	profit -- nonprofit
theory -- reality	in peace -- in war	professional -- charitable
inside -- outside	now -- future	union -- non-union
logical -- illogical	past -- future	open shop -- closed shop
moral -- ethical	young -- old	can -- cannot
ethical -- legal	father -- mother	business -- pleasure
moral -- legal	blue collar -- white collar	parent -- child
personal -- social	honest -- dishonest	adult -- child
single -- group	poor -- rich	employer -- employee
mental -- physical	governmental -- private	employed -- unemployed
for, pro -- against, con	small business -- corporate	military -- civilian
theory -- reality	science -- religion	medical -- psychological
presidential -- congressional	psychological -- physiological	over -- under

WORKING FORENSICS: A Competitor's Guide

IV.

INTERPRETATION EVENTS

GENERAL INFORMATION

HOW TO DO INTERPRETATION

A Brief Overview.. Another Of Many

Just as there is no "one" approach to writing a speech, there is more than "one" approach to doing interpretation. As always feel free to adapt our suggestions to your coach's methods, if they differ.

In this section of the text you will first find a very broad look at what is involved in preparing interpretation. Then you will find guidance in how to both find and select your interpretive material, including how to consider literary merit. Once your have your material, you will read the sections on cutting (trimming) the piece to the time limit and how to put it into script form for your folder. There are many other important aspects of doing interpretation events, so you will also find headings on "HOW TO WRITE INTRODUCTIONS AND TRANSITIONS", "HOW TO CREATE CHARACTERS, and "HOW TO USE FOCUS". Finally, this section ends with some suggestions of what judges are looking for in interpretative events. One thing that we never address specifically (as under a separate "heading") is DELIVERY. An interpreter's delivery is very personal -- a natural extension of their unique personality. [But your style will be developed as you work through the other interpretative processes.] We do address delivery as it relates to other aspects of interpretation.

If you are truly a novice interpreter, you might ask your coach to recommend a good interpretation textbook to fill in any gaps we were unable to cover here -- OR, consider taking a beginning interpretation class. In today's word knowing as much as you can about analysis and presentation of yourself can only be of benefit to you.

AN APPROACH TO LITERATURE : INTERPRETATION IN GENERAL

Oral Interpretation simply means to bring to life a piece of literature by effectively reading it aloud. It is sharing the material that the author has written with an audience, hopefully allowing them to feel what you felt as you read it. Literature is usually divided into three basic types or genres:

POETRY: Any material that is economical in language and written in meter. Some new poems are hard to tell from prose because they are very free in rhythm and language.

DRAMATIC: Usually defined as material that comes from plays, including screen, radio and television, and stage.

PROSE: Any literature that is not a play or a poem. Usually short fiction for the purposes of forensics. But it may be nonfiction works or letters, essays, diaries -- almost anything of literary merit that is not a play or a poem.

It is pretty easy to let interpretation become stilted and unnatural, or even to "put it on automatic pilot" until it becomes slick and "Technique-y". But the best interpretation is natural and conversational and connects real emotions to the literature. The best interpreters seem to enjoy sharing the literature with an audience. Obviously, this is not easy to achieve and doesn't happen overnight. However, the following general tips may help you work more efficiently and get to performance level without too many stumbles:

1. The first tip is to read the whole work...the whole story, play, whatever. Don't try to guess what the selection is about from reading a cutting, a scene, a chapter. Believe it or not, your judge may already know the selection and have a problem with careless interpretation. Believe it or not, you can't possibly give a selection it's full potential without knowing the totality of what it is about.

2. Check with your coach as soon as you locate a possible selection. A coach can save you time by telling you early in your selection process if the piece is worth working on, or if, it just won everything in sight last year, or if it is a "tired old piece.".

3. Real interpretation begins when you understand the text, what the words mean, what you can find out about the author, what the references are, who the speaker is and why the speaker is speaking, who is being spoken to and why. Then, when the words and their intent are easy for you, you can begin to dig for the feeling and the truth. There are **NO SHORTCUTS**.

4. Interpretation is complicated. It involves pacing, rate, focus, placement, characters, imagery, subtext, articulation, and visualization, among other things. **YOU NEED A GUIDE!** Don't cheat yourself by thinking that you can do it just as well on your own. You may be able, but it will take longer and cause lots of discouragement along the way. Don't be afraid to get coaching early-- long before you are "perfect". You don't need a coach when you're perfect! But you need one until you are. Allow your coach to help you be what you want to be...by including your coach early in your process and by continuing to check with him/her regularly as you progress.

5. Never cut something out just because you don't understand it. You may be extracting the heart of the piece, without knowing it. Understand the importance of the deletion -- surgeons do!

6. Interpretation is not the same as acting but, they do share lots of traits (particularly in analysis). Interpretation, unlike acting, requires the use of a script and a somewhat limited use of the body and space.

7. Do not be inhibited by the rhyming pattern of poems. Make it natural. Follow the thought more than the line delineation. Break the rhythmical pattern whenever possible.

8. Make the speaker in the literature real to you. Who is it and who is she/he speaking to? Play "what if". What if you were in this situation and you were the speaker? How would you feel? What would you want people to feel? Put yourself in that place. Paraphrase the piece to make it "yours". Imagine your listeners and try to make them respond through your presentation.

9. Take the piece apart, word by word. Understand everything about it for yourself. Don't be afraid if, later, you discover some revelation in the cutting that makes you change the way you interpret it. Stay flexible, but at the same time, wring the meaning out of every comma and syllable. Having fun?

10. Don't allow yourself to be discouraged because other competitors work at different speeds than you. Everyone does not use the same process or the same speech. Some people **seem** to be quicker than other people at putting competition pieces together. It may be that they work all night at home. Don't worry about them. Worry about you. Let them work at their own pace and you spend your energy working on your own selections in your own way -- with your coaches help, of course.

11. Follow the worksheets included here religiously. The step by step process will help guide you through the interpretation.

12. One of the best tricks that interpreters can use to develop strong openings is creating for themselves a very real "moment before." The more you know about what caused someone to say the first words your about to say, the more real it becomes. You need to know who is speaking, and why! And to whom and why. Imagine a question that your first line will answer. Very few of us just "start talking." There is a reason. Find it.

FINDING AND SELECTING INTERPRETIVE MATERIAL

Finding the right material for competition and for your own style is undoubtedly the most difficult part of interpretative forensics. It takes hours of reading and lots of patience. But hang in there, because the "right" material will make the rest of your job easier.

In General the following hints might help you locate material:

1. Read widely always "keeping an eye out" for good choices of literature or themes...even in textbooks.

2. Keep a file of anything interesting that you do find, regardless of where you find it, or when.

3. Learn to use the library's cross reference file and the indexes for short stories and poetry. They categorize by theme and author.

4. Follow the work of authors you like. Find out what else they have written. Check other genres for their work.

5. Scan openings and closings (paragraphs, chapters, scenes) to see if you are interested.

6. Make it a practice to write down titles, pages, authors of selections that appeal to you.

7. Photocopy the "good" stuff for a file.

8. Keep lists or index cards with ideas and possible material.

REMEMBER you should continue to check back with your coach. You need guidance for what material will work in your region and what has been overdone at tournaments.

SUCCESS IS NEVER FINAL AND FAILURE IS NEVER FATAL.

Anonymous

WORKING FORENSICS: A Competitor's Guide

SELECTION CRITERIA FOR LITERATURE

You are looking for perfect literature that has literary merit. In addition to that, you must consider that you and this selection will be together for a long time. You want literature with "staying power". You have begun your search. Perhaps the following criteria will help you make your selection:

1. Material that reflects universality, individuality, imagery.

    Universality - the quality of having appeal to all kinds of people and a sense of timelessness

    Individuality - the quality of being different and original

    Imagery - the quality of allowing the interpreter **and** the audience to visualize the ideas presented

2. Material must build to a climax with a beginning, and an end. [Some new literature does not have really strong endings, and this may make the audience feel unsatisfied].

3. Material should suit your personality, voice and abilities.

4. It helps if you "love" your selection because you will be living together a long time.

5. The material should be able to hold an audience - over and over again.

6. Your selection should not be too familiar to your competition audience.[40]

7. If you are working on a theme, show more than one view.
    Examples: Show the kinds of approaches: weddings viewed historically, humorously, and then emotionally. Or show different sides of one event: the causes of the civil war as told by a rebel and then as told by a yank. Or view the same side with differing results: Two cases of abused children with one rising above it and the other sinking beneath the weight.

    Go for balance and/or contrast. Find the interest and expand on it.

ONE OF THE MOST DANGEROUS FORMS OF HUMAN ERROR IS FORGETTING WHAT ONE IS TRYING TO ACHIEVE.

Paul Nitze

---

[40] Trust your coaches' judgement here!

The sources for interp selections might be such things as:

1. **Anthologies:** (For those who may not know, anthologies are collections of literature taken from other sources - this includes text books.)

2. **People:** experienced competitors; Faculty--include non-speech faculty such as English or History; All "readers" of your acquaintance. Ask them to watch for you -- tell you about the "best" stuff they read.

3. **Libraries:** faculty, department, other colleges or universities in your area, and the local public library, even inter-library loans.

4. **"Best Of" series:** Best Short Plays; Best in Short Fiction; Best of John Cheever; others

5. **"Scenes-from" books**: Understand that you must go back later and read the entire play or story if you select from this source.

6. **Play productions and acting classes**: Watching such can be a pleasant way to become familiar with writers.

7. **TV shows, movies**[41]: Remember that they may be based on a story in print. Watch the credits.

8. **Magazines:** OMNI, ESQUIRE, various literary magazines and such are good sources of really new works

9. **Bestsellers list**: Check The New York Times or other lists.

10. **Book reviews:** They appear in various papers and magazines. Clip the ones that interest you. OR keep a running list in your calendar.

11. **Material used by other competitors** at tournaments--but, check with coaches on this one. You do not want to steal their material to compete against them. But, you may compete against this school only this one time during the season, or you may find and use a different cutting, or you may want to save it for next year.

---

[41] We do recommend caution in selecting current blockbuster movies.

THE INTERPER'S FIRST SOJOURN INTO THE LIBRARY
A Few Hints for Interpers

If you are ready to look in the library for material, gather up a few dimes, and begin your search.

Get a list of suggestions of titles before you go, from all your literary contacts or your own investigative power.

Don't neglect periodicals. Great prose, poetry and, yes, even drama can be found in magazines.

Look in the poetry indexes, the prose indexes, the short story indexes, etc. They are organized by title, author, first lines, subject matter. Looking under subject will speed up companion piece finding, especially with poetry. Making a list of synonyms for the subject before you go could prove to be valuable. Most libraries mark the books they own in these guides.

If you don't know how to use these index things, get someone to teach you. The librarians will help if you act humble.

HE WHO IS AFRAID OF ASKING IS AFRAID OF LEARNING.

Danish Proverb

Photocopy good stuff (usually, 10 cents per) and write all bibliographic info on the photocopy. You may need to go back to this source later.

Keep a record of where you found all the literature you didn't photocopy. This is just in case you need to find it again at a later date.

Learn to follow the work of authors you like. Read all the titles for your favorite writers. Look at the beginnings and endings of new "possibles". You can tell a lot by how things start and stop. If it appeals to you, check it out further by reading the middle.

Don't judge a selection by it's length alone -- OR flip through for a section that is long enough.

KEEP ALL INFO. What might not be used now, may be used later. This is why you have spent all those years in English class learning to make note cards.

LITERARY MERIT

Literary merit is a very ambiguous term. Even the three authors cannot agree on a definition for Literary Merit. So we chose to each write our own. This fact alone should give you some idea of the subjectivity that is involved in pinning down a precise definition.

Author # 1[42]: Literary merit is intensely personal. Literature should have some value that makes it worth the time of the interpreter and the audience, since both will make an investment of time in the selection.

However, the following guidelines help me determine the literary value of a selection.

1. Do you love it? Is there some feeling of connection? When you read it, did it speak to you?

2. Does it challenge you intellectually? Make you think or feel? Make you re-examine the way you believe or think?

3. Does it have universal appeal?

4. Will it appeal to a broad base of people?

5. Does it violate the conventions of good taste?

6. Is the literature vivid? Does it suggest images in your mind?

7. Does this selection stay in your mind? Haunt you?

Author #2: To compete in interpretive events takes a lot of time and effort. Therefore, you want to make sure the literature you choose has "literary merit". This ambiguous term implies that the literature has value to the above average person.

Frankly, some authors have more credibility than other authors (this DOES NOT imply that unknown authors have no literary quality - many do!) In my opinion, because so much subjectivity is involved it is almost impossible to come up with a clear definition. The best advice is to check your selections with your coach.

---

[42] The names have been concealed to protect the innocent.

Author #3: I desire to be, seek to be, and live to be on the cutting edge of literature.

There have been tomes of treatises written on the literary merit of Dickens, Salinger, Joyce. I do not wish to write about these authors. I leave that to the others.

When I read contemporary literature[43], I <u>feel</u> my way through it. These <u>feelings</u> are my guide to "literary merit". I look for words whose multiplicity of meaning lay like shadows reflected in a house of mirrors below the print. I want thoughts that prick my soul and force me to rethink myself. I desire sentences that cause me to catch my breath--the kind you whisper again and again. The images must be so original that to try to describe them as "like..." anything else is impossible. My conditions for literary merit in contemporary literature are <u>very</u> personal.

I nearly always find that it is writing that is not easy....that often it makes me uncomfortable. It is often wonderful to read, even if I don't understand a word of it. Like music....it dares me to dig into myself for a thread that will link me to the writer...to the creative force.

---

[43] For me this usually means less than 10 years old.

HOW TO CUT
or
SURVIVING SURGERY

Now that you have chosen an event and a selection, you are ready to "cut" to a required length. Cutting is the process of carving a perfect chunk from the masterwork.

The **FIRST** step in this process is to read the ENTIRE selection. Then you can perform this surgery with educated skill.

While you Read the Whole Thing:

1. Do not be too concerned with the length of anything in the beginning. It is better to have too much material as you start to work on a piece.

2. Consider whether one "scene" can be lifted from the whole. If there is one section that especially interests you, mark it by using a place marker or sticky note. OR photocopy it and mark with a highlighter.

3. Consider whether 2 "scenes" can be joined to create one longer cutting. If there are 2 or 3 places that especially interest you, mark them all.

4. Consider cutting extraneous characters without hurting the flow of action. Think of your cutting as a Michelangelo angel inside a block of marble. Your job is to remove every single scrap that doesn't belong to the angel, so that it can stand alone. As an interpreter you want to carefully remove any bit of story, or extra characters or description that gets in the way of the story you are telling. When you remove everything that doesn't relate, only the angel should be left.

5. Consider whether there is material from another source which seems tied to this one in some way. If so, get a copy of it. Even if you don't think you need it, this weeks' prose may be next weeks POI.

6. Consider whether you will need a "companion" piece for variety or length. This frequently happens in poetry -- and, of course, POI.

7. Will your cutting still make sense when you take your "choices" away from the whole of the material? Will a short transition of explanation enable you to fill in the gaps so that it makes sense?

8. One helpful technique is to decide the last line of your cutting and then cut everything that doesn't lead to that last line.

When you have made the decisions about what parts you think you are going to use, you are ready to begin ....

The cutting copy:

1. **ALWAYS** cut from a photocopy or something other than the original source.

2. **Always** keep a clean copy of the **whole** piece for reference later.

3. Make an extra copy for your coach to work from if that should become necessary.

4. Write authors, book titles, piece titles, where found, etc. on the copies.

5. Cutting with pencil is better than with some kind of permanent marker. You might need to put material back. Therefore, on your copy lightly mark all possible cuts in pencil ...PENCIL ...**PENCIL**.

6. Don't be afraid to cut short in length. This way you don't **have** to hurry in performance **or** worry about going overtime.

   NOTE: Completed group selections are called programs; The individual selections are called pieces.

   Pre-timing may be useful. Find out how long it takes <u>you</u> to slowly read a page. If a page takes 3 minutes, 6 pages will take about 18. So, before you cut, determine about what percentage needs to be removed. It saves time.

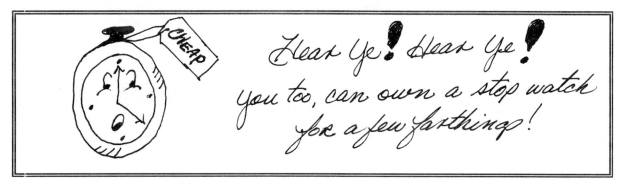

Where possible, cut large segments rather than small bits. Cutting "chunks" is better, if you can do it without harming the selection.

As a novice, please start with a section of a work, not the whole novel or a whole play. Although those can been done, it is a much longer and more complex job.

There may be some instances when certain changes might be made, such as, changing tense, or omitting passages. **But**, before doing much of this, you will want to consult a coach!

Remember, ethics demand that the integrity of the piece remain. Don't twist the authors intent or word to your desire.

Rules of Thumb:

1. Cut minor characters.
2. Cut tag lines such as "he said" wherever possible.
3. Cut out repetitions.
4. Parenthetical expressions can usually go.
5. Try to keep the number of characters (including narrator) down to 3 or 4, or less. This, of course, depends on your ability to "do" characters and the importance of those characters.
6. Minor points or uninteresting side issues/subplots can be easily cut. (Or they may turn out to **be** the cutting)
7. When cutting poetry, be very careful of rhyme, meter and such. In poetry, cut by stanza if at all possible.
8. Remember, you can use transitions to bridge gaps.
9. Of course you must be careful that what is left after you've finished cutting is more than an outline; leave some meat on the bones of the ideas.

After the first cut:

1. Read **aloud** at a reasonable rate and time the reading. [ALOUD TAKES LONGER.]
2. Be certain that neither the author's purpose/central idea nor his style has been distorted by your cutting. Be equally certain that the essence of the characters and their intent is not distorted.
3. Remember: It is important that the audience feel that it is receiving a complete unified experience, not a series of fragments.
4. Does the cutting have a beginning, middle, and end?
5. Does the cutting make sense by itself?
6. Are there "jumps" and "skips"? Fill them in, if possible, or figure out acceptable transitions.
7. If it is a Duo, is the scene balanced between performers?

AFTER THE FIRST TIMED READ-THROUGH:

If you are still overtime, cut some more even it if hurts. A good rule of thumb requires, that each piece be cut one minute under the maximum time. This includes intro and transitions because the tendency in interpretation is that you get slower as analysis gets deeper. So.... Begin again. When you can't cut anymore, get help. Ask a coach to cut on it for a while[44] (expect this process to take at least 2 or 3 days).

---

[44] Before your coach attacks the cutting, warn them of any line without which, you would be in a major funk.

THE PHYSICAL SCRIPT/BINDER
or
HOW TO ASSEMBLE AND TRAIN YOUR NEW BODY APPENDAGE

THE FOLDER:

All prepared scripts for interp events are housed in a notebook/folder which is held during performance. Reading from that script is a part of your overall skill.

Competition folders come in all shapes and sizes. In our part of the world we use the small size, about 6 X 8 X 1.75 inches. They are usually relatively stiff, black and 3 ring. But, these details vary from region to region[45].

The stiffness and small size seems to make the folder easier to handle -- a definite plus. A dark color is preferred in nearly all regions because it is less distracting to the audience. After all, the purpose of the script is not to draw attention to itself. Therefore, help yourself by keeping that binder unadorned, no gold trim or school logo. The folders are 3 ringed because....well, because that is the way they are manufactured most of the time. Your area can have entirely different ideas with rationale that is just as sound. Your coach will know the standard for your region.

No matter what kind of folder you have, if it has a little inside pocket, this is a nice place for keeping notes on schedules of rounds, etc. But, don't pack the pocket with dangerous flying objects. It just doesn't look professional to have your good luck marble fall out and roll across the judges foot. If you don't have a little pocket, you could use a blank first page on which all of your important notes can be written. Just keep the pockets neat and unstuffed. A picture of Jim Morrison taped to the inside is distracting if the audience glimpses it. This helps you look professional.

You might want to keep a small **pencil** or pen in your folder - firmly attached. This way, you'll always have something readily available if you want to jot down a title or author that you like.

Mark your folder. Your name, school name, and a phone number should be written somewhere in/on the folder in a place that will not show as you perform. With 100 or more little black folders at a competition, it gets really hard to find the owner of the script left in the upstairs bathroom of the Science Building, especially if it has no name in it. Never mark it on the outside. NEVER.

Most folders can be purchased at an office supply store or at the college bookstore. Buy a sturdy binder. They get opened and closed a lot. We suggest that when you shop for one, try it on, so to speak. Check how it feels in your hand. Does it flop? Does it feel sturdy? Does it make your hand sweat? Is it easy to grip with one hand? Some are a little too slick and are thus harder to hold when you get a little tense.

Once you own a binder, you will want to practice your interp selections with it as soon as possible. The following page will help you get the material into the script and guide you in its use. From now on, this binder is an inseparable part of you. Use it every time you rehearse. You want to learn to feel that it is a natural extension of your arm.

---

[45]Basic black seems to be universally favored.

ASSEMBLING THE SCRIPT:

There are several thing to consider when assembling your script:

Paper
People use many different types of paper. Some people use notebook paper (lined or unlined), some use typing paper (folded in half for small folders), and some use heavy stationary. Most use both front and back of paper so that there are fewer page turns. Use whatever makes you happiest and is approved by your coach. All of these are acceptable.

Spacing
Your reading can be made easier by controlling the way space is used on the page. Spacing can be what ever you wish but, a space and a half or double space seems to be the norm. This allows you room to mark the script with your personal markings without crowding the text. If you use a small size script, the pages usually have 45 lines per page as a maximum.

By the way, some people hand write their script, but most type. The act of writing the words (in either format) seems to help competitors remember them, so it is best if you do it yourself.

Pagination
This is arranging the words so you can turn the page at the right psychological moment -- as a transition, or after the climax instead of during, for instance. Plan the page turns. Think of appropriate spots. You can destroy a magic moment in your performance with a poorly planned page turn, and you can dramatically build an effect with a well planned one.

Numbering
Numbering the pages is a good idea. You can quickly tell if every page is there and in order. A designation with the number is better: DI-1 or Prose-5, in case they accidentally get shuffled. This is especially true if you are a person who moves material within the folder frequently.

Margin
Don't forget that the margin must be adjusted for the holes in the page, if you do not use plastic page protectors. There will be different margin adjustments for the front and the back of the sheet of paper. And if you do use page protectors, you must allow margin space for them.

Slicks
Plastic page protectors are called "slicks". They are "sleeves" or pockets that you slip your script pages into, and then put into your forensic folder. There are many kinds of slicks: non-glare and foggy; clear and glarey; those with solid bottom; those with bottom and top open; those with reinforced ring holes or without reinforcement. Make your choice according to your own likes and dislikes. This is another personal or team preference choice. However, those with closed bottoms seem to prevent page fallout.

When you purchase slicks: take your folder with you so that you can check hole size and placement of the holes. Some times the holes in the slicks won't line-up with the rings in your folder. You will also need to check that the slick will not stick out when the folder is closed. These things vary and are important when you begin to use the folder.

If you use slicks, consider buying a box and splitting with your teammates. It will take more slicks than you think to house all of your events (and they are much cheaper by the box.)

Slicks are **NOT** essential. Some people do **not** to use them, especially before the selection is completely cut. Some people find it awkward to take pages out of the slicks to make changes. Some find the glare a problem. Some have trouble turning the pages with slicks. They are, however, becoming more and more standard. The main advantage is that they protect your pages from the wear and tear of countless rehearsals. To be slicked or not to be slicked, that is the question. This is something you must decide on your own.

Word processing

The use of word processing is the miracle of the century. It allows for easy changing in your pieces. This means a lot when you are changing versions faster than underwear.

Aside from ease of change, word processing has some unique advantages that some of you may take advantage of. If you have access to a word processor, you can vary the size of the print. For instance, we have used large bold print for dyslexic competitors.

Organization

Some people rearrange the contents of their folders between rounds so that the next event is at the front of their folder. This isn't that important, but some competitors want the script to look "even" in performance. If your folder becomes too bulky, you may need two folders.

Another organization technique is to buy/or make dividers to fit your folder. If you do this, label the event on the tab, then you will always know where each event script is in your folder.

MARKING THE SCRIPT:

Everyone does this to suit themselves. It is very personal. We have however noted some things that seem to be common and are usually helpful. You might find them so.

* Some use different colored highlighters to designate such things as different character's lines.

* Some use the margins to draw little arrows or other such reminders for the locations for focus.

* Some use the margins to write such personal things such: "slow down here"; "begin to build".

* Some use the margins to write motivational notes like: "Go for it"; "You're doing fine".

* Some mark their pages with pronunciations, indications for pauses, emphasized words, inflections.

* Some people put paper clips to mark places so that they can find the correct place to open the folder after having closed it for a transition or introduction.

* Other devices that can be used in the same way are index tabs or sticky notes.

Feel free to try anything that makes working with the script easier for you. After all, it's your script.

USING THE SCRIPT:

Get your script into a folder as soon as the rough cut is approved, so that you can get used to the weight and balance and turning the pages. Of course, you will still have revisions to make in your script, but you need to be learning the physical tricks of using it, at the same time.

You will find your own technique for holding and using your script. Some use two hands: one holds place and the other holds the script. Some hold the folder in their palm. Some hold it with their thumb making a hook at the bottom of the page. Do whatever is most comfortable and allows you to turn pages efficiently.

It is okay, during performance, to switch the hand holding the folder, as long as the exchange is smooth.

SPECIAL NOTE: Check before you get up to perform to see if your script is upside-down.

One of the mystiques of tournament surrounds the opening of the folder. Many forensic squads have signature openings, and many individuals have developed unique styles of their own. But, no matter how you open the folder you should remember that the purpose of opening it is to get the interpretation started. It is the beginning of your interpretation. Therefore, the opening should be consistent with the mood you want to establish. This may seem picky, but it matters and it works.

When using the script....
 ...bring it up, not your head down.
 ...move your eyes down, not your head.
 ...do not bring the script higher up than your heart.
 ...do not flap your script around like a butterfly.
 ...do not let the top droop toward the audience. They do not wish to read it for you.
 ...The audience should never see the written word. This is known as "showing your underwear".

At those times when the script is closed, competitors usually keep it about the waist level. The most important thing is to hold it in a way that is natural looking and comfortable for you. If you don't use markers, use your finger to mark the place. Speak, then hold your pose for a beat, open the folder, look at the page, look at the audience and......begin!

Turning pages should be smooth and usually unobtrusive. If you want to make a statement with a page turn (i.e. time change, location change), be bold and clean.

INTRODUCTIONS AND TRANSITIONS
FOR
INTERPRETIVE EVENTS

INTRODUCTIONS: For forensic contests, an intro MUST include the author and the title. In addition:

It is the audience's opportunity to meet you -- the performer.

It must be delivered naturally -- just as if you were talking to the audience ...a real one-on-one feeling.

It must set the mood.

It is usually short (a minute or less).

It often states a theme (establishing a rhetorical situation).

It is the interpreter's opportunity to convey information to the audience and to prepare them for the selection emotionally.

It must be memorized.

It should be performed with the script closed.

The introduction does not always come at the first of a performance. It can be preceded by a pre-intro. A pre-intro is a snippet of the piece or a "teaser". It is just like movies or TV shows that do a preview before they run the opening credits. Pre-intros are normally less than a minute so that your audience doesn't start to wonder if you forgot to do your intro. At the same time, pre-intros less than 30 seconds may not be worth the effort. They are very effective in some material.

**TO AVOID CRITICISM --
DO NOTHING,
SAY NOTHING,
BE NOTHING.**

Elbert Hubbard

TRANSITIONS:

Transitions are bridges between two parts of a program that MUST include the title and author of the next piece.

IN ADDITION:

They are used to tie together, thematically, two pieces, or to connect two pieces which need explanation such as a time transition.

They must link the last part of one piece to the first part of the next piece--they bridge ideas.

They show how these two go together or why they follow each other, usually through a connecting theme.

They should bind two selections seamlessly.

They should not leave the audience feeling that the mood has been broken from one selection or scene to the next.

They must be delivered naturally-- another chance for the audience to hear you as a real person

They must be performed with the script closed.

They must be memorized.

They occasionally are very long. Sometimes they may be short--one or two sentences. The length is not as important as the effect.

BOTH INTROS AND TRANSITIONS:

They are typed and put into the script when they are new. After they are memorized, they may be removed, but it is a good idea to keep them in your script somewhere.

They are both included in your time limit.

Extemporaneous intros and transitions rarely have the impact of a carefully written, beautifully rehearsed, spontaneous "sounding" one.

As you perform an introduction or transition your folder is closed. Therefore, you would be smart to let your finger hold your place, and/or mark those pages with paper clips or tabs.

CREATING CHARACTERS FOR INTERPRETATION

Occasionally you may hear interpers refer to characters as "voices". This concept seems to encourage interesting voices, but very flat characterizations. It is probably more helpful if you try to develop fully rounded people (or animals or whatever) to put behind those "voices". What you are creating here are tiny jewel-like performances, some of them only a line or two long, that must be distinctive and memorable. The brevity of the role only means that the character becomes more distilled, more concentrated, more perfect.

Once you are very familiar with your selection, you can begin in earnest to develop the characters. One successful method of creating those characters follows:

1. In order to do those thumbnail portraits (on a giant 10 minute canvas) you must first isolate each character. Using a separate piece of paper for each character, identify that character. Be sure to include the narrator of each selection and the person to whom the narrator is speaking (even if that person never speaks).

2. On each character's page, write all the information **that is in the text** about that character. Then expand to include who the character is speaking to, and what propelled him to talk now to this person about this topic.

3. Next, write as complete a **physical** description of each of them as you can. This is probably where you are going to kick in your own imagination.

4. Now gossip! Tell all that you know about this character. Fill the page with what they are doing, with whom and why? Don't leave out any of the juicy details. Tell what they are doing in your selection and why...the amplified version. And what the relationships are with each other.

5. By now, you should be beginning to <u>know</u> these characters. Can you close your eyes and see each one? What do they sound like in your mind? Go ahead. Imagine them speaking. <u>That</u> is the voice you want them to have. It is the one that belongs to them. Relax, don't force it. Let the characters help you make the decisions. It will change subtly as you learn more about them. But, if you can hold this visual image in your mind you will bring the imagined character to life. Don't be afraid to experiment. This is a victory that you will want to share with your coach when you think you have mastered it. Keep that mental image. If your were telling this "story" to a friend, in a lively version, what voice would you use?

6. If you are serious about making "real" rounded characters, continue to build details around them. Form real histories, imagine the details of their day, how they dress, where they live.... Each layer makes them more substantial.

7. Remember that every action is a reaction to something -- something that happened in the moment before. Create a "moment before" for each character. Construct a situation which brought them into the moment of your selection. Then when you perform, you have a firm base for them. It is easier to "find" them if you know where they come from. Some interpreters refer to this as "the spot" or "the place" where they go to "find" their characters. Don't be afraid to experiment. Try the easy and the very far reaches. When you hit the right combination, you will know.

   Remember that visualization and imagination are the most precious tools that an interper has, next to the words of a great writer.

8. Try to physicalize the character. Some physical change or facial change or gestures that suggests the character physically will make him/her more identifiable to the audience and to you.

9. Once the character is firmly developed and easy to visualize, you will find it natural to have a focus and "voice". The work that you have done in building this character will help you create an air of reality for yourself, as well as your characters, that will make them "come alive" for you and your audience. The more details that you add and the more that you rehearse, the easier the characters are to create and control.

THIS ONE STEP --

CHOOSING A GOAL AND STICKING TO IT --

CHANGES EVERYTHING.

Scott Reed

FOCUS IN INTERPRETATION
or
Where Do I Look?

To make literature "come alive" for yourself and your audience, you need to have clear and distinct focus that is appropriate to the literature. By its simplest definition, focus means where you look or place your eyes. But a more in-depth definition would say, focus involves careful analysis of the literature to motivate the reader to focus in a certain place. One of the aspects of focus is that it helps create the reality of multiple characters by enabling the audience to see the different characters through your eyes as you "become" the other character. ...It is similar to watching a child play with an imaginary friend -- the child "looks" at the friend.

There are six types of focus.[46] We will look at each one separately:

1. On stage or direct

2. Inward (reflective)

3. Direct audience

4. Offstage - character placement

5. Offstage - on the action or on an object

6. On script

First, lets look at a description of each of these focuses as they apply to an individual interpreter in forensics and then special hints as to how that specific focus applies in duo interpretation.
However, please understand that focus is sometimes easier to demonstrate than it is to read about. Therefore, you may want to watch demonstrations by fellow seasoned teammates in addition to reading about them. Perhaps the combination of our descriptions and a demonstration will make focusing come into "focus" for you.

---

[46] According to Dr. Vera Simpson, retired Professor of Oral Interpretation, Texas Tech University

1. **ON STAGE (DIRECT) FOCUS**

   This focus is not often used in competition. It is used primarily in the theatre, when one character directly looks at another character while performing a play.

2. **INWARD (REFLECTIVE) FOCUS**

   This type of focus is used anytime the speaker (narrator or character) is thinking reflectively (i.e. talking to him/herself). It does not mean staring in a direction, but more nearly gazing. The direction of the gaze is a tool that is individualized by the interpreter. Consider where you, personally, look when you are contemplating or thinking. You probably use a variety of focuses - so you should with INWARD focus when interpretation asks you to "think".

3. **DIRECT AUDIENCE FOCUS**

   The literature is often written so that the speaker (narrator or character) is talking to the audience. In these instances, the interpreter should choose to look directly at them. You should allow this gaze to move naturally through the audience to make it seem as realistic as possible. [Holding a person's gaze for a few seconds before moving to another person's]   Intros and transitions almost always use direct audience focus.

4. **OFFSTAGE FOCUS - CHARACTER PLACEMENT**

   Offstage focus is used when more than one character is involved in the chosen selection (even if that means the narrator and one other character). You must analyze the literature carefully to determine where each speaker should be placed; which 'speakers' will be placed slightly to the right or left. Try not to place your characters too far apart because your audience would then only see the sides of your face as you shift from character to character, and they begin to feel as if they are at a tennis match, craning their necks from side to side. Remember who you are talking to, how tall they are in relation to this character, etc. As your skill in character development increases, your focus for each character should creep closer and closer to the center until only a slight inclination of angle is left. However, that tiny bit is vitally important. Get it right!

Note: Remember that when you look at people, you don't just look in their eyes. Focus is the same.

In duo interpretation, the two interpreters have two options when using offstage focus:

(1) straight
(2) cross focus

Cross focus is taught in most of the oral interpretation texts, so let's look at it first.

In cross focus, you see your partner as if his/her body were projected in a mirror 2 to 4 feet in front of you. The best way to learn cross focus is to practice 2 to 4 feet in front of a mirror. You stand approximately 10 inches apart and turn ever so slightly toward one another. Obviously there is some room here for creative license, but this is the general beginning - the rest is determined by the literature.

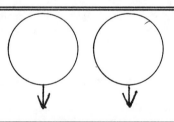

DUO OFF-STAGE CROSS FOCUS

Movement with off stage focus must be done with that mirrored partner, not the one beside you. No fair touching or peeking at the real one. In duo, off-stage focus requires that action also be done in the same "mirror". No touching (In an off-stage kiss, no lips touch.) Respond in a mirror. This is tricky at first and great fun once you get the hang of it.

Straight focus is similar, except that each performer sees his partner in a mirror directly in front of him. The focus does not cross at 2 feet.

DUO OFF-STAGE STRAIGHT FOCUS

5. **OFFSTAGE FOCUS - ON ACTION OR OBJECT**

Descriptive literature often requires an interpreter to either visualize a 'scene' as if it were being reenacted or to visualize an object as if it were real. This focus is similar to INWARD focus, but different, because instead of focusing on nothingness while thinking - you actually project images with your brain that the audience can see. Believe it or not, audiences will see what you see.

6. **ON SCRIPT FOCUS**

Every interpreter should refer to his/her script occasionally. After all, the script is the symbol for interpretation itself. However, a wise interpreter will find appropriate places to look down in his/her script and will not have too much head bobbing (up and down) or too much reliance on the script.

NARRATOR - Inward, direct adience	
NARRATOR + 1 CHARACTER - Inward, direct & off-stage	OR
NARRATOR + 2 CHARACTERS - Inward, direct & off-stage	
2 CHARACTERS - Off-stage	

WORKING FORENSICS: A Competitor's Guide

WHAT JUDGES LOOK FOR IN INTERPRETIVE EVENTS

There are as many styles of judging as there are judges, and each one looks for different things in a performance. This list is an attempt to identify <u>some</u> of those for you:

An introduction that
- ..... catches their attention
- ..... is original
- ..... is not longer than the selection! [usually 45 seconds to 1.5 minutes
- ..... makes you want to hear the selections(s)
- ..... has a natural delivery
- ..... that lets you meet the real person standing there

Transitions that are
- ..... smooth
- ..... not too long, not too short - just right
- ..... natural-- the audience meets a real person
- ..... logical bridges from selection to selection (and continues development of theme
- .....informative

The selection(s) should have:

Action suitable to the demands of the material while being creative and original
Builds in action and emotion that are well planned
Well developed characters
Clear distinction between characters
Correct focus for all characters, including the narrator
Gestures that are not repetitive
A moment before closing folder to briefly hold the mood
Imagery that is apparent--you really see the pictures in your mind
A reason for joining these pieces together (if it is a program)
Killer punch that gives the piece real impact
Enough volume to be easily heard
Strong material choices (difficultly usually counts extra in a tie breaker, this one can make the difference.)
Natural sounding delivery--like you are really talking to us
Not being overtime
Poise and confidence that shows from start to stop
Literature of quality
Real use of your folder; looking at the script; using it as an extension of your performance
Appropriate speed
Enthusiasm
A sense of finality at the end

INTERPRETATION EVENTS

DESCRIPTIONS & WORKSHEETS

INTERPRETATION EVENTS
How to Begin - Phase 1: The Commitment

In this sub-section of Interp Events, you will find general information for each event including: other names that events are known by (AKA), generic rules, and a few additional notes that explain aspects of the event that are worthy of note, and then there will be a set of worksheets (divided into 6 phases).

Before you can truly begin to work on ANY type of interp however, you must first complete PHASE ONE.

PHASE ONE: COMMITMENT

If you have not decided which events in which you wish to compete, NOW IS THE TIME. Quit procrastinating. If you skipped it before, now is the time to turn back and read (or re-read) "HOW TO CHOOSE EVENTS".

.... Now!... .We'll wait for you.

tap tap step-ball-change tap tap step-ball-change shuffle shuffle tap tap tap....[47]

Now, armed with that information, you need to remember that college interp competition comes in many flavors which do not necessarily parallel the high school events with which some of you might be familiar -- so be alerted! The skills involved are the desire to research and find material your love, analyze it, cut it, and analyze some more, getting familiar and practicing until your performance style is easy and natural!

You now have enough knowledge concerning the general procedures for each type of interp. Which one or ones interest you most? You are ready to go to the page that has the event name in bold print and begin. However, ... before you do, let us forewarn you. This Phase One was the easiest phase to read (although, we are well aware that true commitment may be the most difficult to achieve). Phase Two through Phase Six of the worksheets are at times laborious lists. Let us gently remind you (once again) that the title of this text has the word "working" in it. We never said it would be a cake walk? You're not backing out are you? Of course not! You have made a commitment. You want to learn and grow and become an effective interper. Go to your first interp event choice. [By the way, work the phases IN ORDER and don't forget the coaching that accompanies.]

---

[47] OK, OK, so we're not the Rockettes. At least we know how to have fun!

PROSE INTERPRETATION
or
HAVE I GOT A STORY FOR YOU

AKA: Prose; Pro

COMPANION READING:

FINDING AND SELECTING INTERPRETIVE MATERIAL
THE INTERPER'S FIRST SOJOURN INTO THE LIBRARY
AN APPROACH TO LITERATURE - INTERPRETATION IN GENERAL
LITERARY MERIT

GENERIC RULES:

A selection or selections of prose material of literary merit, which may be drawn from more than one source. Play cuttings are prohibited. Use of manuscript is required. Time limit is 10 minutes.

MATERIAL:

Material for this event can include any published literature which is not poetry or drama. This could include: short stories, novels, essays, letters, speeches, or cereal box tops[48].
Whether you cut a chapter, a section, or a whole novel, it must have some kind of beginning, middle and end. It must make sense to someone that has not read it.

Some years, novels are the big deal. Don't let this bother you. Short stories are still very viable as material, as are all the other forms of prose. Go for quality and/or new stuff. The point is that the material should be well written and new enough to hold the interest of a judge that probably reads a lot. Or it can be new-old stuff. Example: a lesser known story by a well known author; a seldom done section of a well known book. Or, if you are really brave, it can be a classic selection--maybe a less familiar section than the obvious choice. Most importantly, the prose should speak to you--have something to say that you think is worth saying.

The Companion Reading will help fill in any holes.

    REMEMBER: CHECK WITH YOUR COACHES AT EACH STEP OF THE WAY.

---

[48] Well, legally cereal box tops **are** prose, but realistically, most don't have enough literary value.

PROSE WORKSHEETS PHASE 2.1

PROSE INTERPRETATION WORKSHEET
Phase 2: SELECTING THE LITERATURE

WHY DO THIS PHASE?

This phase's necessity is pretty obvious: without the hunting and selecting the literature, you don't have the event. It's time to learn how to find material on your own[49].

WARNING: This phase requires either a lot of luck or a lot of what is often very frustrating work. You may stumble across your "perfect" material quickly OR you have to kiss a lot of "literary" frogs to find your royal piece.

COMPANION READING:

FINDING AND SELECTING INTERPRETIVE MATERIAL
THE INTERPER'S FIRST SOJOURN INTO THE LIBRARY
AN APPROACH TO LITERATURE INTERPRETATION IN GENERAL
LITERARY MERIT

FINDING YOUR SELECTIONS:

____ 1. Do you have your library card?

____ 2. Have you collected your dimes for photocopying?

____ 3. Begin a list of your favorite authors and/or stories and/or novels and/or chapters of novels.

____ 4. You may want to check anthologies of <u>contemporary</u> short stories to find authors you like. Then, if you need other literature, look for more works by those writers.

____ 5. Check the Card Catalogue and/or any Short Story or Fiction Guide listed by subject, title, or writer.

---

[49]This comment is addressed to folks who have in the past been "given" their pieces. We know that you, personally have never been in this situation -- you have always said "Coach, I'd rather do it myself".

WORKING FORENSICS: A Competitor's Guide

PROSE WORKSHEETS PHASE 2.2

_____ 6. Check literary magazines like <u>The New Yorker</u>, or even less lofty publications like <u>Redbook</u> or the <u>Hitchcock Digest</u>.

_____ 7. Ask your English teacher or any person who loves to read to give you suggestions of a favorite story or chapter in a longer work.

_____ 8. Have you reviewed "FINDING AND SELECTING INTERPRETIVE MATERIAL?" for the selection criteria?

PROSE WORKSHEETS PHASE 3.1

PROSE INTERPRETATION WORKSHEET
Phase 3: CUTTING

COMPANION READING:

HOW TO CUT

You will find very specific guidelines for cutting in the HOW TO CUT section. This list will help guide you through a double check to be sure you are on track. Check the time limit for the event you are about to cut. Remember that performance of interp takes longer as more analysis is done. So, allow for that. You will also be adding an introduction which will consume time, so cut shorter than you think you need.
Now, complete the following checklist as you cut.

_____ 1. Have you read the entire selection(s)? This is important in order to find the perfect "scene" to give you a grasp of the whole of the literature.

_____ 2. Have you located the part that appeals to you? You are looking for the page or paragraph that really "speaks" to you, touches you in some way, stands out from the rest. When you locate this key passage, look around for what completes it in the whole of the work.

_____ 3. Photocopy those parts which you think will work. All those parts. Even if you aren't sure which ones will go together.

_____ 4. Working from your key passage, is it possible to find a complete "piece" with a beginning, a building climax, and a conclusion. Is it possible to borrow from throughout the entire work to put together the story? Without warping either the character or the authors intent? This is an ethical matter of great importance.

> ### LIFE IS FULL OF THINGS WE DON'T WANT TO DO.
>
> Her Mother

PROSE WORKSHEETS PHASE 3.2

_____ 5. To quickly try to make a coherent entirety, try the "cut and tape" method. Using the photocopies, actually cut out those sections-- (even if its just words or half a sentence) that you want to use and assemble them on a blank piece of paper with tape, in order. [Keep an uncut one!] You can then arrange and rearrange to your hearts content, using a pencil, mark, out things to be omitted.
Look for missing links, try on new endings, whatever is necessary to get it "right." Then photocopy the finished product so you won't be compromised by (bits of script literally falling off your paper) words. This can be your "rough cutting". As you answer the following questions.

    A. Is the cutting complete with a beginning and an ending that is satisfying?
    B. Does the action in the middle build?
    C. Does it make sense without the rest of the story?
    D. Is their a stronger, more interesting opening /closing some other place in the literature?
    E. Will this cutting keep the audience emotionally involved all the way to the end of the performance.
    F. Does this cutting have variety in mood? Can you find a way to give it that variety, either through additions to the cutting or performance?
    G. Does this cutting allow you to spotlight the things that you do best in performance?

_____ 6. Read it out as well as you can at this phase.

Current time of rough cut:_____

If the cutting is still too long:

Review "Rules of Thumb" under **HOW TO CUT** and/or get some help from your coach and/or from a more seasoned teammate.

If the cutting is too short:

Is there another segment you can add in? Does it need a long introduction to give information or set the mood?

Remember to allow time for your introduction and/or needed transitions.

Re-read the rough cutting out loud and re-time it.

Current time of rough cut:_____

WORKING FORENSICS: A Competitor's Guide

PROSE WORKSHEETS PHASE 4.1

PROSE INTERPRETATION WORKSHEET
Phase 4: PRELIMINARY ANALYSIS

WHY DO THIS PHASE?

At this phase of development, you as an interpreter are ready to begin the process of learning all there is to know about the literature you chose because it caused a response in you. In the course of examining it more closely than you have probably ever looked at literature, you will hopefully find that you like it better all the time. Like true love[50].

COMPANION READING:

CREATING CHARACTERS FOR INTERPRETATION
FOCUS IN INTERPRETATION

Write your answers on a separate sheet of paper.

THE AUTHOR:

Frequently background information will give you big clues to understanding the literature, as well as help for writing introductions.

____ 1. Who was the author and why do you think he wrote this selection? Really dig into the motivation for writing as it may open a door to understanding that you can't find any other way.

____ 2. When was this selection written and does that matter? Use some thought on this one! Examine what was happening to the world when it was written. What was happening to the author? How is that reflected in what was written? How does it affect how you feel about the selection? How will you use this to make an audience respond to the literature?

---

[50]Corny analogy, but... true!

PROSE WORKSHEETS PHASE 4.2

THE SELECTION(S):

___ 1. Who is speaking? Be specific–<u>someone</u> is speaking. 'The narrator' is **not** enough. Tell something about him/her.

___ 2. To whom is he/she speaking? Specifically–even if it is the audience. Another use-your-imagination question! Be complete. The best choice is to speak to one person. Someone who matters.

___ 3. When does this story take place? Where?

___ 4. What happens in the action before your selection begins? (The moment before)

___ 5. Describe briefly each character, including their appearance, movement, and voice. Don't shortcut here. You need to be able to visualize these people when you present them to an audience.

___ 6. What is the mood at the opening of the selection? See it as a color, or an image.

___ 7. What is the mood at the end of the selection? Visualize it again.

___ 8. What caused the change?

___ 9. At what point (word/line) does the change take place?

___ 10. What other places in the cutting are pivotal?

___ 11. Current time of cutting:_____

Schedule a coaching session. Please bring worksheet completed to this point, the cutting with any changes copied for coach, & a PENCIL.

PROSE WORKSHEETS PHASE 5.1

PROSE INTERPRETATION WORKSHEET
Phase 5: THE PHYSICAL SCRIPT AND CONTINUED ANALYSIS

COMPANION READING:

THE PHYSICAL SCRIPT
INTRODUCTIONS AND TRANSITIONS FOR INTERPRETATIVE EVENTS

INTRODUCTION:

_____ 1. How much time is left for your introduction? Allow a little (30 seconds, say) for your improvement as a reader and another space (15 seconds, say) to cushion you from the deadly over time problem. What is left is the maximum amount of time you have left for introduction.

_____ 2. If your selection needs more introduction than you have time for, guess where you get it? Yep, back to the cutting board!

_____ 3. Looking at the selection, decide:

    A. What information does the audience **have to have** to understand the piece?
    B. What is the selection (your cutting) about? Write the "theme" in a sentence.
    C. Why should the audience want to hear this selection?
       Understanding? Entertainment? Catharsis?
    D. What mood do you want to create?

_____ 4. Now just tell us the responses to those investigative probes -- as if <u>you</u> were <u>telling</u> us -- only write down what you would have said. This is the beginning of you intro.

_____ 5. Be sure to include author and title in your introduction.

_____ 6. Look at that introduction (rough as it is!) Can you make it more streamlined? Telescope ideas more compactly?

_____ 7. Can you make your first sentence so "something" (intriguing, unique, dramatic, tantalizing) that the audience is captured by it?

_____ 8. This is not your final introduction. It is your working introduction. It will be revised and refined again. But if it fits within your time limit and your coach approves it, memorize it. The introduction will be performed with a closed folder exactly as if you were just sharing your thoughts about the cutting with a few friends.

PROSE WORKSHEETS PHASE 5.2

TRANSITIONS:

A NOTE ABOUT TRANSITIONS: When at all possible, transitions should be a part of the selection, rather than an intrusive message in the flow of prose. When it is impossible to avoid this follow this advice:

_____ 1. Tell the audience what it needs to know.

_____ 2. Tie your theme and selections together.

_____ 3. Mention the title and author of the next piece - if different.

_____ 4. Keep the transition as brief as possible.

CONTINUING ANALYSIS:

_____ 1. **Imagery** involves the reader "seeing" images or ideas as you perform. In order to do that you need to isolate and identify those images. Take you script and look at it (from the first word). On a piece of paper write what you see and when. While you may not have to write all the detail, you should be able to visualize in absolute reality detail. This skill will develop more clearly as you continue to work with the cutting. [I.E. "it was the best of time. It was the worst of times." What is the speaker seeing? The past? The revolution? His family? His own role in what happened? Do you see that the more specific the choice, the more emotional flavor it has?] If you see it, the audience can see it as well.

_____ 2. **Don't throw away any idea.** The audience will notice. Some ideas take more effort than others to unlock.

_____ 3. Work on **motivation** for each character in your selection. Why do they do what they do? Don't take them for granted -- find out.

Read your selection for a small group of persons, maybe your teammates, and note their response.

_____ 1. Where did they get bored?

_____ 2. Where were they interested?

_____ 3. Where did they laugh?

_____ 4. Did they have an emotional response? Where? Was it the response you wanted them to have?

_____ 5. Based on their responses, what changes do you want to make?

PROSE WORKSHEETS PHASE 5.3

Now prepare your performance script as directed in **"THE PHYSICAL SCRIPT"**.

By this time, you should know your piece very well. You might even have it memorized. However, you must appear to be actually reading when you compete. So...

____ 1. Mark in different color highlighter when different characters speak.

____ 2. Mark the script so that you look down at the right places. Can you make that glance a part of the action?

____ 3. Practice "acting" like you are reading every time you rehearse.

____ 4. Practice page turns. Make them part of the performance. When can you "add something" with a page turn.

PROSE WORKSHEETS PHASE 6.1

PROSE INTERPRETATION WORKSHEET
Phase 6: POLISH AND TAPE

COMPANION READING:

SOME NOTES ON MEMORIZING
PRACTICE PRACTICES
WHAT JUDGES LOOK FOR IN INTERP EVENTS

Make a video tape of your performance, from entering the room to returning to your chair. Watch your own performance critically. If video is not available, make an audio tape.

_____ 1. Do you enter the room like a "champion"?

_____ 2. Do you look natural and comfortable in performance?

_____ 3. Do you look professional in appearance from start to finish?

_____ 4. Each thought and word must be given appropriate weight and meaning. Is your energy maintained consistently?

_____ 5. Does the tempo vary? Enough? Are there effective pauses?

_____ 6. Does the intensity vary?

_____ 7. Do you have distracting mannerisms that need to be axed?

_____ 8. Is there a "dead zone" where the attention wanders? This may be because you don't understand that passage. Don't skip it. Take that section apart and dig into its meaning. It may also be a place where your concentration is weak for some reason. Can the problem be corrected? How? Do you understand how the speaker "feels"?

_____ 9. What changes in volume should occur that didn't? Why?

_____ 10. Is your focus distinct for each character (if you have any)? Are the focuses too far apart? This makes your audience feel as if they are watching tennis!

_____ 11. If you have characters, have you found them physically and vocally? Are there physical differences?

WORKING FORENSICS: A Competitor's Guide

PROSE WORKSHEETS PHASE 6.2

_____ 12. Is your articulation clear and understandable?

_____ 13. Is your imagery clear? Do you really see the images?

_____ 14. Note the mood changes from beginning to the end of the piece. Are they in the appropriate places? Are they strong enough? Too strong?

_____ 15. What is the current time of your piece? _____

After completing the worksheets to this point, the interpreter should continue to rehearse and polish. Work to make each performance consistent, so that you can do the selection perfectly every time. You are never finished. Continue to read out loud daily, to find new audiences (they will teach you new things about your cutting). The coach is still a powerful partner in perfecting this event. So keep going for regular coaching sessions.

POETRY INTERPRETATION

or
STANDING WITH THE STANZAS

AKA: Poetry; Poe.

GENERIC RULES:

A selection or selections of poetry of literary merit, which may be drawn from more than one source. Play cuttings are prohibited. Use of manuscript is required. Time limit is 10 minutes.

WHAT IS IT?:

All of the material in this event is poetry--ANY poetry. This does not mean it has to rhyme, be American, or from a specific era. Just poetry. This includes any work designated as poetry which is imaginative literature arranged in rhythmic structure and usually rich in figures of sound and sense. Poetry with strong dramatic content or poetry that tells a story frequently works well. It is also helpful if the rhyming pattern can be de-emphasized. Sing-song poems rarely do well in competition. Traditionally contemporary poetry seems to fare better than historic poetry (the old stuff). Some contests require that the poetry or poet be published, some do not. Beyond following the rules, what is important is that you like the poetry and feel strongly about what it says.

Poetry is usually selected because it has a strong appeal for the reader, or because it develops his/her theme or provides contrast to other poems in a thematic program.

A program can be one or more pieces of poetry unified by theme. If you use two or more poems, it becomes a program with transitions. A program should have universal appeal, logical sequence, a clear theme, balance, contrast, and a uniqueness. Because poetry tends to be more abstract and/or use more elevated language, the interpreter must be absolutely sure of the meaning. Therefore, this event will require finding poetry that speaks to you, analyzing and rehearsaling... and more rehearsaling.

CHECK WITH YOUR COACH AT EACH STEP OF THE WAY.

POETRY INTERPRETATION WORKSHEET
Phase 2: SELECTING THE LITERATURE

WHY DO THIS PHASE?

This phase's necessity is pretty obvious: without the hunting and selecting the literature, you don't have the event. It's time to learn how to find material on your own[51].

WARNING: This phase requires either a lot of luck or a lot of what is often very frustrating work. You may stumble across your "perfect" material quickly OR you have to kiss a lot of "literary" frogs to find your royal piece.

COMPANION READING:

FINDING AND SELECTING INTERPRETIVE MATERIAL
THE INTERPER'S FIRST SOJOURN INTO THE LIBRARY
AN APPROACH TO LITERATURE INTERPRETATION IN GENERAL
LITERARY MERIT

FINDING YOUR SELECTIONS:

____ 1. Do you have your library card?

____ 2. Have you collected your dimes for photocopying?

____ 3. Begin a list of your favorite poets and/or poems. You may want to make this list a permanent on going one to guide both competition selection, but also your own reading habit.

____ 4. You may want to check anthologies of <u>contemporary</u> poetry to find poets you like. Then, if you need other poetry, look for more works by those poets.

____ 5. Check the Card Catalogue and/or any Poetry Guide listed by subject, title, or poet.

---

[51]This comment is addressed to folks who have in the past been "given" their pieces. We know that you, personally have never been in this situation -- you have always said "Coach, I'd rather do it myself".

POETRY WORKSHEETS PHASE 2.2

____ 6. Check literary magazines like <u>The New Yorker</u> or <u>The Poetry Review</u>.

____ 7. Ask your English teacher or any person who loves to read to give you suggestions of a favorite poem or poet.

____ 8. Have you reviewed "FINDING AND SELECTING INTERPRETIVE MATERIAL?" for the selection criteria?

SELECTION CHOICES:

Fill in these blanks with the literature you want to use for poetry interpretation.

TITLE(S)   POET

_____   _____
_____   _____
_____   _____

Now check with your coach to see if the literature selected is acceptable.

Ready? Answer the following questions:

____ 1. Have you read the entire poem? Or every poem (if you've chosen more than one).

____ 2. Have you made two photocopies of every poem that you are considering in your "program"? [Hereafter, we will talk about the completed group of selections as the "program". The individual selections we will call "pieces".] One copy goes to your coach, one copy you will use to work on.

____ 3. Have you double checked the specific time limits and requirements for the tournaments that you are considering? Remember that they might vary slightly.

4. Do you have...(choose one)

   ____ A. One selection which is long enough and able to sustain the audiences' interest? OR

   ____ B. An interesting poem which needs to be longer? OR

   ____ C. A theme which interests you but can be approached in many different directions with various poems?

WORKING FORENSICS: A Competitor's Guide

POETRY WORKSHEETS PHASE 2.3

If you selected "A" (<u>one selection</u>) check the following items:

_____ 1. Does the poem seem complete (with a beginning and a climax)?

_____ 2. Does it have a strong opening that will make the audience want to hear more?

_____ 3. Does the poem have strong imagery?

_____ 4. Does the poem keep the audience emotionally involved to the end?

_____ 5. Does it have a variety of moods?

If you selected "B" (<u>an interesting poem that needs to be longer</u>) consider:
if your poem is only a tiny bit too short, you might lengthen the introduction. But most likely you will need to find an additional selection (companion piece) to round out your program.
For instance, <u>Casey at the Bat</u> needs a short companion piece. You might want to select the lyrics of one stanza of <u>Take Me Out to the Ball Game</u>[52].

Once you have found possible companion piece(s), complete the following check list:

_____ 1. What is the theme of your original selection? Or the theme to which you wish to link the poems?

   _____

_____ 2. Does the companion piece(s) tie strongly to your theme?

_____ 3. Does it compliment or contrast the theme?

_____ 4. Does it amplify the meaning of the theme?

_____ 5. Can you find another selection that states the theme better?

_____ 6. Do the pieces flow together?

_____ 7. Are they different enough to provide contrast?

_____ 8. Is the shorter selection more effective as a "teaser" (a pre-introductory piece)?

---

[52]Note: 2 of the 3 authors think this is a bad example. Don't ask which one because we promised not to confirm which of us has questionable taste.

170   *WORKING FORENSICS: A Competitor's Guide*

POETRY WORKSHEETS PHASE 2.4

Now, complete the following questions for each piece in your program.

_____ 1. Does the poem seem complete (with a beginning and a climax)?

_____ 2. Does it have a strong opening that will make the audience want to hear more?

_____ 3. Does the poem have strong imagery?

_____ 4. Does the poem keep the audience emotionally involved to the end?

_____ 5. Does it have a variety of moods?

If you selected "C" (a theme which interests you but can be approached in many different directions with various poems) an example might be: Mary Had a Little Lamb, Little Lamb Who Made Thee by Bobbie Burns, and Baa Baa Black Sheep as a short program of poetry with the theme of sheep: showing their social relevance, their religious heritage, and their economic value[53].

Now you need to go to any of the poetry guides, looking under thematic listings, be especially watchful for listings of contemporary poetry, although they are rarely extensively listed. Before you go, you might make a list of synonyms for your theme. Example: Your theme is ghosts. You might look under ghosts, specters, haunting, etc..

After you have selected your companion poems for the program, check the following items:

_____ 1. Does the program build tension toward a conclusion?

_____ 2. Does the program have variety (i.e. humor, pathos, anger)

_____ 3. Does the program catch the audience's attention immediately?

_____ 4. Do they want to hear more after every piece?

_____ 5. Do the selections represent a variety of styles?

_____ 6. Is the order strong or would the intensity build better with a different arrangement?

_____ 7. Have you made 2 photocopies of each poem?

_____ 8. Have you cleared these pieces with your coach?

---

[53] Note: all 3 of the authors thought this was a bad example, but it was fun...!

POETRY WORKSHEETS STEP 2.5

Now read your poetry aloud, as well as you can, and time it.

Current time of each piece:_____, _____, _____, _____.

Total time of your program:_____

Current selection titles, in order, with poets' names:

1._____

2._____

3._____

POETRY WORKSHEETS PHASE 3.1

POETRY INTERPRETATION WORKSHEET
Phase 3: CUTTING

COMPANION READING:

HOW TO CUT

You will find very specific guidelines for cutting in the HOW TO CUT section. This list will help guide you through a double check to be sure you are on track. Check the time limit for the event you are about to cut. Remember that performance of interp takes longer as more analysis is done. So, allow for that. You will also be adding an introduction which will consume time, so cut shorter than you think you need.

NOTE: Poetry is more difficult to cut than many forms of literature because of the rhythm and rhyme.

_____ 1. Double check the time limit for poetry at each contest.

_____ 2. Is there a whole section or stanza that has a subplot or unnecessary description that can be cut?

_____ 3. Can any internal phrase be cut without destroying the flow of the line?

_____ 4. Can parallel cuts be made to keep the structure in line? Remember, if you cut one line you will usually have to cut at least 2 lines in rhymed poetry.

> EXAMPLE: Mary had a lamb
> White as snow
> Everywhere Mary went
> The lamb would go.

_____ 5. Can halves of stanzas be joined to create a new stanza?

_____ 6. Can you begin later than the first line in the poem, omitting some of the first lines?

* Now, re-read your poetry aloud and time it.

Current time of each piece:_____, _____, _____, _____.

Total time of your program:_____

* If it still seems too long, take it to your coach or a seasoned teammate for more individualized help.

POETRY WORKSHEETS PHASE 4.1

POETRY INTERPRETATION WORKSHEET
Phase 4: PRELIMINARY ANALYSIS

WHY DO THIS PHASE?

At this phase of development, you as an interpreter are ready to begin the process of learning all there is to know about the literature you chose **because** it caused a response in you. In the course of examining it, more closely than you have probably ever looked at literature, you will hopefully find that you like it better all the time. Like true love[54].

COMPANION READING:

CREATING CHARACTERS FOR INTERPRETATION
FOCUS IN INTERPRETATION

THE AUTHOR:

Frequently background information will give you big clues to understanding the literature, as well as help for writing introductions.

_____ 1. Who was the poet and why do <u>you</u> think he/she wrote this selection? Really dig into the motivation for writing as it may open a door to understanding that you can't find any other way.

_____ 2. When was this selection written and does that matter? Use some thought on this one! Examine what was happening to the world when it was written. What was happening to the poet? How is that reflected in what was written? How does it affect how you feel about the selection? How will you use this to make an audience respond to the literature?

_____ 3. Express the message of this poem in one sentence.

---

[54]Corny analogy, but... true!

POETRY WORKSHEETS PHASE 4.2

SELECTION(S):

NOTE: Poetry is not all that different from other types of literature as far as the analysis is concerned. It, too, has builds, stories (implied, if not stated), moments before, etc. So, the following questions will work very well IF you can shake that stereotypical image of poetry from your head.

____ 1. Who is speaking? Be specific--<u>someone</u> is speaking. 'The narrator' is **not** enough. Tell something about him/her.

____ 2. To whom is he/she speaking? Specifically--even if it is the audience. Another use-your-imagination question! Be complete. The best choice is to speak to one person. Someone who matters.

____ 3. When does this story take place? Where?

____ 4. What happens in the action before your selection begins? (The moment before)

____ 5. Describe briefly each character, including their appearance, movement, and voice. Don't shortcut here. You need to be able to visualize these people when you present them to an audience.

____ 6. What is the mood at the opening of the selection? See it as a color, or an image.

____ 7. What is the mood at the end of the selection? Visualize it again.

____ 8. What caused the change?

____ 9. At what point (word/line) does the change take place?

____ 10. What other places in the cutting are pivotal?

____ 11. Pay particular attention to title, allusions and the duality of words in poetry. There, perhaps more than in any other literature do they have more importance.

____ 12. Current time of cutting:_____

Now is a good time to show off for your coach. Dazzle them with the clarity of your characters[55], then amaze them with analysis, and pound them with your preparation. It will feel good.

Schedule a coaching session. Please bring worksheet completed to this point, the cutting with any changes copied for coach, & a PENCIL.

---

[55]Remember, even in poetry, you will have at least one character -- the narrator.

WORKING FORENSICS: A Competitor's Guide

POETRY WORKSHEETS PHASE 5.1

POETRY INTERPRETATION WORKSHEET
Phase 5: PHYSICAL SCRIPT AND CONTINUED ANALYSIS

WHY DO THIS PHASE?

While your analysis of the cutting in on-going, other work needs to be done to get you ready for competition. The most pressing of these concerns is an introduction that presents your cutting perfectly. By creating the right mood and giving the audience the information that they need to appreciate your selection, you can insure the attention of your listeners. So follow the worksheet through writing an introduction and further analysis toward poetic perfection.

COMPANION READING:

THE PHYSICAL SCRIPT
INTRODUCTIONS AND TRANSITIONS FOR INTERPRETATIVE EVENTS

INTRODUCTION:

_____ 1. Time the poetry. How much time is left for your introduction? Allow a little (30 seconds, say) for your improvement as a reader and another space (15 seconds, say) to cushion you from the deadly over time problem. What is left is the maximum amount of time you have left for introduction.

_____ 2. If your poetry needs more introduction than you have time for, guess where you get it? Yep, back to the cutting board!

_____ 3. Looking at the poetry, decide:

    A. What information does the audience **have to have** to understand the poetry?
    B. What is the poetry (your cutting) about? Write the "theme" in a sentence.
    C. Why should the audience want to hear this poetry?
       Understanding? Entertainment? Catharsis?
    D. What mood do you want to create?

_____ 4. Now just tell us the responses to those investigative probes — as if <u>you</u> were <u>telling</u> us – only write down what you would have said. it will be the beginning of your intro.

_____ 5. Be sure to include poet(s) and title(s) in your introduction.

_____ 6. Look at that introduction (rough as it is!) Can you make it more streamlined? Telescope ideas more compactly?

_____ 7. Can you make your first line so "something" (intriguing, unique, dramatic, tantalizing) that the audience is captured by it?

POETRY WORKSHEETS PHASE 5.2

_____ 8. This is not your final introduction. It is your working introduction. It will be revised and refined again. But if it fits within your time limit and your coach approves it, memorize it. The introduction will be performed with a closed folder exactly as if you were just sharing your thoughts about the cutting with a few friends.

TRANSITIONS:

Transitions are usually used in poetry to connect selections of poetry. The idea of a transition is to link one thing to the next. It is a bridge to help the audience cross from idea to idea. The method is usually to take a thought or reflection from selection A, tie it securely to your theme then link it to a thought which leads into selection B. Remember to state the author and title of B.

_____ 1. What does the audience need to know in order to understand what is happening?

_____ 2. Did you tie your theme and your selections together?

_____ 3. Did you include the title and author?

_____ 4. Is the transition as brief as possible?

CONTINUING ANALYSIS:

_____ 1. **Imagery** involves the reader "seeing" images or ideas as you perform. In order to do that you need to isolate and identify those images. Take your script and look at it (from the first word). On a piece of paper write what you see and when. While you may not have to write all the detail, you should be able to visualize in absolute reality detail. This skill will develop more clearly as you continue to work with the cutting. [I.E.[56] "It was the best of time. It was the worst of times." What is the speaker seeing? The past? The revolution? His family? His own role in what happened? Do you see that the more specific the choice, the more emotional flavor it has?] If you see it, the audience can see it as well.

_____ 2. **Don't throw away any idea.** The audience will notice. Some ideas take more effort than others to unlock.

_____ 3. Work on **motivation** for each character in your selection. Why do they do what they do? Don't take them for granted -- find out.

---

[56] We know the example is from prose! We just wanted to see if you were paying attention.

WORKING FORENSICS: A Competitor's Guide

POETRY WORKSHEETS PHASE 5.3

Read your selection for a small group of people, maybe your teammates, and note their response.

_____ 1. Where did they get bored?

_____ 2. Where were they interested?

_____ 3. Where did they laugh?

_____ 4. Did they have an emotional response? When?

_____ 5. Based on their responses, what changes do you want to make?

Now prepare your performance script as directed in **THE PHYSICAL SCRIPT**.

By this time, you should know your program very well. You may even have it memorized. However, you must appear to be actually reading when you compete. So...

_____ 1. Mark the script so that you look down at the best places. Can you use that glance at the script as a part of the action?

_____ 2. Then practice "acting" like you are reading every time you rehearse.

_____ 3. Practice page turns. Make them part of your performance.

_____ 4. Mark each "character" in a different color highlighter (if more than narrator).

POETRY WORKSHEETS PHASE 6.1

POETRY INTERPRETATION WORKSHEET
Phase 6: POLISH AND TAPE

COMPANION READING:

SOME NOTES ON MEMORIZING
PRACTICE PRACTICES
WHAT JUDGES LOOK FOR IN INTERP EVENTS

Make a video tape of your performance, from entering the room to returning to your chair. Watch your own performance critically. If video is not available, make an audio tape.

_____ 1. Do you enter the room like a "champion"?

_____ 2. Do you look natural and comfortable in performance?

_____ 3. Do you look professional in appearance from start to finish?

_____ 4. Each thought and word must be given appropriate weight and meaning. Is your energy maintained consistently?

_____ 5. Does the tempo vary? Enough? Are there effective pauses?

_____ 6. Does the intensity vary?

_____ 7. Do you have distracting mannerisms that need to be axed?

_____ 8. Is there a "dead zone" where the attention wanders? This may be because you don't understand that passage. Don't skip it. Take that section apart and dig into its meaning. It may also be a place where your concentration is weak for some reason. Can the problem be corrected? How? Do you understand how the speaker "feels"?

_____ 9. What changes in volume should occur that didn't? Why?

_____ 10. Is your focus distinct for each character (if you have any)? Are the focuses too far apart? This makes your audience feel as if they are watching tennis!

_____ 11. If you have characters, have you found them physically and vocally? Are there physical differences?

POETRY WORKSHEETS PHASE 6.2

_____ 12.   Is your articulation clear and understandable?

_____ 13.   Is your imagery clear? Do you really see the images?

_____ 14.   Note the mood changes from beginning to the end of the piece. Are they in the appropriate places? Are they strong enough? Too strong?

_____ 15.   What is the current time of your piece? _____

After completing the worksheets to this point, the interpreter should continue to rehearse and polish. Work to make each performance consistent, so that you can do the poetry perfectly every time. You are never finished. Continue to read out loud daily, to find new audiences (they will teach you new things about your cutting). The coach is still a powerful partner in perfecting this event. So keep going for regular coaching sessions.

DRAMATIC INTERPRETATION

or
ONE-MAN SHOW

AKA: Dramatic Interp; DI

GENERIC RULES:

A cutting which represents one or more characters from a play or plays of literary merit. This material may be drawn from stage, screen or radio. Use of manuscript is required. Time limit is 10 minutes.

A FEW WORDS ABOUT DRAMATIC INTERPRETATION (DI):

DI is an event in which the interpreter "reads" a cutting (usually) from a play or plays but sometimes (depending on the contest rules) from any dramatic material. This event is not acting[57] -- the performer remains relatively stationary. In this event a script **must be used**. In this event the character placement is shown through focus, as well as voice and body.

DI may involve the interpreter portraying more than one character of either or both sexes. It occasionally combines more than one cutting into a program around a central theme and frequently features a number of characters. Doing more than one character allows you to show your virtuosity and usually makes the performance more challenging. But, in spite of that, the event is also successful with interpretation using only one character. This seems to be a matter of current trend. Some years, one; some years, multiple. Whatever you choose for material, invest your best effort in bringing it to life. Don't try too hard to figure out a formula.

I CAN GIVE YOU A SIX-WORD FORMULA FOR SUCCESS:

THINK THINGS THROUGH - THEN FOLLOW THROUGH.

Eddie Rischenbacher

---

[57] We're not _even_ going to begin to discuss the "fine line" between acting and interp. If you feel like being confused, go pick up any interp text or ask your coach to explain the artificial boundaries.

Since there is usually no narration in dramatic material, the content of the piece and the introduction must establish place and time. The audience must be able to distinguish between characters by your voice and character physicality. You may help by letting them meet the characters in the introduction but usually you just need to perfect the full characterization within your piece. At any rate, this event takes lots of imaging or visualization ("seeing" it in your mind).

If you select movie/TV scripts, it usually pays to avoid the latest blockbuster. Your performance will be compared to the film by fans. Most of you are not Al Pacino or Meryl Streep—yet. And it is hard to avoid impersonating those performances instead of doing original work. Develop your own style!

It is possible that a DI in the fall will become a duo interp or POI in the spring. Check the conflict patterns for spring tournaments.

REMEMBER: CHECK WITH YOUR COACHES AT EACH STEP OF THE WAY!

DI WORKSHEETS PHASE 2.1

DRAMATIC INTERPRETATION WORKSHEET
Phase 2: SELECTING THE LITERATURE

WHY DO THIS PHASE?

This phase's necessity is pretty obvious: without hunting and selecting the literature, you don't have an event. It's time to learn how to find material on your own[58].

WARNING: This phase requires either a lot of luck or a lot of what is often very frustrating work. You may stumble across your "perfect" material quickly OR you have to kiss a lot of "literary" frogs to find your royal piece.

COMPANION READING:

FINDING AND SELECTING INTERPRETIVE MATERIAL
THE INTERPER'S FIRST SOJOURN INTO THE LIBRARY
AN APPROACH TO LITERATURE INTERPRETATION IN GENERAL
LITERARY MERIT

FINDING YOUR SELECTIONS:

____ 1. Do you have your library card?

____ 2. Have you collected your dimes for photocopying?

____ 3. Begin a list of your favorite writers and/or plays and/or scenes. You may want to make this list a permanent on-going one to guide not only competition selection, but also your own reading habits.

____ 4. You may want to check drama publishers catalogue (like Samuel French or Baker or Dramatists -- short descriptions of plays).

____ 5. Check the Card Catalogue and/or any Drama Index listed by subject, title, or writer.

---

[58] This comment is addressed to folks who have in the past been "given" their pieces. We know that you, personally have never been in this situation -- you have always said "Coach, I'd rather do it myself".

WORKING FORENSICS: A Competitor's Guide

DI WORKSHEETS PHASE 2.2

____ 6. Check theatre magazines like *American Theatre* for one-acts or play reviews.

____ 7. Ask your English teacher[59] or any person who loves to go to the movies or theatre for suggestions.

____ 8. Have you reviewed "FINDING AND SELECTING INTERPRETIVE MATERIAL?" for the selection criteria?

---

[59] OF COURSE, other kinds of teachers go to the movies and theatre... BUT as a group, in a very informal survey, we discovered that many English teachers are movie and theatre fans.

DI WORKSHEETS PHASE 3.1

DRAMATIC INTERPRETATION WORKSHEET
Phase 3: CUTTING

COMPANION READING:

HOW TO CUT

You will find very specific guidelines for cutting in the HOW TO CUT section. This list will help guide you through a double check to be sure you are on track. Check the time limit for the event you are about to cut. Remember that performance of interp takes longer as more analysis is done. So, allow for that. You will also be adding an introduction which will consume time, so cut shorter than you think you need.
Now, complete the following checklist as you cut.

_____ 1. Have you read the entire selection? This is important in order to find the perfect "scene" to give you a grasp of the whole of the literature.

_____ 2. Have you located the parts that appeal to you? You are looking for the page or paragraph that really "speaks" to you, touches you in some way, stands out from the rest. When you locate this key passage, look around for what completes it in the whole of the work.

_____ 3. Photocopy those parts which you think will work. All of those parts. Even if you aren't sure which ones will go together.

_____ 4. Working from your key passage, is it possible to find a complete "piece" with a beginning, a building climax, and a conclusion. Is it possible to borrow from throughout the entire work to put together the story? Without warping either the character or the authors intent? This is an ethical matter of great importance.

_____ 5. To quickly try to make a coherent entirety, try the "cut and tape" method. Using the photocopies, actually cut out those sections-- (even if its just words or half a sentence) that you want to use and assemble them with tape on a blank piece of paper, in order. You can then arrange and rearrange to your hearts content, using a pencil, mark, out things to be omitted.

Look for missing links, try on new endings, whatever is necessary to get it "right." Then photocopy the finished product so you won't be compromised by (bits of script literally falling off your paper) words. This can be your "rough cutting". As you answer the following questions.

    A. Is the cutting complete with a beginning and an ending that is satisfying?

    B. Does the action in the middle build?

    C. Does it make sense without the rest of the story?

WORKING FORENSICS: A Competitor's Guide

DI WORKSHEETS PHASE 3.2

      D. Is their a stronger, more interesting opening /closing some other place in the literature?

      E. Will this cutting keep my audience emotionally involved all the way to the end of the performance.

      F. Does this cutting have variety in mood? Can you find a way to give it that variety, either through additions to the cutting or performance?

      G. Does this cutting allow you to spotlight the things that you do best in performance?

_____ 6. Read it out loud -- as well as you can at this phase.

      Current time of rough cut:_____

If the cutting is still too long:

Review "Rules of Thumb" under **HOW TO CUT** and/or get some help from your coach and/or from a more seasoned teammate.

If the cutting is too short:

Is there another segment you can add in? Does it need a long introduction to give information or set the mood?

Remember to allow time for your introduction and/or needed transitions.

Re-read the rough cutting out loud and re-time it.

Current time of rough cut:_____

DI WORKSHEETS PHASE 4.1

DRAMATIC INTERPRETATION WORKSHEET
Phase 4: PRELIMINARY ANALYSIS

WHY DO THIS PHASE?

At this phase of development, you as an interpreter are ready to begin the process of learning all there is to know about the literature you chose because it caused a response in you. In the course of examining it more closely than you have probably ever looked at literature, you will hopefully find that you like it better all the time. Like true love[60].

COMPANION READING:

CREATING CHARACTERS FOR INTERPRETATION
FOCUS IN INTERPRETATION

THE AUTHOR:

Frequently background information will give you big clues to understanding the literature, as well as help for writing introductions.

___ 1. Who was the author and why do you think he wrote this selection? Really dig into the motivation for writing as it may open a door to understanding that you can't find any other way.

___ 2. When was this selection written and does that matter? Use some thought on this one! Examine what was happening to the world when it was written. What was happening to the author? How is that reflected in what was written? How does it affect how you feel about the selection? How will you use this to make an audience respond to the literature?

> **DON'T CONFUSE FAME WITH SUCCESS.**
> **MADONNA IS ONE -- HELEN KELLER IS THE OTHER.**
>
> Erma Bombeck

---

[60] Corny analogy, but... true!

WORKING FORENSICS: A Competitor's Guide

DI WORKSHEETS PHASE 4.2

THE SELECTION:

____ 1. Who is speaking? Be specific--<u>someone</u> is speaking. 'The narrator' is **not** enough. Tell something about him/her.

____ 2. To whom is he/she speaking? Specifically--even if it is the audience. Another use-your-imagination question! Be complete. The best choice is to speak to one person. Someone who matters.

____ 3. When does this story take place? Where?

____ 4. What happens in the action before your selection begins? (The moment before)

____ 5. Describe briefly each character, including their appearance, movement, and voice. Don't shortcut here. You need to be able to visualize these people when you present them to an audience.

____ 6. What is the mood at the opening of the selection? See it as a color, or an image.

____ 7. What is the mood at the end of the selection? Visualize it again.

____ 8. What caused the change?

____ 9. At what point (word/line) does the change take place?

____ 10. What other places in the cutting are pivotal?

____ 11. Current time of cutting:_____

Schedule a coaching session. Please bring worksheet completed to this point, the cutting with any changes copied for coach, & a PENCIL.

DI WORKSHEETS PHASE 5.1

DRAMATIC INTERPRETATION WORKSHEET
Phase 5: PHYSICAL SCRIPT AND CONTINUED ANALYSIS

COMPANION READING:

THE PHYSICAL SCRIPT
INTRODUCTIONS AND TRANSITIONS FOR INTERPRETATIVE EVENTS

INTRODUCTION:

_____ 1. How much time is left for your introduction? Allow a little (30 seconds, say) for your improvement as a reader and another space (15 seconds, say) to cushion you from the deadly over time problem. What is left is the maximum amount of time you have left for introduction.

_____ 2. If your selection needs more introduction than you have time for, guess where you get it? Yep, back to the cutting board!

_____ 3. Looking at the selection, decide:

   A. What information does the audience **have to have** to understand the piece?
   B. What is the selection (your cutting) about? Write the "theme" in a sentence.
   C. Why should the audience want to hear this selection? Understanding? Entertainment? Catharsis?
   D. What mood do you want to create?

_____ 4. Now just tell us the responses to those investigative probes — as if <u>you</u> were <u>telling</u> us -- only write down what you would have said. It is the beginning of your intro.

_____ 5. Be sure to include author and title in your introduction.

_____ 6. Look at that introduction (rough as it is!) Can you make it more streamlined? Telescope ideas more compactly?

_____ 7. Can you make your first sentence so "something" (intriguing, unique, dramatic, tantalizing) that the audience is captured by it?

_____ 8. This is not your final introduction. it is your working introduction. It will be revised and refined again. But if it fits within your time limit and your coach approves it, memorize it. The introduction will be performed with a closed folder exactly as if you were just sharing your thoughts about the cutting with a few friends.

WORKING FORENSICS: A Competitor's Guide

DI WORKSHEETS PHASE 5.2

TRANSITIONS:

Transitions are rarely used in DI. They are sometimes needed to bridge a gap in the cutting, or to connect two selections. In order to write them, please answer the following questions.

_____ 1. What does the audience need to know to understand what is happening? How can you compress that information?

_____ 2. Did you tie your theme and selections together?

_____ 3. Is the transition as brief as possible?

_____ 4. Is there a clever way to include this information without breaking the mood of the piece?

_____ 5. Did you mention the title and author of your next selection?

CONTINUING ANALYSIS:

_____ 1. **Imagery** involves the reader "seeing" images or ideas as you perform. In order to do that you need to isolate and identify those images. Take you script and look at it (from the first word). On a piece of paper write what you see and when. While you may not have to write all the detail, you should be able to visualize in absolute reality detail. This skill will develop more clearly as you continue to work with the cutting. [I.E. "It was the best of time. It was the worst of times." What is the speaker seeing? The past? The revolution? his family? His own role in what happened? Do you see that the more specific the choice, the more emotional flavor it has?] If you see it, the audience can see it as well.

_____ 2. **Don't throw away any idea.** The audience will notice. Some ideas take more effort than others to unlock.

_____ 3. Work on **motivation** for each character in your selection. Why do they do what they do? Don't take them for granted -- find out.

DI WORKSHEETS PHASE 5.3

Read your selection for a small group of people -- maybe your teammates. Note their response.

_____ 1. Where did they get bored?

_____ 2. Where were they interested?

_____ 3. Where did they laugh?

_____ 4. Did they have an emotional response? When?

_____ 5. Based on their responses, what changes do you want to make?

Now prepare your performance script as directed in **THE PHYSICAL SCRIPT**.

By this time, you should know your DI very well. You may even have it memorized. However, you must appear to be actually reading when you compete. So....

____ 1. Mark in different color highlighter when different characters speak.

____ 2. Mark the script so that you look down at the right places. Can you make that glance a part of the action?

____ 3. Practice "acting" like you are reading every time you rehearse.

____ 4. Practice page turns. Make them part of the performance. When can you "add something" with a page turn.

____ 5. What physical actions can you do that will enhance the words?

____ 6. Can you find imaginative ways to use the folder to enhance what is happening. [The folder might become a mirror or a package.] Use discretion. Too much is too much.

____ 7. Is your character placement and focus distinct and clear?

WORKING FORENSICS: A Competitor's Guide

DI WORKSHEETS PHASE 6.1

DRAMATIC INTERPRETATION WORKSHEET
Phase 6: POLISH AND TAPE

COMPANION READING:

SOME NOTES ON MEMORIZING
PRACTICE PRACTICES
WHAT JUDGES LOOK FOR IN INTERP EVENTS

Make a video tape of your performance, from beginning in your chair before you perform, to returning to your chair at the end of your performance. Watch your own performance critically. If video is not possible, use audio tape.

_____ 1. Do you look natural and comfortable from the time you leave your chair until you return? Do you enter the room like a "champ"?

_____ 2. Do you look professional in appearance from start to finish? Each thought and word must be given appropriate weight and meaning. Energy must be maintained.

_____ 3. Does the tempo vary? Enough? Are there effective pauses?

_____ 4. Does the intensity vary? Are your focuses too far apart, clear -- distinct?

_____ 5. Is there a "dead zone" where the attention wanders? This may be because you don't understand that passage. Don't skip it. Take apart that section and dig into its meaning. It may be a place where your concentration is weak for some reason. Do you not like this section? Love the next one? Have weak images? Do you understand how the character feels? Can the problem be corrected? How?

_____ 6. Is your physical movement distracting or helpful? Be honest now....

This is only the beginning. Now you begin to perfect the DI. Keep working out loud, stand up, with a coach.[61] The hard work is to keep it "real". Avoid the auto-pilot. Trust your coach.

---

[61] Actually, the coach can sit.

DUO DRAMATIC INTERPRETATION
or
THIS IS NOT ACTING

AKA: Duo Interp; Duo; DID (Dual Interp Drama)

GENERIC RULES:

A cutting from a play, humorous or serious, involving the portrayal of 2 or more characters presented by 2 individuals. This material may be drawn from stage, screen, or radio. This is not an acting event. Thus, no costumes, props, lighting, etc., are to be used. Presentation is from the manuscript and the focus is off stage. Time limit is 10 minutes.

MATERIAL:

The selection may or may not be taken from a play. Check the rules at each contest. While plays may be used more frequently at competitions, do not let this stop you from using other forms of dramatic literature that you like and that will fit into the event, if the rules permit. (Occasionally, duo's come form other genres of literature such as prose.)

A Duo scene/selection should be reasonably balanced so that each interpreter shares the material as equally as possible. It is best if a story of some kind is told, with the good ole beginning, middle and end. The cutting should have audience impact, grab their attention and have potential for some physicality within the context of the scene.

Duo dramatic is **the** event where interpreters get to play together. Two interpers read dramatic literature as partners. This is a relatively uninhibited event where lots of activity is implied and some limited movement is allowed. While the actors employ off stage focus, great emphasis is placed on "honesty" in performance.

NOTE:

It's possible for one or both of you to "play" multiple characters, but the character change must be extremely clear to the audience.

PICKING A PARTNER

The perfect marriage of material and partners is the key to success in duo, so choose carefully. It **is** possible to select your cutting without a partner. Or, you can choose a partner first and then the two of you select a cutting together. If choosing literature is easier than choosing people, you may want to get your coach's help. He/she may have a system that works of which you could be the beneficiary. No matter who picks the partners, picking a partner is tricky business. The following things should be considered:

? Can he/she act/interpret or, have the potential to do so?

? Do you both have the same level of dedication?

? Do your schedules match well enough for adequate rehearsal time?

? Is he/she going to be in the activities that limit time and commitment for this event (such as a play or work)?

? Is he/she going to qualify for this tournament in all the other ways required on your team?

? Will he/she fit the other character(s) in the cutting?

? Do you really want to do a duo with your best friend JUST because they are your best friend?

? Do you really want to do a duo with your S.O. (significant-other) just because they are your S.O.? And what happens if you break up[62]?

? Do you really want to spend this much time with this person?

? Do they value your opinion? Do you value theirs?

? Can you work together comfortably, talk openly, accept criticism from each other, trust one another?

Will it be possible to find a selection that fits both of you?

If a person asks you to work with them and you do <u>not</u> feel they meet these criteria, politely say, "No, I don't think I can." It is a sign of maturity. You don't have to give a reason or rationale.

Regardless of how your partner is chosen, you both must be committed to the event. PHASE ONE is essential!

---

[62] Authors' personal note: Most of the S.O. duos we've coached have not lasted the entire year, either as partners or S.O..

DUO WORKSHEETS PHASE 2.1

DUO INTERPRETATION WORKSHEET
Phase 2: SELECTING THE LITERATURE

COMPANION READING:

FINDING AND SELECTING INTERPRETIVE MATERIAL
THE INTERPER'S FIRST SOJOURN INTO THE LIBRARY
AN APPROACH TO LITERATURE INTERPRETATION IN GENERAL
LITERARY MERIT

FINDING YOUR SELECTIONS:

____ 1. Do you have your library card?

____ 2. Have you collected your dimes for photocopying?

____ 3. Make a list of your favorite authors and/or plays and/or movies.

____ 4. You may want to check anthologies of <u>contemporary</u> plays to find authors you like. Then look for more works by those writers. Or you may want to look again at some forgotten classic playwrights.

____ 5. Check the Card Catalogue and/or any Drama Index listed by subject, title, or writer.

____ 6. Check the drama publishers catalogues (like Samuel French or Baker or Dramatists-- short descriptions of plays).

____ 7. Ask any person who loves to read and/or go to the theatre or movies to give you suggestions of a favorite play or scene.

____ 8. Have you reviewed the selection criteria in FINDING AND SELECTING INTERPRETIVE MATERIAL?

WORKING FORENSICS: A Competitor's Guide

DUO INTERPRETATION WORKSHEET
Phase 3: CUTTING

COMPANION READING:

HOW TO CUT

You will find very specific guidelines for cutting in the HOW TO CUT section. This list will help guide you through a double check to be sure you are on track. Check the time limit for the event you are about to cut. Remember that performance of interp takes longer as more analysis is done. So, allow for that. You will also be adding an introduction which will consume time, so cut shorter than you think you need.
Now, complete the following checklist as you cut.

_____ 1. Have you read the entire selection? This is important in order to find the perfect "scene" to give you a grasp of the whole of the literature.

_____ 2. Have you located the parts that appeal to you? You are looking for the act or scene(s) that really "speaks" to you, touches you in some way, stands out from the rest. When you locate this key passage, look around for what completes it in the whole of the work.

_____ 3. Photocopy those parts which you think will work. All those parts. Even if you aren't sure which ones will go together.

_____ 4. Working from your key passage, is it possible to find a complete "piece" with a beginning, a building climax, and a conclusion. Is it possible to borrow from throughout the entire work to put together the story? Without warping either the character or the authors intent? This is an ethical matter of great importance.

_____ 5. To quickly try to make a coherent entirety, try the "cut and tape" method. Using the photocopies, actually cut out those sections-- (even if its just words or half a sentence) that you want to use and assemble them on a blank piece of paper, in order, with tape for securing same. You can then arrange and rearrange to your hearts content, using a pencil, mark, out things to be omitted.
Look for missing links, try on new endings, whatever is necessary to get it "right." Then photocopy the finished product so you won't be compromised by (bits of script literally falling off your paper) words. This can be your "rough cutting". As you answer the following questions.

   A. Is the cutting complete with a beginning and an ending that is satisfying?

   B. Does the action in the middle build?

   C. Does it make sense without the rest of the story?

DUO WORKSHEETS PHASE 3.2

   D. Is there a stronger, more interesting opening /closing some other place in the literature?

   E. Will this cutting keep my audience emotionally involved all the way to the end of the performance.

   F. Does this cutting have variety in mood? Can you find a way to give it that variety, either through additions to the cutting or performance?

   G. Does this cutting allow you to spotlight the things that you do best in performance?

_____ 6. Read it out loud -- as well as you can at this phase.

   Current time of rough cut:_____

If the cutting is still too long:

Review "Rules of Thumb" under **HOW TO CUT** and/or get some help from your coach and/or from a more seasoned teammate.

If the cutting is too short:

Is there another segment you can add in? Does it need a long introduction to give information or set the mood?

Remember to allow time for your introduction and/or needed transitions.

Re-read the rough cutting out loud and re-time it.

Current time of rough cut:_____

DUO WORKSHEETS PHASE 4.1

DUO INTERPRETATION WORKSHEET
Phase 4: PRELIMINARY ANALYSIS

WHY DO THIS PHASE?

At this phase of development, you as an interpreter are ready to begin the process of learning all there is to know about the literature you chose because it caused a response in you. In the course of examining it more closely than you have probably ever looked at literature, you will hopefully find that you like it better all the time. Like true love[63].

COMPANION READING:

CREATING CHARACTERS FOR INTERPRETATION
FOCUS IN INTERPRETATION

Write your answers on a separate sheet of paper.

THE AUTHOR:

Frequently background information will give you big clues to understanding the literature, as well as help for writing introductions.

_____ 1. Who was the author and why do you think he wrote this selection? Really dig into the motivation for writing as it may open a door to understanding that you can't find any other way.

_____ 2. When was this selection written and does that matter? Use some thought on this one! Examine what was happening to the world when it was written. What was happening to the author? How is that reflected in what was written? How does it affect how you feel about the selection? How will you use this to make an audience respond to the literature?

---

[63] Corny analogy, but... true!

DUO WORKSHEETS PHASE 4.2

THE SELECTION(S):

____ 1. What happens in the action before your selection begins? (The moment before)

____ 2. What is the relationship between these characters. Write separate histories for each character. Discuss them. Then find a mutual history for them together.

____ 3. Who is speaking? Be specific--<u>someone</u> is speaking. 'The narrator' is **not** enough. Tell something about him/her.

____ 4. To whom is he/she speaking? Specifically--even if it is the audience. Another use-your-imagination question! Be complete. The best choice is to speak to one person. Someone who matters.

____ 5. When does this story take place? Where?

____ 6. What happens in the action before your selection begins? (The moment before)

____ 7. Describe briefly each character, including their appearance, movement, and voice. Don't shortcut here. You need to be able to visualize these people when you present them to an audience.

____ 8. What is the mood at the opening of the selection? See it as a color, or an image.

____ 9. What is the mood at the end of the selection? Visualize it again.

____ 10. What caused the change?

____ 11. At what point (word/line) does the change take place?

____ 12. What other places in the cutting are pivotal?

____ 13. Current time of cutting:_____

Schedule a coaching session. Please bring worksheet completed to this point, the cutting with any changes copied for coach, & a PENCIL.

DUO WORKSHEETS PHASE 5.1

DUO INTERPRETATION WORKSHEET
Phase 5: PHYSICAL SCRIPT AND CONTINUED ANALYSIS

COMPANION READING:

THE PHYSICAL SCRIPT
INTRODUCTIONS AND TRANSITIONS FOR INTERPRETATIVE EVENTS

INTRODUCTION:

_____ 1. How much time is left for your introduction? Allow a little (30 seconds, say) for your improvement as a reader and another space (15 seconds, say) to cushion you from the deadly over time problem. What is left is the maximum amount of time you have left for introduction.

_____ 2. If your selection needs more introduction than you have time for, guess where you get it? Yep, back to the cutting board!

_____ 3. Looking at the selection, decide:

    A. What information does the audience **have to have** to understand the piece?
    B. What is the selection (your cutting) about? Write the "theme" in a sentence.
    C. Why should the audience want to hear this selection?
       Understanding? Entertainment? Catharsis?
    D. What mood do you want to create?

_____ 4. Now just tell us the responses to those investigative probes --- as if <u>you</u> were <u>telling</u> us -- only write down what you would have said. It is the beginning of the intro.

_____ 5. Be sure to include author and title in your introduction.

_____ 6. Look at that introduction (rough as it is!) Can you make it more streamlined? Telescope ideas more compactly?

_____ 7. Can you make your first sentence so "something" (intriguing, unique, dramatic, tantalizing) that the audience is captured by it?

_____ 8. This is not your final introduction. It is your working introduction. It will be revised and refined again. But if it fits within your time limit and your coach approves it, memorize it. The introduction will be performed with a closed folder exactly as if you were just sharing your thoughts about the cutting with a few friends.

DUO WORKSHEETS PHASE 5.2

TRANSITIONS:

A NOTE ABOUT TRANSITIONS: When at all possible, transitions should be a part of the selection, rather than an intrusive message in the flow of prose. When it is impossible to avoid this follow this advice:

_____ 1. Tell the audience what it needs to know.

_____ 2. Tie your theme and selections together.

_____ 3. Mention the title and author of the next piece - if different.

_____ 4. Keep the transition as brief as possible.

CONTINUING ANALYSIS:

_____ 1. **Imagery** involves the reader "seeing" images or ideas as you perform. In order to do that you need to isolate and identify those images. Take you script and look at it (from the first word). On a piece of paper write what you see and when. While you may not have to write all the detail, you should be able to visualize in absolute reality detail perfect. This skill will develop more clearly as you continue to work with the cutting. [I.E. "It was the best of time. It was the worst of times." What is the speaker seeing? The past? The revolution? His family? His own role in what happened? Do you see that the more specific the choice, the more emotional flavor it has?] If you see it, the audience can see it as well.

_____ 2. **Don't throw away any idea.** The audience will notice. Some ideas take more effort than others to unlock.

_____ 3. Work on **motivation** for each character in your selection. Why do they do what they do? Don't take them for granted -- find out.

Read your selection for a small group of persons, maybe your teammates, and note their response.

_____ 1. Where did they get bored?

_____ 2. Where were they interested?

_____ 3. Where did they laugh?

_____ 4. Did they have an emotional response? Where? Was it the response you wanted them to have?

_____ 5. Based on their responses, what changes do you want to make?

DUO WORKSHEETS PHASE 5.3

Now prepare your performance script as directed in **"THE PHYSICAL SCRIPT"**.

By this time, you should know your piece very well. You might even have it memorized. However, you must appear to be actually reading when you compete. So...

_____ 1. Mark in different color highlighter when different characters speak.

_____ 2. Mark the script so that you look down at the right places. Can you make that glance a part of the action?

_____ 3. Practice "acting" like you are reading every time you rehearse.

_____ 4. Practice page turns. Make them part of the performance. When can you "add something" with a page turn.

DUO WORKSHEETS PHASE 6.1

DUO INTERPRETATION WORKSHEET
Phase 6: POLISH AND TAPE

COMPANION READING:

SOME NOTES ON MEMORIZING
PRACTICE PRACTICES
WHAT JUDGES LOOK FOR IN INTERP EVENTS

Make a video tape of your performance, from entering the room to returning to your chair. Watch your own performance critically. If video is not available, make an audio tape.

_____ 1. Do you enter the room like a "champion"?

_____ 2. Do you look natural and comfortable in performance?

_____ 3. Do you look professional in appearance from start to finish?

_____ 4. Each thought and word must be given appropriate weight and meaning. Is your energy maintained consistently?

_____ 5. Does the tempo vary? Enough? Are there effective pauses?

_____ 6. Does the intensity vary?

_____ 7. Do you have distracting mannerisms that need to be axed?

_____ 8. Is there a "dead zone" where the attention wanders? This may be because you don't understand that passage. Don't skip it. Take that section apart and dig into its meaning. It may also be a place where your concentration is weak for some reason. Can the problem be corrected? How? Do you understand how the speaker "feels"?

_____ 9. What changes in volume should occur that didn't? Why?

_____ 10. Is your focus distinct for each character (if you have any)? Are the focuses too far apart? This makes your audience feel as if they are watching tennis!

_____ 11. If you have characters, have you found them physically and vocally? Are there physical differences?

WORKING FORENSICS: A Competitor's Guide

DUO WORKSHEETS PHASE 6.2

_____ 12. Is your articulation clear and understandable?

_____ 13. Is your imagery clear? Do you really see the images?

_____ 14. Note the mood changes from beginning to the end of the piece. Are they in the appropriate places? Are they strong enough? Too strong?

_____ 15. Do you relate to each other in the most effective way?

_____ 16. Can you vary your positions in a way that enhances the meaning without actually moving a great deal?

_____ 17. What is the current time of your piece? _____

After completing the worksheets to this point, the interpreter should continue to rehearse and polish. Work to make each performance consistent, so that you can do the selection perfectly every time. You are never finished. Continue to read out loud daily, to find new audiences (they will teach you new things about your cutting). The coach is still a powerful partner in perfecting this event. So keep going for regular coaching sessions.

PROGRAM ORAL INTERPRETATION
or
A LITTLE BIT OF THIS; A LITTLE BIT OF THAT

AKA: POI; OI; INT; Mixed; Program Oral Interpretation; Oral Interpretation; Mixed Genre Interpretation

GENERIC RULES:

A program of thematically linked selections of literary merit chosen form two or three recognized genres of competitive interpretation (prose, poetry, drama). A substantial portion of the total time must be devoted to each of the genres used in the program. Different genres mean that material must appear in separate pieces of literature (e.g. A poem included in a short story that appears only in that short story does not constitute a poetry genre.) Us of manuscript is required. Maximum time limit is 10 minutes including original introduction and/or transitions.

A FEW BITS OF WISDOM:

POI is essentially a theme or idea expressed in more than one genre: poetry, prose or theater. These can be selected from such literature as: short story, novel, play, screenplay, TV script, poetry, song lyrics, speech, letter, essay.

The program can run chronologically: for example, the feelings of Native Americans from the first contact with whites to present state in the white man's world. They can run a spectrum of emotions: for instance, three ways to react to adultery. They could explore one theme of a writer in different mediums: the escape theme in Sam Shepard's poetry and his plays. They could explore relationships such as mother/daughter, father/son, writer/works. They can explore themes: death, misfits, ugliness, fairy tales -- as long as they do so in more than one genre.

You could begin with a piece you love which is too short, one that won't fit another category, or one which inspires a question to be answered. The seed could come from anywhere. It could evolve from another program of a now "dead" event. You may simply discover 2 selections that you love which seem to "belong" together.

The program should have universal appeal, logical sequence, a clear theme, two or more kinds of literature, balance, and a uniqueness. When finished, it should look more like a mosaic than a collage.

After assembling the material you want to use, bring it to your coach. Explain how you intend to put it together. They will advise you whether you are on the right track, ways to assemble, ideas for transitions, or whether you need a different kind of piece, other material, etcetera. Example: All of your material may be saying the same thing in the same way. You might need to look for an opposing view or a contrasting light piece. Some of your material may have been overused. Then you would have to look for the same idea, different material.

When the material is okay, you may want to play with the order of the material. Remember that the program should catch the audience early, should flow smoothly, should have a strong piece at the end, and the program needs to build in intensity for dramatic effect.

With the material arranged in an order that seems right, try the transitions to see if you can make it link. The transitions may be original or literary, but they must reinforce the theme (See Phase 5 under "TRANSITIONS" for fuller explanation. Then read it aloud to see if the POI makes sense. When the POI gets shakily on its legs, time the whole thing together. Even if the pieces/program has rough spots, read it to a coach. Get advice and/or ideas. Then you will probably have to cut it again. This is VERY normal.

You will rewrite transitions, re-cut, rearrange, re-time, and regret a lot before it is ready to polish. You will fall in and out of love with material. So, what else is new!?

*** WARNING! WARNING! ***

It could be that none of the above is necessarily true. Sometimes the programs just fall together like people in love. Sometimes this kind of program just "does itself". But, don't bank on it. This is an exception when it happens.

POI is a very challenging event for interpers. It is also stimulating and wonderful. Have fun!

POI WORKSHEETS PHASE 2.1

PROGRAM ORAL INTERPRETATION WORKSHEET
Phase 2: SELECTING THE LITERATURE

WHY DO THIS PHASE?

This phase's necessity is pretty obvious: no literature, no event.

WARNING: This phase require either a lot of luck or a lot of what is often very frustrating work. You may stumble across you "perfect" material quickly OR you have to kiss a lot of "literary" frogs to find you royal piece.

COMPANION READING:

FINDING AND SELECTING INTERPRETIVE MATERIAL
THE INTERPER'S FIRST SOJOURN INTO THE LIBRARY
AN APPROACH TO LITERATURE INTERPRETATION IN GENERAL
LITERARY MERIT

FINDING YOUR SELECTIONS:

____ 1. Do you have your library card?

____ 2. Have you collected your dimes for photocopying?

____ 3. Begin a list of your favorite authors and/or stories and/or novels and/or chapters of novels.

POI is going to test your ability to find material and synthesize it. Most people begin with one selection that they love that is unsuitable by itself. It may be an event which can no longer be used, or maybe it is too short. Sometimes, POI competitors simply have a theme they want to explore -- like "ghosts of the past". Once in awhile, in searching for other literature, someone will find two pieces from separate genres, that just seem to belong together. Voila! That is a POI. That's how they are born.
If you read a wide range of literature, you are ahead in this event, because you may be able to identify quickly a chapter or sub-story which blends perfectly into your theme.
If you aren't lucky enough to have more than one piece yet, this phase is about finding those companions.

____ 4. You may want to check anthologies of classic, modern and <u>contemporary</u> work to find writers you like. Then look for more work by those writers.

____ 5. Check the Reader's Guides and/or Indexes for literature listed by subject, title, or writer. If you have trouble, ask the information librarian for help.

POI WORKSHEETS PHASE 2.2

_____ 6. Check current literary periodicals like <u>The New Yorker</u>.

_____ 7. Ask your English teacher or any person who loves literature to give you suggestions.

_____ 8. Don't be afraid to lift material which doesn't **seem** to be representative of the work. EX. <u>Cujo</u> has a wonderful 3 minute section about loneliness.

_____ 9. Have you reviewed the selection criteria in FINDING AND SELECTING INTERPRETIVE MATERIAL?

SELECTION CHOICES:

Fill in blanks with the literature you want to use. Don't worry. At the end of the season some of these <u>will</u> probably change.

TITLE(S)	AUTHOR
_____	_____
_____	_____
_____	_____

Now check with your coach to see if the literature is acceptable.

POI WORKSHEETS PHASE 3.1

PROGRAM ORAL INTERPRETATION WORKSHEET
Phase 3: CUTTING

COMPANION READING:

HOW TO CUT

You will find very specific guidelines for cutting in the HOW TO CUT section. This list will help guide you through a double check to be sure you are on track. Check the time limit for the event you are about to cut. Remember that performance of interp takes longer as more analysis is done. So, allow for that. You will also be adding an introduction which will consume time, so cut shorter than you think you need.
Now, complete the following checklist as you cut.

_____ 1. Have you read the entire selection(s)? This is important in order to find the perfect "scene" to give you a grasp of the whole of the literature.

_____ 2. Have you located the parte that appeal to you? You are looking for the page or paragraph that really "speaks" to you, touches you in some way, stands out from the rest. When you locate this key passage, look around for what completes it in the whole of the work.

_____ 3. Photocopy those parts which you think will work. All those parts. Even if you aren't sure which ones will go together.

_____ 4. Working from your key passage, is it possible to find a complete "piece" with a beginning, a building climax, and a conclusion. Is it possible to borrow from throughout the entire work to put together the story? Without warping either the character or the authors intent? This is an ethical matter of great importance.

_____ 5. To quickly try to make a coherent entirety, try the "cut and tape" method. Using the photocopies, actually cut out those sections-- (even if its just words or half a sentence) that you want to use and assemble them on a blank piece of paper with tape, in order. You can then arrange and rearrange to your hearts content, using a pencil, mark, out things to be omitted.

Look for missing links, try on new endings, whatever is necessary to get it "right." Then photocopy the finished product so you won't be compromised by (bits of script literally falling off your paper) words. This can be your "rough cutting". As you answer the following questions.

A. Is the cutting complete with a beginning and an ending that is satisfying?

B. Does the action in the middle build?

WORKING FORENSICS: A Competitor's Guide

POI WORKSHEETS PHASE 3.2

      C. Does it make sense without the rest of the story?

      D. Is their a stronger, more interesting opening /closing some other place in the literature?

      E. Will this cutting keep my audience emotionally involved all the way to the end of the performance.

      F. Does this cutting have variety in mood? Can you find a way to give it that variety, either through additions to the cutting or performance?

      G. Does this cutting allow you to spotlight the things that you do best in performance?

_____ 6. Read it out loud as well as you can at this phase.

      Current time of rough cut:_____

If the cutting is still too long:

Review "Rules of Thumb" under **HOW TO CUT** and/or get some help from your coach and/or from a more seasoned teammate.

If the cutting is too short:

Before you decide it IS too short, remember that you may have transitions between each segment.....

Is there another segment you can add in? Does it need a long introduction to give information or set the mood?

Remember to allow time for your introduction and/or needed transitions.

Re-read the rough cutting out loud and re-time it.

Current time of rough cut:_____

POI WORKSHEETS PHASE 4.1

PROGRAM ORAL INTERPRETATION WORKSHEET
Phase 4: PRELIMINARY ANALYSIS

WHY DO THIS PHASE?

At this phase of development, you as an interpreter are ready to begin the process of learning all there is to know about the literature you chose because it caused a response in you. In the course of examining it more closely than you have probably ever looked at literature, you will hopefully find that you like it better all the time. Like true love[64].

COMPANION READING:

CREATING CHARACTERS FOR INTERPRETATION
FOCUS IN INTERPRETATION

Write your answers on a separate sheet of paper.

THE WRITERS:

Frequently background information will give you big clues to understanding the literature, as well as help for writing introductions.

_____ 1. Who are the writers and why do <u>you</u> think they wrote these selections? Really dig into the motivation for writing as it may open a door to understanding that you can't find any other way.

_____ 2. When were this selections written and does that matter? Use some thought on this one! Examine what was happening to the world when it was written. What was happening to the author? How is that reflected in what was written? How does it affect how you feel about the selection? How will you use this to make an audience respond to the literature?

THE SELECTIONS: Do this for each selection in the program.

_____ 1. To whom is each speaking? Specifically--the audience can be an answer. This is another "use-your-imagination" question.

_____ 2. When does this story/poem/play take place? Where?

_____ 3. What happens in the action just before each of your selections begins? (The moment before)

---

[64]Corny analogy, but... true!

POI WORKSHEETS PHASE 4.2

____ 4. Describe briefly each character, including their appearance, movement, and voice.

____ 5. What is the mood at the opening of each of your selections?

____ 6. What is the mood at the end of each of the selections?

____ 7. What caused the change?

____ 8. At what point (word) does the change take place?

____ 9. Are there small "builds" within each of the pieces? Where?

____ 10. Current time of cutting:_____

REMEMBER: This cutting is no longer a part of the whole work. Any information that the audience needs must be contained in the performance.

Schedule a coaching session. Please bring these materials: completed worksheets completed to this point, the cutting with any changes copied for coach, and a PENCIL.

POI WORKSHEETS PHASE 5.1

PROGRAM ORAL INTERPRETATION WORKSHEET
Phase 5: PHYSICAL SCRIPT AND CONTINUED ANALYSIS

COMPANION READING:

THE PHYSICAL SCRIPT
INTRODUCTIONS AND TRANSITIONS FOR INTERPRETATIVE EVENTS

INTRODUCTION:

The introduction of a POI is especially important. This is the place that you must tell us your theme and its significance, preview for us how each selection will enhance our understanding of the theme and set up your first selection. If you have used a pre-intro, you will also have to tie that selection into the whole. And your time will be limited by the size of your program. Good Luck!

_____ 1. Read and time the pieces. How much time is left for your introduction? Allow a little (30 seconds, say) for your improvement as a reader and another space (15 seconds, say) to cushion you from the deadly over time problem. What is left is the maximum amount of time you have left for introduction.

_____ 2. If your program needs more introduction than you have time for, guess where you get it? Yep, back to the cutting board!

_____ 3. Looking at the program, decide:

   A. What information does the audience **have to have** to understand the program?
   B. What is the program (your cutting) about? Write the "theme" in a sentence.
   C. Why should the audience want to hear this program? Understanding? Entertainment? Catharsis?
   D. What mood do you want to create?

_____ 4. Now just tell us the responses to those investigative probes (#3 above) — as if you were telling us -- only write down what you would have said. It is the beginning of the intro.

_____ 5. Be sure to include author/s and title/s in your introduction.

_____ 6. Look at that introduction (rough as it is!) Can you make it more streamlined? Telescope ideas more compactly?

_____ 7. Can you make your first sentence so "something" (intriguing, unique, dramatic, tantalizing) that the audience is captured by it?

WORKING FORENSICS: A Competitor's Guide

_____ 8. This is not your final introduction. It is your working introduction. It will be revised and refined again. But if it fits within your time limit and your coach approves it, memorize it. The introduction will be performed with a closed folder exactly as if you were just sharing your thoughts about the cutting with a few friends.

TRANSITIONS:

The key to making a POI work is connection. Making it easy for the audience to follow the flow from one piece to another. The secret, if there is one, is tying each piece tightly to the theme. Now there **two techniques** for making the POI transition. Your choice will depend, at least in part, by the rules of the tournaments you plan to attend (their specific rules).

Transitions can be like mini-introductions, linking the previous selection to the theme and then the theme to the next election. This is a traditional form which does allow you as a performer to "set up" each selection; to have input at each junction; and to give the author and title just before their appearance , so to speak. **OR** you can set each piece well in the slightly longer introduction, and **weave** the selections -- put them together without close-the-book transition. Or you can weave by using a "common thread" piece -- like, a poem or song lyric of which you use a small section between each of your longer pieces. The resultant program is a "blended program" and should be identified as such in your intro [i.e. "In this blended program I will....."]. These could be called literary transitions.

ADVICE: Please do not weave/blend for the sake of doing so. The choice of the method should not be because everyone else is doing it[65] IF the theme and the program is strengthened by weaving, then weave. If there is nothing gained by weaving then DON'T WEAVE. One of the possible hazards involved with presenting blended programs is that some judges are negative toward programs in which they are not **clearly aware** of when new selections begins. The regular audience, too, needs a sense of knowing where you are in the program. Both of these "hazards" depend on the introduction, more than anything else, to prevent disaster. Remember, one of the goals of the event is to present different genre and different views -- if it all sounded like one voice, then perhaps you weren't where you needed to be.

Once you have decided which style will work for your tournament schedule, your style, your material, your coach, using sketched out rough transitions or using the "literary" ones ask yourself:

_____ 1. What does the audience need to know in order to understand what is happening?

_____ 2. Did you tie your theme and selections together?

_____ 3. Did you include the title and author?

_____ 4. Is the transition as brief as possible?

---

[65] After all, what would your mother say if you used that excuse?

POI WORKSHEETS PHASE 5.4

CONTINUING ANALYSIS:

_____ 1. **Imagery** involves the reader "seeing" images or ideas as you perform. In order to do that you need to isolate and identify those images. Take you script and look at it (from the firsy word). On a piece of paper write what you see and when. While you may not have to write all the detail, you should be able to visualize in absolute reality detail perfect. This skill will develop more clearly as you continue to work with the cutting. [I.E. "It was the best of time. It was the worst of times." What is the speaker seeing? The past? The revolution? His family? His own role in what happened? Do you see that the more specific the choice, the more emotional flavor it has?] If you see it, the audience can see it as well.

_____ 2. **Don't throw away any idea.** The audience will notice. Some ideas take more effort than others to unlock.

_____ 3. Work on **motivation** for each character in your selection. Why do they do what they do? Don't take them for granted -- find out.

Read your selection for a small group of persons, maybe your teammates, and note their response.

_____ 1. Where did they get bored?

_____ 2. Where were they interested?

_____ 3. Where did they laugh?

_____ 4. Did they have an emotional response? Where? Was it the response you wanted them to have?

_____ 5. Based on their responses, what changes do you want to make?

Now prepare your performance script as directed in **"THE PHYSICAL SCRIPT"**.

By this time, you should know your piece very well. You might even have it memorized. However, you must appear to be actually reading when you compete. So...

____ 1. Mark in different color highlighter when different characters speak.

____ 2. Mark the script so that you look down at the right places. Can you make that glance a part of the action?

____ 3. Practice "acting" like you are reading every time you rehearse.

____ 4. Practice page turns. Make them part of the performance. When can you "add something" with a page turn.

POI WORKSHEETS PHASE 6.1

POI INTERPRETATION WORKSHEET
Phase 6: POLISH AND TAPE

COMPANION READING:

SOME NOTES ON MEMORIZING
PRACTICE PRACTICES
WHAT JUDGES LOOK FOR IN INTERP EVENTS

Make a video tape of your performance, from entering the room to returning to your chair. Watch your own performance critically. If video is not available, make an audio tape.

_____ 1. Do you enter the room like a "champion"?

_____ 2. Do you look natural and comfortable in performance?

_____ 3. Do you look professional in appearance from start to finish?

_____ 4. Each thought and word must be given appropriate weight and meaning. Is your energy maintained consistently?

_____ 5. Does the tempo vary? Enough? Are there effective pauses?

_____ 6. Does the intensity vary?

_____ 7. Do you have distracting mannerisms that need to be axed?

_____ 8. Is there a "dead zone" where the attention wanders? This may be because you don't understand that passage. Don't skip it. Take that section apart and dig into its meaning. It may also be a place where your concentration is weak for some reason. Can the problem be corrected? How? Do you understand how the speaker "feels"?

_____ 9. What changes in volume should occur that didn't? Why?

_____ 10. Is your focus distinct for each character (if you have any)? Are the focuses too far apart? This makes your audience feel as if they are watching tennis!

_____ 11. If you have characters, have you found them physically and vocally? Are there physical differences?

POI WORKSHEETS PHASE 6.2

_____ 12. Is your articulation clear and understandable?

_____ 13. Is your imagery clear? Do you really see the images?

_____ 14. Note the mood changes from beginning to the end of the piece. Are they in the appropriate places? Are they strong enough? Too strong?

_____ 15. What is the current time of your piece? _____

After completing the worksheets to this point, the interpreter should continue to rehearse and polish. Work to make each performance consistent, so that you can do the selection perfectly every time. You are never finished. Continue to read out loud daily, to find new audiences (they will teach you new things about your cutting). The coach is still a powerful partner in perfecting this event. So keep going for regular coaching sessions.

V.

SURVIVAL SKILLS

WHY SURVIVAL SKILLS?

Forensics activities involve a **big** commitment of time and energy. In order to participate in these activities, most of you may need skills to help you survive the non-forensic parts of your life. We want you to survive[66], so we would like to share with you some basic survival skills. We believe that general how-to-juggle-your-life skills are essential, so we've included information on time management and on the use of a portable calendar. Obviously, you are also going to need (or at least, most students do!) some advice in surviving in the academic world. So, we have also included a big hunk about writing term papers (as our extended example of time management) and advice on how to make and keep positive relationships with teachers (good old fashioned "apple-polishing" that hones your interpersonal and learning skills) and we even throw in, at no additional cost, some suggestions of how to do better during exams. The better you can control your life (including your classes) the more concentration you can give to forensics. If you can feel secure about your time and your grades, have strong relationships with the significant people in your life, and have a minute or two for yourself, you should be able to handle forensics without a problem.

We always assume that academics are your first priority, so we have several skill lessons to help you learn to control those activities -- like time management.

THERE IS MORE TO LIFE THAN INCREASING IT'S SPEED.

Ghandi

---

[66] So you will live long enough to buy the 3rd Edition of this text and pay off your student loans [Live long and prosper!]

TIME MANAGEMENT

To be successful in forensic activities, do well in school, (i.e. keep your grades up), and maintain a reasonably happy personal life, you must learn to manage your time wisely. As the new saying goes, "We all have the same 24 hours each day. It's how we use them that makes a difference." So, let us share with you some suggestions about how you can set priorities, some tips on how to use time effectively, and some suggestions about maintaining good grades and good relationships with your instructors.

TIMELY TIPS:

1. ***Discover and protect your most creative/productive time of the day.*** (Know your work habits. Do the most important/difficult jobs when you are at your best.)

2. Combine tasks when possible - this is called ***"double dipping"*** (reading and highlighting a history chapter while you do the laundry, for instance)

3. ***Learn to say "No"*** to long-winded telephone callers and other time wasters, earlier rather than later in the conversation. Learn to say "no" to people who tempt your with activities that pull you away from your goals.

4. ***Plan for the unexpected: don't schedule every minute.*** Be reasonable in your plans. During especially stressful/packed times, think of tomorrow only and decide that you will concentrate on doing the most important things first. ***You really can't do it all in one day***.

5. Avoid being a perfectionist. ***Perfectionism can be procrastination in noble disguise.***

JUSTIFYING A FAULT DOUBLES IT

---

6. **Examine your response to priority tasks**. If you habitually put off certain chores, analyze why -- and what you can do to make priority work less routine. Try doing that task first.

7. **Keep lists**. Time management experts recommend keeping a master list, and a shorter daily list of crucial tasks

8. **Doing the "hardest" (or least favorite) thing first makes everything else on your list easy.**

9. **Don't put "riders" on your goals.** Promising to study for a test after you memorize your new speech is just avoiding the job.

10. ***Don't agonize -- organize!!***

    a. **Define your goals** - Be specific, visualize them and write them down. "Get more money" is a wish. Writing and mailing a resume is a goal.

    b. Break each goal up into smaller **sub-goals** (steps or parts). Example: if you have a research paper due, divide it into topic selection, finding resources, researching, making biblio cards, outlining, writing, editing.

    c. Create a timetable for each step of the goal. Example: research done by February 16th. ***Caution...if you spend hours and hours organizing, you may be procrastinating.***

    d. Once you have created the timetable, ***do only one step at a time*** - don't worry about the next step. You are supposed to be using the timetable as a tool, not racing against it as though it were the enemy.

    e. Consider how much your time is worth. Is everything you do worth the same? ***Don't spend dollar time on penny items.*** Don't spend your most productive time doing such things as reorganizing your sock drawer. Put non-think jobs in a time slot in which you couldn't think if you had to.

    f. Decide what is really essential. Is every part of every step essential? ***Concentrate on essentials.*** Example: A few years ago one of our students discovered that if you wear sweaters over your shirts, you only need iron the part of the shirt that showed. This wasn't slovenliness. He just made the decision based on the amount of time he had available.

11. Give yourself time limits and then stop - **don't steal time** from your next project.

12. Remember, you can't master time until you master your thoughts - **learn to concentrate**. Don't say, "I can't" - try!!

13. ***Make Time Deposits.*** Save time when possible.
    Example: <u>Use waiting time</u>. Short spans of time such as before classes start, at the doctor's office, between customers at work, are valuable as times to work on updating your list/schedule, writing outlines, writing introductions, memorizing lines, etc. One of our acquaintances does her reading in the bath tub -- hard on books but a great use of time.

14. **Don't make excuses** - excuses just waste more of your own time as well as the time of the person to whom you are making the excuse.

15. **Be flexible**, but stick to your priorities. Remember that **priorities may change** from one day to the next or even from one hour to the next. But....be careful, if you change too often, it may be your way of procrastinating.

YOUR LIFE MANAGER: THE PORTABLE CALENDAR

The **MOST IMPORTANT** thing a forensic person should have is a calendar. It should be one that you can keep with you at all times.[67] Then fill it in as each item arrives.[68] Even tentative dates will be better than no dates at all. So get one and then.....

Include on the calendar:

tourney dates (include travel time as soon as you find out)
work schedule
finals times
meetings
doctor/dentist appointments
family gatherings
due dates and "back-timing" for class papers/projects
personal recreation time
shopping/laundry/cleaning times
production schedule for plays if you are involved
performance dates

holidays (real-world and school)
class schedules
midterm grade days
rallies
coaching times
test times
lab times
study time
teaching conference times
audition dates/time
rehearsal times

Keep with your calendar:

phone numbers of offices and libraries
hours of libraries, teachers, coaches, counselors
the names and phone numbers of at least one "good" student in each of your classes
 If you have a forensic partner or extemp, impromptu, or debate mates, you need their hours/schedules and phone number(s) handy.
 Keep a writing utensil with your calendar.
Some people also use their calendar as a place to keep lists:
goals
shopping
to-do
projects
class work breakdowns
questions to ask of whoever.

Now you are ready to look at your calendar. DON'T PANIC. It can probably all be done. The questions is, do you want to do it all. Now is a good time to think about priorities. No one can or should be all things to all people. Consider whether you want to spread yourself out or give your various preferred commitments more time by eliminating some activities. It is wise and prudent to make those decisions about what to prune or eliminate, now.

---

[67] There are many styles available at most college bookstores and/or office supply stores.

[68] Not just at the first of the year, but religiously throughout the year. It should be your constant companion.

WORKING FORENSICS: A Competitor's Guide

The Time Managers Motto:
Divide and Conquer!

We assume academics are the reason you go to college. It is high priority. But it may be that you can ease the stress by **deciding** a few things concerning your class work. Our experience is that speech/theater students are usually bright, alert people who tend to do well at school, once they figure out how to organize their lives efficiently. Therefore, look at the work patterns of each class. Which classes might you need to get a jump on because of requirements later in the semester? Decide if you may need a tutor. Decide if that class is needed or is it something you could live without. Are you willing to put forth the effort and time for an "A" or will a "B" do just as well?
If you have not already done so, consider the following in reference to your college classes.

1. It is wise to have your heaviest academic load in your lightest forensic semester (usually the first semester).
2. Before you register, if possible, find out which instructors are more tolerant of absences because of forensics. Your fellow competitors will gladly share their experiences, if you ask them.
3. Try to avoid early morning Monday or late Friday classes because of tournament traveling. These may be your least productive times.

BACK-TIMING & YOUR CALENDAR

Back-timing is a radio term. ***Simply put, in order to see where to start, you begin at the end.*** In order to illustrate how this principle works, we have chosen to back-time the dreaded "term paper" to examine how this is entered on your calendar, and in your life as a frantic forensic slave. Of course, writing a paper is a perfect example for forensic student because it's just like writing a speech.

First you need to read "TAKING STEPS TO WRITE A TERM PAPER"[69].

To back-time your paper, get out your calendar and insert the paper's due date. Then look at step 23. Figure how you plan to sub-divide that step. Going from due date backward, plug in the last part of step 23 in the first available slot. Then go to the step before that. Plug it into the calendar. Proceed this way until you have plugged/scheduled part one of step one.

You can adapt this technique for Christmas shopping, preparing forensic events, studying for tests, cleaning the house, or just about anything a good time manager can conceive.

> **Personal moment:** One of our favorite moments in any day is announcing a schedule change and then watching all the calendars get whipped out to record the change. ... It takes so little to warm our hearts. What can we say... we are easily amused.

ALL GREAT ACHIEVEMENTS REQUIRE TIME.

David Joseph Schwartz

---

[69] Turn the page!

TAKING STEPS TO WRITE A TERM PAPER

ONE EXAMPLE OF TIME MANAGEMENT[70]

Step 1 *Generate a list of possible topics*: brainstorm and then narrow the topic list to the top 3 contenders.
(Approx. time needed: 10-30 minutes)

Step 2 *Go to the library and scan* the card file, periodical guides, microfilm index, etc. for availability of material on those top 3 topics. You may wish to jot down where you looked and make some notes on the good, the bad and the ugly but mainly what you are doing here is seeing if there is any hope of finding anything. DON'T WRITE ANYTHING DOWN AT THIS POINT - as far as the paper itself is concerned. Don't spend time on something that hasn't been approved yet. (Allow 1-3 hours)

Step 3 Eliminate any topics without enough available material. Of the remaining topics: prioritized according to personal preference. (Allow about 5 minutes.)

Step 4 Take these topics to instructor for approval. You don't have to wait for next class period. Go to the instructor's office. If your instructor is not there, leave a note and copy of topics. Note <u>specific</u> time when you will return or call for a response. (Time needed varies with the verbosity of the instructor. In the best of all possible worlds, it should take no more than 15 minutes.)

Step 5 *Once the topic is approved, write a thesis statement.* Example: "There are three main factors in the behavior of Thoreau which prove he was an existentialist". This thesis is your constant guide. It reminds you what you are writing about. Refer to it often. It will keep you from wasting time researching non-essential material. (Approx. time: 1 hour)

Step 6 Now, **make lists**: questions for which you need answers in order to write the paper; sub topics to be addressed; headings to look under; places to look.
Make these lists at lunch, between classes, (Approx. time needed 10-15 minutes per list)

SUCCESS IS
1% INSPIRATION and 99% PERSPIRATION.

Thomas Edison

---

[70] Also works for speech writing

Step 7   **Get ready to go to the library.** Things needed: your lists from step 6; your thesis statement; knowledge of the available library hours; your library card(s); enough EXACT change for photocopier; index cards, post-its, legal pads, pencils, pen; information on data needed for bibliography. (Allow from 30 seconds to 30 minutes. It depends on how good a time manager you have become.)

If you can't handle being in the library for an extended period of time, plan to divide it up. For example: one visit you can look at card file and at another visit look in the periodical guide. If you are forcing yourself past your library limit, the time spent becomes non-productive.

Step 8   Off to the library. Scan (rather than read) material looking for key words and phrases. Stick a post-it on the pages that look "promising". You may want to note a key word or phrase on that post-it. After you have post-it noted the available sources, proceed to the copier (about an hour before you have scheduled yourself to leave the library). Copy all the tagged information being sure that you note all the biblio information on the photo copy. Also number and name each page. You could drop them and never be able to put them back together again in their proper order. (Approx. total time 4-10 hours depending on how fast you scan) REMEMBER: You can do this in small increments and not necessarily in a library marathon.

Step 9   After all the library research has been completed [with your thesis statement in front of you] highlight all pertinent information. Make a note in the margin about the area of the paper into which each piece of material may go.

Remember you can divide this step into small increments of time. Keep some of the material with you and work on it in odd moments. (This close reading and highlighting will take approx. 5 minutes per page.)

Step 10 If you are required to turn in a set of cards with your bibliographic information on them before you write your paper, you do that at this step. If not, go to step 11.
Making biblio cards: Again, subdivide the work. Double check the bibliographic form before you begin so that you will not have to re-write 153 cards. (A card will take about 3 minutes.)

Step 11 **Now transfer the highlighted material to note cards.**
This is the cards with quotes on them. Again, check the form so that you will not have to re-do them. Remember that if it is one <u>idea</u> per card a 3 sentence quote could require 6 cards. Again divide into itty bitty chunks. (Approx. 3 minutes per card)

Step 12 Arrange the note cards as you think they will appear in the paper. Now **look for the black holes** in your research. Look to see if the points you wish to make need more facts to substantiate. If you need to change your approach and/or go back to the library, now is the time. (Approx. 1-3 hours) If the cards look good arranged as they are take a pencil and lightly number the order (this way you can erase the numbers before you turn the cards in).

Step 13 If all the information is there, use the arranged note cards to write your **rough outline**. (Approx. time 1 hour)

Step 14 Get that outline approved. See step 5.

Step 15 Make corrections on outline and get a clean copy ready. (Approx. 1 hour)

Step 16 **Write your first rough draft** and turn it in, if required. Some of you will do this on computer while others will chose to do it in longhand. If you compose on computer, the rewrites and final printing will take a lot less time. You could subdivide this work using the sections as in the outline. (Approx. time 4-6 hours)

Step 17 Rewrite, rewrite, rewrite until the paper says exactly what you want it to say---like a good speech. (Approx. total 4-6 hours)

> Perfection is made up of trivial things
> but...
> Perfection is not trivial.
>
> **Michelangelo**

Step 18 We now suggest that you go through the paper checking for one or two of the **Final Edit Check** items at a time (see next page for list). These can be divided up and done at different times but overall it takes (get ready for this) about 6 hours.

Step 19 Type/print the final clean corrected copy. (Approx. total time with computer is about 5 minutes to print. We haven't done it manually [from long hand to typewriter or from long hand to computer] in so long that we can't guess at the time, but it will take considerably longer.) **Check for typos**. You need to do this even if your word processor has a spell check. The machine may not know that you meant "their" instead of "there".

Step 20 Write endnotes; biblio sheet; title page. (Approx. time about 5 minutes per item)

Step 21 Check spelling, form, punctuation on endnotes; biblio sheet; title page. (Approx. range is wide but about 30 minutes total should do it.)

Step 22 **Make 2 clean copies--a photocopy will do for you.** (Time here depends how many corrections need to be done. I would guess that even with corrections it shouldn't take more than an hour total.)

Step 23 Put paper in appropriate cover with any cards that are required and turn it in.[71] (Approx. time... wing it!)

TREAT YOURSELF TO A MOVIE, A NIGHT ON THE TOWN, A SUNSET, OR WHAT EVER REWARD WORKS FOR YOU. YOU DESERVE IT.

---

[71] We presumed you wanted an "A" paper. The steps are about the same for a lesser grade, but the time spent and the attention to detail is less.

Final Edit Check List

___ Check to see if the paper is too long or too short. If you make major changes because of length, check them against your outline.

___ Look for smooth transitions from paragraph to paragraph. Does the last sentence in paragraph A flow into the first sentence in paragraph B? It is often a common word in each sentence that makes this happen.

___ While looking at thesis statement, have you told them what you said you would tell them?

___ Check the form: double spaced? correct margins?

___ Check form: footnotes? endnotes?

___ Check form: page numbering? number placement?

___ Go back and check for transitions from sentence to sentence within each paragraph

___ Look for variety of vocabulary and proper word usage

If everything above checks out:

___ Check punctuation

___ Check for sentence fragments

___ Check for tense agreement

___ Check for slang and contractions

___ Check spelling

A Man's Mistake is to Believe He is Working for Someone Else.

TIPS FOR IMPRESSING INSTRUCTORS

Teachers, being rare humanoids[72], are pleased to think that students like them and their classes and that they find the class material interesting and valuable. They are often found to be kindly creatures and like to reward students who put forth extra effort. They, as a rule, are eager to help people who demonstrate a willingness to participate and who have good habits in class. They respond to good treatment.

Since forensic students frequently have to miss a lot of class, it is perhaps wise (even more so than regular students) to keep in good stead with your teachers. It might therefore behove you to follow these few pointers.

1. **GO TO CLASS EVERY TIME.** Be on time and be PREPARED. There will be tournament days when you can't be there. Protect your image with good attendance.

2. **Talk to your instructors**. Ask to complete make-up work before rather than after you go to tournament. You'll feel better and they will feel better.

3. Take all tests on time or at your agreed-upon make-up time. **Never, never stand a teacher up.**[73]

4. If they give you an extension, don't push the limit. Get the completed work in as soon as possible. Never ask for an extension on an extension.

5. **Don't waste their time**. Before class or before a conference, make a list of questions to be answered and/or things what you need to talk about.

6. **Sit at the front** of the room. This is a sign of that eagerness that they love so well, and it helps them know your face [which makes you a real person and thus opens up the door to interpersonal communication].

7. Offer to **perform for class** - English teachers love interp; government teachers may like that speech. You will benefit from the audience, they will reinforce their image of you as a bright, involved student.

8. **Thank the teachers** for their willingness to help you. And really <u>be</u> grateful.

9. Enter into **class discussion**.

10. *Do not ask, "Do I have to know this for the test?"*

11. Pay attention in class and take good notes--teachers notice. **Use good active listening skills**.

12. *Never use forensics as an excuse.*

---

[72]Yes, it is true. Teachers are human. This has been documented.

[73]Unless they fall down.

HINTS FOR DOING BETTER IN CLASS

1. Read all the assigned material. If you can't get it read before class, at the very least, **read first and last paragraphs in chapters, because they sum-up the material.**

2. If there are end-of-chapter questions, read them first. Then you can **read to find the answers**. This helps retention and comprehension.

3. When reading material, look at subheadings first. Then, as you read, try to answer Who, What, When, Where and Why as it concerns those subheadings. Reading with a purpose aids retention. Example: If the subheading is "The Battle of New Orleans", you might want to read to find the answers to who fought?; what was the result?; when did it happen?; why did they fight?

4. **Highlight** as you read.

5. **Outline** in the margins.

6. **Annotate** in the margin.

7. If you look up words - write the definition in the margin.

8. Re-write your class notes as soon as possible after class. This cements the information in your head and forces you to organize the material. This way, if you missed something in your notes, you can ask for clarification at the <u>beginning</u> of the next class period[74].

9. Try to **organize the class notes in a list form.** Lists are easier to remember. Example: 6 causes of the Civil War, 5 reforms caused by the Civil War, 7 types of igneous rocks, etc.

10. Make charts, time lines, graphs, etc., when possible. The very act of doing so helps you remember and the visuals are easier to review for final exams.

11. If items you must learn have several things in common, **concentrate on the differences.** Example: Let us say that you must memorize the definitions of 6 classes of plants. You make a list of the main points in each definition. When you look at the lists you find the first 3 main points of all of the definitions are the same. So you memorize the first 3 points only once instead of 6 times. Then you concentrate on the differences for each definition. This can work for terms of treaties, steps of processes and such. Knowing the difference often helps with multiple choice questions easier.

12. Take 5-10 minutes to review the last class session notes or material right before the next class begins. This also further cements the information.

13. During class, highlight or star anything an instructor places special emphasis on -- or repeats as many as three times.

---

[74] Or outside of class, if you really want to impress that teacher.

14. Use a tape recorder for notes, with permission. The tape can be transcribed to set the information and organize it in your mind as with written class notes. The advantage is that if you are taping you can listen better, not having to worry about getting all the words on paper. You can also play back the tape for information reinforcement[75]. Many people actually comprehend better by listening.

15. If you need a tutor - get one early, before the problem compounds. Your school may offer them free of charge in some kind of peer tutoring exchange. Check it out!

16. If a subject has traditionally given you trouble, consider scheduling it in a Summer Session. It goes very quickly--over faster. Too, concentrating on one subject is easier than concentrating on 4 or 5.

17. **If you have a learning disability DON'T hide it.** Get Help. Many very intelligent students are learning disabled. Programs are available that will make your life and studying easier. Get with the programs.

> # ARGUE FOR YOUR LIMITATIONS,
> # AND SURE ENOUGH,
> # THEY'RE YOURS.
>
> Richard Bach

---

[75] Long car trips home are a good time.

A FEW HINTS ABOUT TESTS

First of all you should know that **test taking is a skill that can be learned and improved.** There are far too many things we could say about test taking than we care to put in this book. Indeed, many books have been written on the subject. So, we have gleaned only a few of our tried and true ones to put here. We recommend that if you are a victim of testaphobia or if you simply wish to make that part of your life easier you should visit the learning/counseling centers on your campus. They often have handouts or video instruction that will be of help. In addition, many schools offer learning skills classes.

1. *Begin to prepare for tests on the first day of class by:*

    A. Keeping all notes ORGANIZED

    B. Getting in the habit of reviewing all material on a daily and weekly basis.

2. Play Teacher: "If I were writing this test, what would I ask?"

3. Remember where the emphasis was placed in class discussion.

4. Try to **think of discussion questions ahead of time** and mentally outline the 3 major points.

5. Ask the teacher WHERE to place the emphasis of studying.

6. Ask the teacher for the parameters of the material to be studied.

7. Take the advice from the memory section of this book.

8. **Don't study what you already know.**

9. Look at the questions at the end of chapters.

10. Check notes and make flash cards.

DURING THE TEST:

1. When you get the test read/scan each section. Find out what percentage of the grade that each section counts. Look at the time and schedule for each section according to its relative worth. Read the instructions <u>carefully.</u>

2. First, answer the short answer questions of which you are sure. CAUTION: In multiple choice questions, don't answer too soon. Remember, you are looking for the <u>best</u> answer. Don't stop reading the possibilities because you came to an answer that "would do".

3. Second, go to the essay section and jot down a short <u>outline</u> for the answer. If you run out of time, you can sometimes get partial credit for the outline. With most essays it is who, what, where, when, and why, or it is persuasive with no less than 2 and no more than 3 points as proof. Write the essential stuff. By and large teachers are not impressed with BS. They just want the <u>answer</u> in clear simple sentences.

4. Third, go back and answer all unanswered short-answer questions.

5. Make educated guesses. **NEVER** leave an answer blank. Only on a few standardized tests will it "cost" you to guess. Those tests will tell you if it hurts to guess--in those cases, don't guess.

6. When "guessing", your first response tends to be correct.

7. If you don't know a word, dissect it. Look for prefixes, suffixes, word roots.

8. Look for give-aways in grammatical construction: agreement of verb and noun, etc.

9. Look for the clue words in true/false questions such as always, never, all -- they are usually in "false" answers. Such words as some, most, etc. are usually found in "true" answers.

10. In true/false questions: if the question has 2 clauses, both must be true for the statement to be true.

11. Use what you learn from previous questions.

12. Be careful to place answers in the proper place. This is ESPECIALLY true if using separate answer sheets. Keep double checking.

13. Remember to use the answer that the <u>teacher</u> supports. A test is no place to debate the issue.

14. You can over-think. You can make a case for nearly any answer if you think long enough. Be careful.

15. Keep an eye on your watch. Leave 3-5 minutes to go over your answers. Time and time again, it has been proven that this can mean points added to your grade. Make sure you have answered every question -- there may be one you were going to come back to but forgot.

16. Don't change your answer unless you really know the new one is correct. Doubt is not enough reason to change.

VI.

GETTING READY TO GO TO TOURNAMENT

SOME NOTES ON MEMORIZING

One of the basic skills needed for competition is memorizing. It is a requirement. Competitors must memorize intros, speeches, transitions, and often, long passages when looking at the page will break the mood. They frequently, through long hours of practice, end up memorizing whole interp events! However, few things scare people more than the task of committing to memory a great deal of material. Take heart! It is a skill that can be learned.

One of the things that memory experts have told us is that our memorizing styles are different. For that reason, you need to experiment with different methods and discover which work best for you. It takes time, concentration and positive thinking. Usually, it takes a place where you can concentrate without interruption. Some of these methods/ideas will work for you, others will be less successful. For most people the more memorizing you do, the better and faster you get. We make no guarantees.

ANALYSIS: Nothing is as successful for memorizing as analysis. Learn what the words mean, why they are in that order. Really take the words apart and put them back together. Understand them inside and out, text and subtext, and you will be amazed at how easy it is to remember them. Some people find that after they have worked with material for a while and with some consistency, they have already memorized most of it without consciously trying. This will not all happen in a single session nor will it happen if coaching is the only place that you think about the material. This is really homework, and hard, but you will find that you really begin to make your material or speech come alive ONLY when you have already memorized it.

Mnemosyne was the Greek goddess of memory and mother of the muses.
Mnemonics is the science or art of improving the memory, as by the use of certain formula.
Mnemonician is an expert in systems of memory.

CONCENTRATION: Concentration is the key to memorization. Whatever interferes with attention will interfere with remembering. When you are able to use total concentration, you will be able to remember totally. This explains why you can often remember lines at home, alone, and then not in a classroom full of tension and distraction. Over-learn, and work hard to develop strong powers of concentration. Concentration is one of the most useful skills you will ever develop and one of the most difficult. It is, however, well worth the effort.

KINETIC: Many of us are kinetic learners. We learn words in association with actions. For those people, it is useful to practice the motions as we practice the words. This is one reason that if you need a prop or visual aid, you will probably need to work with it early. It is often found that the motion, or physical placement will trigger the memory of the line. Of course, it requires lots of practice to teach the brain to associate the specific action with the word, but it will happen with adequate rehearsal. Kinetic learners should physically re-write material to be learned.

AUDITORY: Many of us are auditory learners. That is why so many classes are taught by lecture. If you are one, the use of a tape will be beneficial to you in memorizing. Put your performance pieces or speeches on audio tape and play them as often as possible: in the car, in your sleep, while you work, while you jog. You will get it in your brain just like you do the top 40 hits. Repetition and auditory reinforcement work for many. Be sure that when you record you use good vocal techniques and not a lot of corrections (stammers, starts and stops) because this method of memory will pick up not only the line, but the quality. You will tend to sound like the tape. So be warned.

In partnered events, once all the lines are basically secure, you may want to make a tape that is just your cues with a blank space for you to insert your lines. This way you can practice without your partner being physically present.

TIME: Short practice sessions accomplish more than a single long one. That is why we stress driving time, shower time, lunch time, work breaks. You learn best at the beginning of your learning period; second best at the end. So, short sessions work best by giving you more "best" periods.

SLEEP: Yes, you can learn in your sleep. Rewrite what you plan to learn just before you go to sleep. If you don't have time, then re-read it just before lights out. Some people make and play tapes of their work-in-progress as they go to sleep. The sub-conscious will work hard to tuck those words in your head while you sleep.

SCRIPT: Always begin memorization work with a clean copy of the piece or speech. If you have arrows and scratch outs, or changes in the margin, you will have trouble remembering the content clearly. You will tend to visualize the confusing page with its jumps and garbage. The memorized material in your mind may be as jumbled as the source of the words.

CARDS: Some people use cards to help them in early stages of learning. Speakers frequently put key phrases or outlines on cards and use them to reinforce the organization. Some people make "flash cards" with cues on one side and lines on the other. Still others use cards to cover the text, uncovering to check themselves. Don't expect miracles. This is hard work. It takes some time.

LINKING: People normally tend to learn in chunks and/or in patterns. Your brain is aided by the meaning of the words. You can reason **why** two chunks belong together. Understanding the link from idea to idea helps you build a bridge. Then we can relate new words/sentences to what we already remember. It is like building a wall of ideas. When you hit a snag, try to mentally make a link between those ideas.

PARTNERS: In a partnered session, nothing is as helpful as the partners working together to learn lines. Running lines without regard for interpretation is a useful technique for memorization. Frequently, running lines as fast as possible not only aids the memorization, but also teaches you to pick up your cues. This, however, should not be the only way you rehearse these events.

CUES: Use other people to "cue" you or to "hold book" for you (follow along with your manuscript/speech in their hands). Remind them that you want it letter perfect, if that is what you want. Or, tell them that you want to struggle until you get it, and not to help you until you ask (or raise your hand). This will probably depend on where you are in the process of memorizing. You may ask that they mark "the book" with pencil so that you can check your errors after you have done. Or you may prefer that they make a card with all your errors listed on it. Or they may simply stop you with corrections. You choose.

ROTE: Learning by rote (repeating over and over) will work. But, it is usually the least effective method of learning material. Besides, it takes too long.

STUMPER: If you have a section that seems to stump you every time you come to it, take the time to stop and re-analyze that section. Why doesn't it seem to fit? Why don't you remember it? It probably is eluding you because you don't understand it as well as the other sections. Try to analyze how it develops from the section before it, and why it is followed by the next section. Build yourself an idea bridge that will carry you from one idea to another. Imagine what happens that has caused this line to be written. Or visualize each word in the sentence. Or make up a rhyme with the first letters of each section or----or-----

In the case of speeches, it may be that your words are hard to memorize because they are not as clear as they could be, or the transition is not that smooth, or because the sentence is too awkward or too long. If this is the case, fix it.

INTERRUPTION: If you always start at the beginning, but usually get interrupted (or stumped at the same place)...try beginning in the middle sometimes or some other spot. Memorizing can get "lopsided" (you know one part very well and the other part is shakier). When you keep going back to the beginning and then getting stumped or interrupted at the same spot, the interruptions become part of what is memorized. Or, you never get the other sections down as strong as the beginning. So mix it up to even it out.

Some people like to memorize the most difficult parts first. If you divide memorizing into sections, always put the break of the sections **after** the transitions (the link), so that one idea is connected to another. Otherwise you tend to memorize from one section to another without the links, which hampers the flow of ideas in continuity, when you try to repeat them.

REPEAT: Once you have committed the lines to memory, go over them **EVERY DAY** to reinforce the learning. Rehearse aloud as if performing. If this is not always possible, you may have to practice silently, but never stop. Just before a tournament it is a good to re-<u>read</u> the speech/material to correct any "glitches", and to set it absolutely in your mind. This is called "going back to the script".

SCHEDULE: Most people are helped if they have a realistic schedule for memorizing and stick with it. Memorizing does involve some time and should be started as soon as you get the material ready. Remember, as you analyze the work, you are memorizing. Apply your mind to the task from the beginning. If you only use half of your concentration to work on material, you are adding time to the amount that will be needed to memorize. Watching TV as you memorize your speech, more than doubles the time required. Maximize your effort, concentrate 100%.

EMOTION: Emotion has a strong effect on memory, both good and bad. Panic can erase a memory, strong positive emotion can burn things into your brain. Feel the emotion. Use it. Make the words mean something that will cause them to live with you.

SOBRIETY: It is a scientific fact that we remember best when we memorize clean and sober, and deliver the memorization the same way.

TRICKS: Memory <u>devices</u> are tricks of the trade that do work for those impossible spots. Such as: setting that line to a tune, or using acronyms, or making up silly rhymes. Most of these are usually more helpful with such things as the original 13 colonies than they are to forensic pieces, but if the need exists....

PRACTICE PRACTICES
or
HOW TO USE YOUR PRACTICE TIME TO BEST ADVANTAGE

It is no secret that the most valued commodity of any working competitor is time. They never have enough time of any sort, especially practice time. In order to help you use the practice time that you do have to best advantage, we would like to give you some helpful tips.

SOME NOTES ON PRACTICING:

One of those tired old things that coaches hear year after year[76] is, "I never practice. I'll be fine in performance." Or "I am always better at home." Years of experience prove that almost EVERYONE is better in performance, IF they have done the proper amount of rehearsal in front of some kind of knowing audience before that performance. Even if you are one of those who "kick in" when you perform "for real", it is not going to be good enough by the end of the season -- maybe not good enough by the second round at the first tourney of the season. Rehearsal can make your final product consistently fabulous. So, some attention must be paid to getting the most from your practice sessions.

There are many different techniques of practice and successful students may use any or all of them. Therefore, it will be helpful if you try many different ways to perfect the product. You will find the most useful techniques through many hours of (You guessed it!) practice. You may also find that the best methods are different for different events. This is very personal, so experiment.

Don't forget, the coach needs to see your pieces periodically (**especially** before it is perfect). If you are having trouble getting the event to work, they can save you lots of time and frustration.

There is really no substitute for hard work, and those teams with winning records prove that fact over and over. If you want to shine in performance, you cannot practice enough, nor can you begin too early. Great work can seldom be done in the last week before a contest.

Some of the methods that might be useful to you are detailed on the following pages.

---

[76] Usually from first semester students

A PLETHORA OF PRACTICE PLANS

Practice, which is sometimes called rehearsals, can be:

SOLITARY...... by yourself, the most common and fruitful of rehearsal techniques

MECHANICAL.... with the help of a tape or video recorder

COACHED....... with the help of your forensic coach or your teammates or another audience, such as a class

There are tricks to getting the most out of each of them, which will be discussed in a page or so.

Practice sessions should begin as soon as you have selected the material and should continue until your last performance is finished. It is the way that the performer and the material become one unit...a marriage if you will...and it is one of the most powerful secrets to success. The practice sessions may last only as long as it takes to run one small section of your piece, or it may last for hours if you are really involved in what you are doing.

REMEMBER:

As soon as you have the cutting in a workable form, it is a good idea to put the material in the folder and to practice standing up and using the notebook. Or, if you're practicing a speech, put it onto note cards, stand up, and begin.

REMEMBER:

Time the event as often as you can.

REMEMBER:

Practice as though it were real. Visualize the room, the audience, the judge, etc. This means that you are creating for yourself the reality of a competition round. Practice it all -- what you do before and after your performance. Give 100% effort. Do the best work that you can do -- even if your only audience is your stuffed giraffe or a poster of your current hero. This applies even when you are doing only a section or an intro.

METHODS OF PRACTICE

SOLITARY:

The most frequently used rehearsal method is practicing alone. It is the most popular form because it can be done late at night or as the sun rises -- any time that is convenient to you. Actually, most of the best work is done by the eager student on his own. This is the time to analyze, reflect, research (yes, in the library), work on motivation, work for fluency, and practice correcting the things that you have mis-learned through other methods. Working on your own is a habit you should cultivate. If you will only practice for an audience, let's face it -- you lack discipline and will lack polish. Some competitors make solitary rehearsal a part of their bedtime ritual--some make it a morning wake-up exercise. But, having a regular time seems to work best. Make rehearsal a habit -- not just running through the event, but really "working". Finding the missing motivation, analyzing the grey area, thinking about (or researching) the weak spot, turning the phrase, learning the gesture, how to effectively close the folder -- in short, rehearsing EVERYTHING!.

MECHANICAL:

Using the audio and video recorder can be the fastest way of perfecting your performances, because it allows you a certain amount of objectivity about yourself. By hearing and/or seeing yourself as others will, you can spot and correct your problems quickly. You tend not to repeat that awful face you make once you have seen it on video tape. In addition, it provides you **and** your coach with a record of your progress. This can be very valuable because, it helps to check previous good performances to see what it was you "used to do" that you aren't doing now. This is especially helpful if you've forgotten something wonderful. Hopefully your school has both types of recorders available for your use. Check into this.

Special notes on Videotaping: Obviously, it is a little unnatural to talk to a machine, so it may help if you invite a small audience (especially the first few times you videotape). Other potential "tapers" are good choices.

The real value of the tape comes in watching and/or listening to the finished tape. This may be done privately or with a coach. Don't be afraid to stop-start and replay the tape in order to find out exactly what is and what isn't working. Notice as you watch when **your** attention (as an audience member) wanders--Why? Watch the tape as many times as you need to.

It may be best for all concerned if you bought a video tape of your own on which to record your performances but, sharing is okay. Either way, do not tape over other performances. The past record is as valuable as the current one. Consider dating each performance on the tape -- either mechanically, if your recorder has an automatic date stamp or just verbally state the date before you begin your performance. Be particularly careful of other performers work, if sharing a tape.

Please be certain to turn the machines off when you are finished. When you finish watching your tape, it will help if you do not rewind it. Then the tape is cued up and ready for the next performance.

ASSISTED PRACTICE:

Many times in your practice, you will feel the need for another opinion...

>Is the new thing working?

>Does it make sense?

>What is keeping it from "jelling"?

>Is your body helping or hurting the message?

...things that you simply can't judge for yourself. During those times, one of the first choices is to find a trusted coach, if there is one available.

Another good choice is a seasoned competitor...one with competition experience. They can give you a good idea about what they think is working and not working with your performance.

When seeking student advice, remember that it is just that...student advice. Many times you will get excellent and helpful information that you can use, but if you hear anything that discourages you or that you aren't certain about, take your problem to a coach <u>at once</u>. They will give you an honest, definite answer. Even seasoned competitors sometimes give absolute answers--that are absolutely wrong.

Another choice is to ask anyone that you trust to give you that information. Note: It is a good idea to ask them to watch for specific things. That way you won't get information that you don't want at this time and they have some idea about what you want them to hone in on. Otherwise they may not notice the problem you want addressed at all.

Friends who have no forensic training are still a good audience because they know what they like and if it holds their interest. If it doesn't, something may need to be changed. Ask them to be specific (rather than critical) about why they did/didn't like it. Having non-forensic friends watch your performance has an added bonus. You may be a teacher of forensic appreciation to your friends.

3 X 3 is another plan that works. At the end of your performance, ask your "audience" to tell you 3 things that worked and 3 things that didn't work.

COACHED PRACTICE:

This is the preferred method of practice. Unfortunately, there are so many of you and so few coaches that this method isn't possible all the time. If you are planning to work only in the presence of a coach, drop out now and save everyone some time. Coached rehearsal is for refining material that you have prepared yourself. Coaches **are** problems-solvers and time-savers **but** will not do for you the things that you must do for yourself. Working the worksheets between coaching sessions will help you <u>and</u> the coach use the time wisely.

Coaches will help get you started. They will tell you what material and style is acceptable in your region. They must be consulted very early about material, speech topics, etc. so that they can tell you if it is appropriate and if it has winning potential. If you work without this approval, you are running a risk of not qualifying for tournament and of losing valuable time. Once you have the material approved by your coach, you are on your own for a little while.

Many coaches assign time or post some sort of schedule for student rehearsal times. Schedule time with your coach and keep that appointment. If for any reason you have a problem, please have the courtesy to call and cancel as soon as possible. Remember that it is wise to allow enough time between coaching sessions to work on the suggestions made by your coach in the prior session.

Before a coach works with you, they will probably ask you about the running time of your piece/speech. It is your job to see that the piece/speech is **undertime**. Unless time **is** your problem, coaches will probably not want to work on a selection that is still overtime.

Coached practice is valuable assistance in making your speech work, as well as for evaluating your progress, polishing, and directing. From these practice sessions come the information that helps decide the slate of competitors. Coaches are aware that growth is essential to good performance and one of their criteria for performers is usually the amount and quality of the development of a performer or event. So it is essential that they see your "Stuff" as it develops. Later, when they evaluate your progress and assess your ability to compete, their first hand knowledge of your work ethic and growth will be a big bonus for you. At the same time, coaches are aware that these are working rehearsals and are not expecting perfection...yet! So, don't wait until you are "perfect" to perform for your coach.

ODDS AND ENDS ABOUT PRACTICE

1. It is normal for students to feel awkward and nervous when rehearsing in a coach's office. Coaches will try to make you feel more comfortable, but you should remember that they are trying to help you become what you want to be. The more time that has to be spent coaxing you, the less time that can be spent actually working with you.

2. Many students find it helpful to practice offstage focus in a mirror. The focus is like viewing your partner in the mirror. Maybe your school has a dressing room with lots of room and big mirrors. Refer to "FOCUS IN INTERPRETATION"

3. Some facilities have practice rooms (i.e. soundproof rooms in the library, music practice rooms) that can be used to practice forensics. These are usually secluded and quiet and no one knows where to find you.

4. Interpers: The script should be a part of your performance. Use it as you would a part of your arm. Practice page turns, looking up, practice standing and sitting with script, etc..

    Speakers: Always practice with your visual aids. They need to become very natural for you. Practice with the same easels, too.

5. If your selection calls for alternate characters (voices), begin to use them aloud with the first rehearsal so that you're not self-conscious about them later. Feel free to experiment until they are right. It is easier if you think of them as characters, rather than disembodied "voices". Refer to "CREATING CHARACTERS FOR THE INTERPRETATION".

6. Written criticism should be kept and studied. Critiques (ballots) from coaches and judges are written for the education of performers. Soooo...be educated by them.

A HEALTHY COMPETITOR IS A HAPPY COMPETITOR

There is probably nothing on earth harder on your body than competition. Stress, strain, travel, and bad eating habits combine to sabotage you just at the moment you need to be 100% fit. Therefore, guarding your health has to start **now** and continue as long as you compete. Energy, endurance, and sparkle are **crucial to success. So, well in advance of the tournament:**

1. **Eat right.** Not just on competition days, but every day. Junk food and fad diets will rob you of the **steady** flow of energy that is essential. Get some veggies, some green things (besides mold), some meat/protein. They are needed for basic energy building. This building of an efficient system cannot be postponed until the last minute. Carbohydrates (like pasta) are an excellent tournament food choice, as they provide a steady flow of energy. For more detailed information read "FOOD AND FORENSICS".

2. **Control the sleep.** This takes time management and self discipline. The body needs a certain amount of sleep every 24 hours. You know how much is necessary to make you think best and sparkle most. If you don't know how much sleep you need, discover it soon. Not everyone requires 8 hours. Many do better with less and some require more. Sleep researchers tell us that one of the keys to feeling "rested" is a consistent sleep pattern that includes almost always the same number of hours. Get it...no matter what...on a regular basis.

3. **Avoid** germ laden situations. Don't share food and drink. Kissing is optional. You are in charge of yourself.

4. If you get sick, just before a tourney, **get medical help.** Your forensic future depends on it. If you don't have a doctor, ask the school nurse or your coach for a recommendation.

5. **Take vitamins**...regularly. They help. BUT, they don't help your tournament activity if you wait until departure to start them. Two weeks before tournament is a minimum for real help.

6. Try to **control the stress** level in your life. For many people, stress attacks the throat. This can be fatal for a competitor. Controlling stress is very difficult, but by being smart, you can reduce it. The following will go a long way to avoid stressful situations in a competitor's life:

    A. **Be straight with your teachers.** Tell them very early that you compete and will have to miss some classes. Let them help you plan a course of action...Get them on your side. Visit with them when you return. Share the educational benefits of competition and how it furthers your own career goals.

    B. Go to class **every time** that you're not on a forensic trip ...and be on time. Then you won't have to worry about trips making your absence record look like a basketball score. Your teachers will love you for it. (Well, at least respect you.)

    C. **Offer to do make-up work in advance.** Do assignments ahead. Go the extra mile. Then you can relax. Prepare big assignments (i.e. themes) over a long period of time, well in advance of the due dates. It's much easier to come back to class with everything done than with everything late and hanging over your head.

    D. **Prepare** your forensic events well in advance and over-rehearse them. Get **READY** well ahead. This will give you control of your time and energy.

7. There are also ways to **help yourself** when stress does occur, once you have learned to recognize it. As you begin to understand more about how stress affects you as an individual, you will come up with your own ideas of helping to ease tensions. But here are some suggestions[77]:

   A. **TRY PHYSICAL ACTIVITY** — Pressure can often times be released through exercise or physical activity. Playing sports, jogging, walking or dancing are just some of the activities you might try. Physical exercise helps relieve that "up tight" feeling and relaxes you! Exercise also builds endurance, breath control, a sense of well being. Relieving stress is a bonus.

   B. **SHARE YOUR STRESS** — Often just talking to someone about your concerns and worries will help you see your problem in a different light. Friends, family members, teachers, or counselors may help. If the problem is serious, seek professional help. Knowing when to ask for help may avoid a more serious problem later.

   C. **MAKE TIME FOR FUN** — Play can be as important to your well being as work. Everyone needs a break from daily routines to just relax and have fun. Too, it is a scientific fact that laughter heals and that imagination grows with use. So, one way to have fun may just be having a good case of the sillies or day dreaming.

   D. **BE A DUCK** — If something which is causing you stress is beyond your control and cannot be changed at the moment, don't fight it. Learn to accept what is -- for now -- until you can change it. A duck lets water roll off its back. If it soaked it up, the duck would drown.

   E. **ITS OK TO CRY** — A good cry can be a healthy way to bring relief to anxiety (physical and psychological). Actually, a "good cry" might can often **prevent** a headache or some other physical consequences of stress. Too, taking slow deep breaths can release tension.

   F. **CREATE A QUIET SCENE** — Visualize a peaceful, serene setting (such as a country side, the mountains or the sea). If you can't physically "get away", taking a mental vacation for a few minutes can relax you. Often reading a good book or playing beautiful music can create a sense of peace and tranquility. Remember that the mind controls the body -- if you think you are in a peaceful place, your body will (if you let it) react as if it were in a peaceful place.

   G. **AVOID SELF-MEDICATION** — Although some drugs[78] (both legal and illegal one) can relieve stress temporarily, they do not remove the conditions that caused the stress in the first place. Drugs may also be habit-forming and thus create more stress than they take away. Taking illegal drugs definitely increase overall stress levels -- just by the fact that they are illegal and socially unacceptable. Prescription drugs should only be used as prescribed. Avoid playing doctor. Don't assume you know how to increase your dosage safely.

---

[77] These suggestions are only a BROAD overview gleened from many different sources -- including our own experience with forensic situations.

[78] We assume that you, as an educated person, know that alcohol is a drug. Remember alcohol poisoning can kill...

H. **CHECK OFF YOUR TASKS** — Trying to take care of everything at once can seem overwhelming and, as a result, you may not accomplish anything. Making lists of tasks you have to do, giving priority to the most important one, doing them one at a time, and checking them off as they['re completed, is more satisfying -- and thus stress is held at bay. For extra help on those days when the world keeps you from doing what was on the list, write down what you did do and then proudly check it off -- it really helps!

I. **FOCUS ON "I CAN" AND GET RID OF "I CAN'T"** — Is there any logical reason why other can accomplish their goals, but you can't? Of course not! But often, we program our subconscious mind to accept that, for whatever reason, we "can;t." This is a false, self-limiting belief. We're much less stressed out if we learn to embrace the idea of "I can" or even "I must." The truth is, you really are in control of your life -- total control. Learn to approach life positively.

The best strategy for avoiding stress is to learn how to release. Find activities that give you pleasure and that are good for your mental and physical well-being. This will help you be a more successful competitor, student and overall person. We should never forget to be good to ourselves!

HEALTH WHILE ON A TOURNAMENT:

1. **Stay calm**, cool, and collected. Don't use your energy foolishly.

2. Remember, in traveling, that bus talk is **hard on the throat**...go easy on it. If you are not practicing put on your headset, plug in some stress release music, and close your eyes.

3. **Keep up your good habits**: vitamins, sleep, diet.

4. **Keep alert for your body signals about energy**. When it dips, do something. Find an energetic friend, or eat some high energy snack food.

   Some people are not a good judge of their own energy levels. They think they are "fine" when they are really drooping. A competitor of our acquaintance thought her energy level was fine as long as she had any energy at all. It took us a long time to convince her that when we said it was time for her to eat (in order to sustain/raise her fuel tank level) that she MUST EAT right then.

   Speaking of food and energy, it should be noted that sugar gives a quick high followed by a low -- not always a good combination. An old favorite that you might consider in lieu of that Snickers is peanut butter and crackers.

   What ever you use, remember that food takes at least 15-30 minutes to start working. [Often your energy levels will have a pattern. If you learn that pattern, you can cut the energy slump off at the pass.] For more detail read "FOOD AND FORENSICS".

   While at tournament, it is probably not a good idea to nap when your energy drops. It takes too long to get the energy level back up when coming out of sleep mode. Instead, DO something -- walk or talk or find an energy filled person and interact with them.

5. **Get sleep at tournaments**, and let others do so as well. It is sad to hear competitors say that they weren't at their best because they stayed up and played the night before. Worse yet, that they lost because their **former** friends and/or roomies stayed up and played.

6. Remember that tournaments are won in the **tough times**: in the last round after a grueling day; late at night when most normal people have tired themselves out. Plan well in advance so that you will still be fresh in that final round, when all around you people are collapsing. Guarding your health will pay off here.

LIFE IS WHAT HAPPENS WHILE YOU ARE MAKING OTHER PLANS.

John Lennon

7. Remember that hot tea (especially herbal without caffeine) is good to help loosen your throat. Stay away from milk and milk shakes when you have a **glunky throat**—they may feel good, but in actuality they just make the voice worse. Lemon juice, lemon drops, honey and lemon, and some medicines, are much better.

8. Keep your own medicines with you: an aspirin or two, a cough drop, an antacid (even an extra pair of contacts or eyeglasses). If you need them, you have them. This is not, however, a good time to resort to chemicals to give "energy" or an "edge". Chemical advantage is very dangerous and control is quickly out of hand.

    If you are taking medication for some continuing condition, i.e. diabetes, epilepsy, hyperactivity, tournament time is not a good time to experiment with quitting or changing dosages.
    If you are prone to a medical need, i.e. cluster headaches, migraines, etc., take along a small emergency supply of that medication.

    If your baby is due any day, please tell your coach.[79]

---

[79] Don't laugh. They need to know. This example we did not make up.

FOOD AND FORENSICS

You might ask yourself, "What does diet have to do with forensics?" The answer is simple. Your dietary condition is reflected in any activity that involves your body. You really ARE what you eat. The people who fall asleep during rounds, who have that "pasty look", who lose energy in the middle of a tourney, most likely have a dietary problem. In a tournament, especially a swing (back-to-back tourneys), you must have stamina. If your body is not trained along with your events, you will be facing some frustration which could be avoided with a CONSISTENT dietary program.

To achieve maximum results, it is imperative you take good care of yourself. Get plenty of sleep and eat 3 balanced meals a day.

Well... okay, that last sentence reads like your mother's or maybe your grandmother's advice. Before you flip the page, having decided that we're just old fogies who don't understand, let us qualify. Not everyone needs 3 meals a day -- many people do better with 2 a day and a few with one a day -- and some people eat small amount of food 6 - 10 times a day. What's important is to eat enough to keep a consistent energy level. And by the way... "meal" does not have to mean sit down at a table with entree, veggies, drink, etcetera. A "meal" may be peanut butter and crackers, an apple and water or even a nutrition drink or countless other healthy choices.

Just as with your sleep requirements, you need to figure out how your body best functions with food. An important key is to eat when you are hungry. If you tend to get hungry at the same time every day then you could be really smart and eat about 30 minutes before you actually get hungry or before you KNOW you are going to need a lot of energy. In any case, do not wait so long that your energy level is depleted.

Tournament, of course, is a meal of a different color. At a tournament, when you're on a schedule, you may need to eat BEFORE you are hungry because you may not get another chance until it is too late.

When you eat, one good choice is to eat plenty of carbohydrates that have a nutritional bonus, such as fruits and vegetables. These give sustained, even-flow energy which keep you at your best for a sustained period of time. If you ever need a quick boost of energy [which will not create a rapid descent afterward], honey or another food stuff that has fructose (not sucrose) as a main ingredient is recommended. Fructose is easily digested and will not create a "sugar low" after it is metabolized.

Be careful of your dairy product intake. The lactose will build up in your body and will slow your reaction time and thicken your mucosa and saliva. This could take a bit of the edge off your performance, and possibly give you a good case of cotton mouth or clogged nasal passages.

Drink plenty of water and juices (no sucrose additives). This will allow your body to dispose of toxins, keep the saliva and mucosa levels at a functioning level, and keep the body functioning at a more effective level.

Junk food will meet the immediate needs of "something in your stomach", but it is nutritionally only hollow food stuff. It will cost you loss of stamina and power when you reach your final rounds. Junk food will give a good boost of energy, but it will bring about an even faster deficit. Your body will soon tell you it's hungry again -- gaining momentum with each candy bar. You loose health, stamina and maybe the final round.

PRE-TRAVEL CHECKLIST

THIS IS JUST A BEGINNING...

    IT WILL PROBABLY NOT COVER ALL YOU NEED TO DO, BUT HAVE YOU:

____ Picked up excused absence sheet and given it to each instructor (If your school uses this system)?

____ Discussed class work, for missed class time, with each instructor?

____ Arranged to get someone's class notes from each missed class?

____ Gotten the phone numbers of person from whom you have planned to get the class notes?

____ Arranged your absence at your job? Smiled and told them "Thank You"?

____ Found out where the team will load the vehicles; whose vehicle you are in; the departure and return times?

____ Given info about your destination to those concerned?

____ Arranged for transportation from campus to "home" upon your return?

____ Given your coach a phone number to call if you are delayed, or if unscheduled changes come up?

____ Finished all intros and transitions and memorized them?

____ Video taped your selections...and watched them?

____ Made "good" (clean and current) copies of your scripts, intros, and transitions?

____ Assembled all your working supplies in "carry-on luggage". Such as:

    ____ Note cards
    ____ Highlighters
    ____ Flashlight
    ____ Batteries
    ____ Scissors
    ____ Cat Cases (with everything filed and in order)
    ____ Paper, pens, pencils, reinforcements
    ____ Stop watch
    ____ Script/folder
    ____ Speech scripts

____ Labeled your VA cases, packed your VAs, cover sheets, tripods?

____ Discreetly labeled your script/folder with identification of owner?

____ Checked out consolidation of your stuff with your roomies?

____ Checked the weather at the destination...Will you need an umbrella, coat?

____ Checked to see if there is a need for "special occasion" clothes?

____ Chosen your clothes, shoes, accessories for tournament and pared it down to a minimum?

____ Washed your clothes; picked up the cleaning?

____ Gathered all personal supplies needed: razor, deodorant, energy food, medication, contact lens stuff, etc.?

____ Gotten money, Travelers checks?

____ Packed like a good competitor?

____ Checked the tournament schedule and made a fill-in-blank sheet for the front of your script leaving a place for room numbers and speaker positions?

EXAMPLE:

DATE	TIME	RD #	EVENT	ROOM #	SPKR #	JUDGE

PACKING LIKE A PROFESSIONAL COMPETITOR
or
THE ANCIENT ART OF SUITCASE CONTROL

This art is learned quickly by **good** forensic folks... OR ELSE!

A few words about your clothes:

Dress should be **neat** at all times (after all, you are representing your school!) While traveling you are generally allowed to wear jeans or sweats....casual. However at contests, suits or dress slacks and dress shirts/sweaters/ties are the appropriate attire for men. Women generally wear dresses or suits while performing. "Sunday best" is a good description. Your dressing should compliment, not detract from, your performance. It is hard to take a speech on the Effects of Agent Orange seriously if the speaker is clad in lemon yellow slacks. It clashes. This applies to anything: makeup, ties, fingernails, jewelry that dangles, jingles, or draws attention to itself and away from your material.

You should have your own "look". Just make sure it is **tasteful and professional**. Make sure that your clothes are clean, pressed, fit properly.

For non-competition time, bring clothes that are casual--NOT SLOPPY. Your judges will be seeing you. Forensics squads tend to stay at the same hotels. you will be seen, and an impression will be made - conscious or not.

Competition shoes deserve great consideration. You will be on your feet for 12 or more hours a day. You will climb stairs, cross campuses, and generally do a lot of walking back and forth. Your concentration is affected by feet. You lose all chance for professionalism by going bare footed or limping painfully on blistered feet. Somehow, it doesn't quite make the impression you want. Suggestion: pick comfortable shoes first. Then make the wardrobe fit the shoes. Enough said.

Mixing and matching is a good solution for longer tournaments. This means wearing the same clothes in different configurations. Keep it simple. (Mixing and matching with team mates is even a consideration.) Women might try one-piece non-crushable knit dresses or combinations of skirts, sweaters, jackets. Then use scarves, or simple jewelry to dress them up and change the mood. Men can achieve the same effect by a change of tie, vests, or maybe even suspenders! Men should wear slacks and dress shirts. If you don't own a jacket, wear ties and sweaters that look dressy and professional. Remember that dark colors usually hide stains and compliment many styles of programs. Decide on your ensembles **before you go**. Make a choice.

Additional information about packing:

One small suitcase or hanging bag, and one tote is the usual limit per team member. There is very limited space in school vehicles and crowded hotel rooms. Pack together if possible (especially in hanging bags). Note: your luggage will probably take a beating, so no priceless gator bags.

Share hair dryers, irons, shampoo, toothpaste, etc. Your roomies should be assigned early enough to decide which things can be co-used. If you borrow things: **RETURN THEM PROMPTLY!!**

Women: pack an extra pair of neutral hose. Men: pack dark socks.

Some smart cookies bring their own clothes hangers and towels (complete with plastic take home bag). It is up to you, but it may sometimes help.

Check the seams, the buttons, the fit of your clothes **before** you get to the tournament. And then pack safety pins and sewing gear anyway.

You bring it, you usually carry it. So, light is better. Southern belles who think the "gentlemen" should help, usually end up wishing they were at Tara, not on a forensic team.

Backup eye gear [contacts, glasses] is helpful, if your are handicapped without it.
If you must carry your sound machine, make it a small one, limit the musical choice, and above all, bring head sets or leave the whole system at home.

Check out the climate/weather at your destination. You do not always stay indoors at a tourney. Therefore, sweaters, coats, umbrellas or rain wear are always a consideration.

Don't forget allergy medicine, etc. if you are prone. While it should be common knowledge, keep in mind that you should never share ANY prescription medicine, and be exceptionally careful even with over-the-counter stuff.

Note: If you have special medical situations, let your coach know. Are you on medication? Do you have severe allergies? Do you have seizures, asthma attacks, etc. The coaches need to be prepared for such emergencies. It will not become public knowledge.

NEVER pack your scripts. Keep them with you at ALL TIMES. For working as you travel, have close at hand: your flashlight, batteries for that flashlight, pencil, paper, highlighters and any working materials you might need.

EMERGENCY SUPPLIES

At almost every tournament, someone on the squad will have an "emergency". Whether it is a real or an imagined one, temporary or permanent, here is list of items that we suggest that someone (not everyone) bring to each tournament to assist in repairs, cures or whatever:

[Note: You could divide the list or designate a "supplier".]

____   **Scissors**

____   Cellophane tape (excellent for hem repairs)

____   Needle and assorted thread

____   Lip balm

____   Clear nail polish and polish remover pads (the polish for runners and the remover for chipped nails

____   Nail clippers

____   Tweezers

____   Hole punch

____   Extra highlighters

____   Cough Drops, Lemon Drops

____   Masking Tape (Keeps slippery VA easels on tables)

____   Safety pins (in an emergency, remember to check clothes that have been to the cleaners)

____   Reinforcements for page holes

____   Small First Aid Kit (Band Aids, aspirin, antacid, eye wash)

____   Extra folder

____   Extra slicks (if used)

____   Paper clips

____   Feminine hygiene products

____   Male hygiene products (lest anyone think we are sexist)

ROOMIES
or
HOW TO LIVE WITH STRANGERS AND SURVIVE

You usually have no control over who you get as roomies, but you can request a change from your coach in advance, if you have a good cause. Be prepared -- even a "good cause" may not be enough.

At most motels and on many squads, the rule is four to a room. Economy is the phrase to live by. Get used to it. Occasionally you may find more than four! Sleeping bag city! But even if your are only sharing a room with one other person you still need to know roommate survival.

Find out who among your roomies is a morning bather, who is a night bather, who takes the longest to do hair, to dress, to wake up, and to be civil. This is not a gender issue. Everyone does hair and becomes civil. Then plan when to get up, and the order of rising. Remember, if it takes longer for Go-Slo Flo or Sleepy-head Ed to get ready, allow for it. Plan ahead! Make sure she gets up and gets going. There is no second chance to be on time.

Never borrow anything unless you need to. Never borrow anything without asking the owner. Never be offended if someone says "No." Never be afraid to say "No." Pre-planned sharing is not the same thing as borrowing.

Be aware that we all have our little quirks. Don't gripe. Be sensitive. If the quirk is more than you can handle, given the stress that the occasion brings, talk it out. This does not mean explode. Respect each other's work process and nerve endings. There is plenty of tension at a tournament without adding roommate trouble to it.

Obviously, it is helpful if smokers and non-smokers can be segregated for room assignment at the hotel. If that is not possible, we assume you smokers are courteous enough to go away from the non-smokers room to indulge in your habit.

Be aware of other people's work habits. Some folks practice and/or warm up in the morning. Some go over everything at night. Some have a special psyche system. Try to allow for it and respect each other's rights at the same time. Some people NEED sleep. If you want to rehearse and your roomies want to sleep, go into the bathroom, close the door and rehearse. Let them sleep.

If you are a night owl and your roomie is an early-to-bed person, respect it. Bring a quiet thing to do while they are asleep. Find out if the light bothers them (book lights or your trusty flashlight might help).

Do not be offended if your roomie is a "Morning Monster" or if they are a "Happy-and-Bursting-with-Song Person". Do not push your luck if you fall into one of these categories.

If you have a REAL wake up problem, discuss it with your roomies. Tell them how you need it handled. You may ask the "morning person" to take you on as a challenge. No matter what, deal with what can turn out to be a real problem.

Use headsets for your music. Not only must you consider your roomies but you must consider the people next door (one of your judges may be trying to sleep on the other side of the wall).

Neatness counts. Keep your gear together and tidy. It will expedite many things: packing, finding lost items, keeping tempers, leaving on time.

Share the space. Don't hog all the counter; all the closet; all the drawers; all the bed. If you have a legitimate need for a bed by yourself – discuss this with your coach as soon as possible. Then you may need to explain to your roommates as well.

Remember that each of you has to be at your best every competitive morning. Rounds start early! Be smart <u>and</u> considerate.

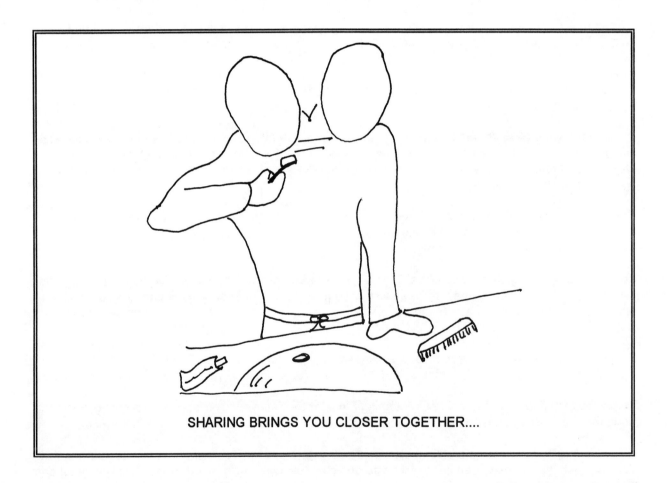

SHARING BRINGS YOU CLOSER TOGETHER....

ON THE ROAD
or
TRAVEL GUIDE FOR NOMADIC COMPETITORS

COMPANION READING:

PACKING LIKE A PROFESSIONAL COMPETITOR
ROOMIES
TOURNAMENT BEHAVIOR

BEFORE YOU GO, TAKE CARE OF YOUR CLASSES:

Discuss attendance with each of your teachers as early as possible in the semester. You might warn them that some absences will be forthcoming. Offer to "make up " your work in advance. Inform all of your teachers of your plans before you leave. (Some schools will provide you with an excuse form that you are required to give to your instructors.) Share with your teachers when you get back so that they feel like a part of your team.

It is a good idea to spot (and make friends with) one or two of the best students in class. Get their phone number. Ask them to help you catch up when you miss, by keeping notes and assignments for you. Be certain to thank them and return the favor when possible. It might be nice to give them a small thank you note at the end of the semester.

THEN:

Pack like a professional competitor.

Find out the "game plan":
    LEAVING TIME, WHERE TEAM IS MEETING, INFO FOR PARENTS, RETURNING TIME, etc..
    Write it down. When your team posts a leaving time, they **will** usually leave then--with or without you.

If you are involved with driving or picking up the vehicles, it is <u>your</u> responsibility to check with your coach for special information anywhere from a week to two days ahead.

HE WHO LAUGHS, LASTS.

Mary Poole

ON T-DAY (TRAVEL DAY):

Be early, packed, ready to go!. Have your luggage there in time to have the vehicles packed before leaving time -- whether you are there that early or not!

Most teams travel in cars, vans, etc. in caravan style. Unless you have special permission, you go <u>with</u> the squad. Coaches generally decide who rides with whom and who drives. The grouping has to do with getting forensic work done on the way to the tourney. Fuel stops give you a chance to change configurations. Its kinda like educational chinese fire drills. **Note**: Coaches assign students to ride in particular vehicles for various reasons.

Generally everybody helps load the vehicles, make a pit stop, and then gets into their assigned vehicles.

Many coaches get testy if you try to get on the van without your final intros and transitions written and memorized. Don't laugh. An irate forensic coach is a terrible thing to witness.

If any car needs to stop for an emergency, the driver should signal other vehicles by flashing lights, blinkers, etc. Watch for these signs when you are in a caravan.

Don't stop unless the other vehicles do; if there is an emergency; or if you can no longer see the vehicle behind you. If traveling in a caravan, stay close enough to be easily seen but do not ride the bumper of the vehicle in front of you. A steady speed seems to work best for vehicles traveling together. Allow plenty of time for changes of lanes, of turns, etc.. Multiple vehicles are not as flexible as one vehicle.

BRIEF stops for bathroom and drinks will be taken, of course. That is unless your coach is really miffed. When traveling a squad usually make as few stops as possible, therefore, when you stop—go whether you need to or not. "Tiny tanks" should restrict fluid intake at stops. Teams generally stop to eat major meals together because it is the fastest way.

WHEN YOU ARRIVE:

Teams often arrive at motels late at night. So, be tolerant of people in the motel by being courteous and quiet.

It is usually the coach's responsibility to register the team and distribute room assignments and keys. The team then drives to the rooms, which for some inexplicable reason are always at the back of the motel and on the upper floors. Quickly and quietly, unload your gear and go to your rooms.

Note: Unless you have a real physical need for help, you carry your own junk - all of it.

Once in your room, quickly unpack, check to make sure you have enough towels, set alarms and/or leave a wake-up call. If you are smart, you will get out your clothes for tomorrow (press, assemble). Then, depending on the hour and the schedule, you will either practice, go to the tournament, or go to bed.

GOING HOME:

Check-out times vary, but you usually have to be packed and/or the vehicles loaded on the morning of your last day--BEFORE you leave to compete for the day. Baggage may be loaded on the vehicle, or placed in **one particular** room. Do this efficiently and allow plenty of time.

If you are going to change clothes for the trip home, you should put your traveling clothes in your tote, or where you can get to them easily.

Be sure that you carefully check to see that you have left nothing behind: stuff on the back of the bathroom door, under the bed, on the night stand, in the drawers.

Rooms should be left in a reasonably tidy state. You are less likely to leave something behind if you tidy before you go. Be sure that you have your good-luck pillow, the extemp files, your car keys!

Keys generally go to the coach (before you check out...not 60 miles down the road).

After the awards assembly, you usually change clothes QUICKLY. Then hit the road. Some teams, of course, change to travel clothes before the assembly--another personal preference that your coach will clarify for you.

On the way home, teams often: review critiques; talk about the tourney; study; begin to discuss strategies for the next tournament; sleep the sleep of a proud/exhausted competitor.

When you arrive back home: everyone helps unload, call for rides if necessary[80], and drags their weary behinds home.

No matter how late they arrive home, professionals DO NOT miss class the next morning. **Never** use forensics as an excuse. It makes the next trip very difficult. Stay up and stay awake in class. Forensics tends to attract the best, the brightest, the motivated. Prove it!

---

[80]If you call as soon as you get back, your ride will be there by the time you unload -- hopefully. This way no one has to wait with you when they would much rather be home in their own bed.

VII.

AT THE TOURNAMENT

TOURNAMENT BEHAVIOR
or
HOW TO LOOK AND ACT LIKE THE WINNER YOU ARE

GENERAL BEHAVIOR

This behavior is a question of image, both for you and your team, as well as, the school you represent. The rules for behavior will be a matter that will ultimately be given to you by your coach. BUT, there are some rules we think each competitor should adhere to. We insist on them for our squad. We share them with you...

1. Remember that you go to contests to perform well and to learn. Both of these require work, dedication, and proper rest. Therefore, no "partying" is allowed until AFTER the contest is over.

2. Most schools have a policy that makes drugs or alcohol a no-no on school sponsored trips. Either of these indulgences will hamper a good performance--not to mention endangering your possibility of ever going on another trip! This has nothing (or little) to do with legality. It has a lot to do with cash investment in your tournament performance and some big words like: **responsibility** and **professionalism.**

3. Most teams practice while in route to contest (unless you suffer car sickness!) and while in the motel rooms and you should be willing to do so. Come prepared to practice: flashlights (for driving in the dark), pencils, paper, and scripts.

4. Be courteous to your roommates--Refer to "ROOMIES".

5. Maturity in all aspects of your behavior is a must. You are a responsible adult representing a fine school, so act like it.

6. **Punctuality:** Be on time **always**. It is your responsibility to know when the cars are leaving, when your round starts, etc. Know, and be there. Don't oversleep. Don't expect others to wait. You will probably be disappointed. You will probably not be forgiven. An anxious squad waiting for one late member is not a pretty sight!

7. You cannot rationalize bad behavior. Don't make excuses.

DON'T ACCEPT YOUR DOG'S ADMIRATION
AS CONCLUSIVE EVIDENCE
THAT YOU ARE WONDERFUL.

Ann Landers

BEHAVIOR AT THE TOURNAMENT

1. **Be professional at ALL times.**

2. Learn and practice the professional way to wait your turn, to approach the front of the room with confidence and return to your seat with confidence. This is more important than you can imagine!

3. Follow the Golden Rule of Forensics:

> LISTEN TO OTHERS AS YOU WOULD HAVE THEM LISTEN TO YOU.

In other words, be a courteous audience. Don't silently practice your own selection; don't chew gum; don't ransack you purse or knapsack or briefcase; don't file or clean your fingernails; don't do anything that could be distracting to other competitors **or the judge!** If you cause a distraction in a round, your team might pay with reduced points from an angry judge. NEVER leave a round unless you are cross-entered This goes for audience members as well! If you serve as an audience, please be equally kind to all competitors: applaud, laugh, etc. for competitors other than your own teammates.

> **NEVER look for small advantages.**
> **If you seek quick result, you will not attain the ultimate goal.**
> **If you are led astray by small advantages, you will never accomplish great things.**
>
> **CONFUCIUS**

4. Find out about your competition rooms **EARLY** by going to the posting area. Write down the time, building, room number, and speaker position. Then locate the room.

   When it is about 10-15 minutes before your round begins, re-check for changes in postings. Your room may have been moved or you may have been re-sectioned at the last minute. It is not personal, so be calm and collected about it.

MORE RULES FOR TOURNAMENT BEHAVIOR

SIGNING-IN -- is the act of putting your name on the blackboard in a round--a roll-call of sorts. On the board there will probably be a list of numbers. When you arrive, you sign-in next to the appropriate slot and add school number and/or contestant number. If XE (cross-entered) you add XE at the end of your name. This lets the judge know that you are coming and/or going. [If your name is there, the judge will wait for you, for as long as the tournament schedule permits.]
DO NOT PUSH YOUR LUCK!

Cross Entering -- If you are cross entered, go to the room in which you will compete last and write the following on the board, next to your speaker position: Name, school number, "XE". This is "signing-in". Then go back to your first room. (If you have a partner, touch base about this plan.)

A typical board may look like this when you enter the room:

```
                        PROSE  RD 2

        1. MEYER 13 XE
        2.
        3. KESTER 12
        4. WILLIAMS 5 TE
        5.
        6. TATE 21
```

You would know that: Meyer from school 13 was cross entered and may or may not be there. Kester from school 12 is there and is not leaving until the round is over. Williams may or not be there but is being braggy by indicating that he is triple entered. That Tate from school 21 is there and is staying. You sign in your name at position 5, as it was posted on the posting list.

Remember that performances may not be in order, because of cross entries. Since current studies indicate that placement has no bearing on win/lose, common practice allows XE performers who are in the room to go ahead of those not cross entered. This absolutely does not enter into a judge's criteria, as long as your are gracious about speeding this process along. Not co-operating makes you look bad. The purpose of "adjusting" the order, in this case, is to let the tournament stay on schedule. This is vitally important.

Extemp is the exception in XE, as the speaking order for extemp is rigidly enforced at every tournament because of the 30 minutes prep rule. [See the Extemp section for more specific information.]

RULES FOR TOURNAMENT BEHAVIOR: PART III........

1. During the round:

    a. A positive attitude is a "must" at all times.

    b. Sign-in, if you haven't already.

    c. Be polite to other competitors and the judge. It is fine to have chit-chat before the competition begins, but keep it friendly. NEVER say anything unkind while at a tournament, about anyone -- including yourself.

    d. Listen to everyone in your round, if at all possible. If you are XE, you will not be able to listen to all competitors. In this instance, you should perform and then after returning to your seat, ask the judge, "May I please be excused, I have another round?" or "I'm sorry, but I'm cross-entered." Then quietly leave, go to your next round's door and listen quietly. Wait until no one is performing, and then slip quietly into the room. Sit. You should already be signed-in. **Those who are cross entered should never draw attention to their coming and going.**

    NOTE: In some regions, it is the custom to go to the board and erase "XE" or draw a line through it to indicate your arrival. If this is your region's or your school's preference, do it quietly and as unobtrusively as possible.

    e. Always act confident (before, during, and after your performance). Fill your head with positive thoughts. Don't judge yourself. Don't be spooked by the other performance.

2. Do **not** ask your judge anything concerning your performance -- before, during, or after.

3. Do **not** discuss your own or any performance that you have heard while you are **at** the tournament. You never know who might be listening (your next judge, a friend of the competitor, etc.). Behind you and around the corner are lots of ears.

4. DON'T WANDER OFF, go shopping, or cruise the campus unless you have more than enough time. If you have that much time, you probably should be supporting your teammates. (See # 5) Make sure that your coach or your teammates always know where you are. Know where you are to meet your teammates between rounds and after competition is over. Be on time at all times!

THE RETURN OF MORE RULES FOR TOURNAMENT BEHAVIOR.....

5. If there is a pattern/time slot in which you are not competing, don't sit around waiting for your next pattern. Instead, choose an event and go listen. Use the time to investigate other events that you might want to do at a later tournament OR support your team (perhaps one of your teammates would like for you to listen to him/her). You can learn a lot by listening to other people.

6. Be one of those wonderful competitors who are noted for being helpful, courteous, and professional.

7. If you have a problem:

    a. Find one of your coaches. If they're not available...

    b. Find an experienced teammate or...

    c. Go to the judges' ballot table and ask for assistance in finding one your coaches **or** tactfully and pleasantly, ask the ballot table people for help.

    Avoid panicking: Remember you need to use your energy for performing, not 'frenzies'. The "panics" will unravel all your hard work--Don't let them.

WATCH FOR

REVENGE OF THE TOURNAMENT BEHAVIOR RULES IX

AT YOUR LOCAL THEATRE

RATED CG-13

No one under 13 allowed in without coach.

BEHAVIOR AT THE AWARDS ASSEMBLY[81]

1. Act like winners--Adult winners. Be positive, supportive, and dignified. Be on time, sit with the squad, and applaud equally for everyone. Professional competitors do not shout or stand-up at awards.

2. If you win: Usually all finalists are called to the front. After receiving your award (applause or hardware) return to your seat. A team sweepstakes is received by the coach or sometimes by a squad captain or designated team member.

3. It is perfectly all right to be surprised or happy to receive hardware. Gratitude and joy are fun if they are honest. It is **not** okay to be angry or show disappointment if you don't get an award you want. Good sportsmanship works both ways. Be gracious and grateful, however it goes. Support everyone--not just your team. Remember that it is a real mark of accomplishment to have won any recognition at a competition.

4. Many teams feel it is more professional to change into your traveling clothes AFTER the awards. Image is often a team matter. Follow the directions of your coach, in this as in all matters.

5. If and when you go to the front of the room to receive another award, leave the ones you are already won. No one is going to steal them.

---

[81] This title is not to be confused with the cult classic series based on Rules for Tournament Behavior. The genres are quite different. Awards Assembly Etiquette does not have the panache of its predecessor.

MAKING IT TO OUT ROUNDS
or
My Name Is Posted on the Wall! Now What?

"Out rounds" is a term which refers to the rounds of competition after preliminaries - quarters, semis, finals. It makes you think of boxing, slugging it out. The terminology is as brutal as the struggle to get here. This honor is sometimes called "breaking", as in breaking away from the pack.

One of the real and most immediate problems with making it to an "out" round is time. You either have too much of it (overnight) or too little of it (ten minutes).

If you have too much time you may decide to change things. Whoa! The fact that you have been singled out means you're doing something right already! So, don't even think of changing it now. Or you decide that they made a mistake in the tab room. Or that you begin to imagine yourself as a midget in the company of giants. You talk yourself into believing that you aren't good enough; you aren't going to succeed.

If you have too little time, it means that just as you read your name you discover that you are to perform in two minutes in a building far, far away. Take a deep breath and remember the judges have to get there too and at their advanced age they can't be that much faster than you are. Adrenalin and youth are on your side.

After the problems with time, the advice is simple. First, don't panic! You broke away from the pack. You impressed _someone_ on the road to this point. You are doing something right. So relax! Have a good time. The less pressure you put on yourself the better you will feel and the better you will perform. Of _course_, you will see wonderful performances in these rounds. [You may also see some things that you don't understand why they have advanced so far.] Enjoy _all_ of them. Learn something from everyone you see perform. Be the best audience that you can imagine being. And as each is finished, mentally decide to be the frosting on the cake; the whipped cream on the top. Use their energy to feed your performance. Far too many competitors defeat themselves before they begin by assessing the competition and assigning themselves last place. No matter what forensic god happens to be in your round, remember that everyone is beatable. Everyone has been defeated at some point or another. So forget the mind games of other competitors and/or their reputations. You are going to get a chance to see what all the talk was about. Learn from it, don't be threatened by it.

And by the way, be complimentary of the good performances that you see. The competitors will be flattered to know that you liked their work, and you may find a new friend or two. It is also true that people you know and like are not nearly as scary or awesome as competitors that you don't know. You may find out that they are afraid of _your_ reputation. Pretty nice, huh?

Time to perform? Remember that consistency in rehearsal means consistency in performance. Check your accessories early....VA's, scripts, whatever. Take a couple of good breaths, walk to the front of the room, and thank God that you are standing there in this room with this bunch of winners instead of at home doing laundry. Then let her rip. This is the gravy, the best of times.

You will feel the charge that comes from having arrived at this time and place. Don't let it push you. Just do what you know how to do. Let the judges sort it out. Feel good about what you are doing. Have the best time you know how to have and forget the crazy win/lose thing. The joy is in the performance. If they want to give prizes for it, great! Take them! But the real reward is in creating that moment that you have been working to create. The real payoff is the performance and the audience response. Make it happen.

WHAT HAPPENS IF
YOUR NAME IS NOT ON THE WALL
or
GOING OUT WITH STYLE

No one likes to lose, so it is a bad moment when the names are posted and yours isn't there. THEREFORE, let's talk about what that means and doesn't mean. **It doesn't mean** that you were not good or that the judge was stupid. (Misguided, maybe.) It means that, no matter how you called the rounds, someone else called them differently. There are lots of lessons to learn before you get your name on that wall consistently. Even then, you have no guarantee. If you will check, you will often find people who have a record of winning this event are not on the wall THIS time. Everybody loses sometime.

Now, **what it means**, unfortunately, is that you will have to wait for the ballots to be reviewed to find out what you did -- right or wrong. It may be that the wise judges liked what you did and you only missed by a hair. It may be that several things need to be corrected that were not caught in rehearsals. Or it may be that the judge hates that author, or that you just weren't as brilliant this time as you usually are. Whatever the cause, nothing can be done about it at this moment. So don't brood, or kick yourself, or talk bad.

If you have another event that is still in the running, rejoice! Forget what is past and devote yourself to the future. Banish negative thoughts. Fill yourself with "Little Engine That Could" thoughts. Drop the disappointment--NOW! This event is gone with the wind. Think only about the event(s) you have left.

If you have now completed the competition phase of this tournament, use the remaining time to learn all that you can, in order to have your name on the wall at the next tournament. Go to watch the people who made it to out rounds of your events. Watch to learn what made these performances work. Is there a trend that you can see? Is there a style that works for them? What are you seeing that you can adapt (not copy) for your own style and material.

Not "getting out" often makes competitors want to trash their material. It is not usually a good idea to scrap your material every time it doesn't win. Instead, use the lessons that you learn to improve the performance the next time that you do it. People who are constantly changing the event or the material rarely have time to get it polished. They are trapped in the early performance stage with each new choice. They don't have *time* to get consistent. Continue to smooth the one that you have, unless you and your coach decide, based on the ballots, that the selection is the problem. Keep working. Don't get discouraged.

Forensic Story: We once had a competitor who worked all year and never won big.....until Nationals. Then she was ranked second place overall speaker at the tournament. Did she get discouraged during the year? You bet! But she didn't quit. She kept working and working and rehearsing and rehearsing. And it paid off big time. [Insert deep voice over] "There are a million stories in the Naked Tournament. This has been one of them."

We know that right now, you don't want to hear success stories. Your name isn't on the wall and you want to feel sorry for yourself. Of course you do, and it's all right to do so....for thirty seconds. The trick is not to show it too publicly. But, no **good competitor** would ever say anything negative in public. Then people would know that you didn't know how to accept disappointment in a socially acceptable manner. They would suspect that you thought your judges were nuts. So, just look at the board, congratulate those who need it, and then slip away to a very private place for thirty seconds to have a pity party. Then go to those out rounds to learn how to improve.

The winningest competitors have learned a secret, and if you ask them they will share it with you. [DRUM ROLL........]

> The secret of winning is in the **ATTITUDE**. The more you concentrate on the joy of performing, the better you do. This means that it really shouldn't matter if you make it to finals or not, as long as you did the best work that you were capable of in that round. We all know that this kind of attitude is hard to come by and harder still to maintain. But, year after year, we have watched it happen to people. Impossible to believe, but some people really DON'T CARE whether their name made the wall or not. And frequently, it does. Defies the imagination, doesn't it? We have watched it work, not only in competition, but in job interviews, auditions, classes. When you give up the mental struggle to win, you win. But for now, just accept the fact that competition is a place to learn. Sometimes we learn through failure and sometimes through success; often through a combination. But winning or losing does not have anything to do with who you are or how good you are. Believe that!

In the moment that you carry this conviction...

in that moment

your dream will become a reality.

Robert Collier

ETHICAL CONCERNS

Ethics has become one of the key words of the decade and may very well remain one into the next millennium. Courses are springing up in universities everywhere to teach ethical behavior in business. And of course, opponents of these classes say that ethics can't be taught. Whatever your belief, your authors firmly believe there are some ethical standards to be applied to forensic work.

We are not going to pretend that we have listed all of them, but here are several for you to consider. We like to call them the THOU SHALL NOTs.

1. THOU SHALL NOT lie to your coach.
2. THOU SHALL NOT flirt with judges.
3. THOU SHALL NOT bad mouth your own coach or teammates to other schools.
4. THOU SHALL NOT be rude to other competitors.
5. THOU SHALL NOT talk loudly in halls during competition time
6. THOU SHALL NOT talk negatively about other competitors or their material for you may be overheard.
7. THOU SHALL NOT purposely "stack" a round with teammates in order to give negative feedback to everyone but yourself.
8. THOU SHALL NOT "MUG" (make faces) while watching other competitors in rounds.
9. THOU SHALL NOT try to "psyche out" other competitors.
10. THOU SHALL NOT say you're "crossed entered" when you are not
11. THOU SHALL NOT fake an excuse to arrive at a room <u>late</u> or to leave a room <u>early</u>.
12. THOU SHALL NOT steal or hide other competitor's property: folders, visual aids, purses, Cat Cases, etc.
13. THOU SHALL NOT take words from a movie and introduce them as coming from the novel.
14. THOU SHALL NOT pass off poetry as prose or prose as poetry, etc.
15. THOU SHALL NOT use the same material or portions from year to year: Neither thy speeches nor thy literature.
16. THOU SHALL NOT plagiarize (copy another's work and not give them credit).
17. THOU SHALL NOT plagiarize in your introduction (pretend you wrote it when it's really from a published source - give them the credit.).
18. THOU SHALL NOT use "canned intros" in unprepared events.
19. THOU SHALL NOT make up information.
20. THOU SHALL NOT incorrectly cite sources.
21. THOU SHALL NOT "steal" pieces from a competitor that you know you will be competing against in that same year.

USING BALLOTS AS A LEARNING TOOL

When the thrill of victory and the agony of defeat have died away and the adrenalin returned to normal, the real work of competing begins: re-working your events. You have done the best work possible at this point and a set of judges have evaluated what they saw. Their evaluation may or may not agree with what you know and believe, but you can still learn from them if you:

1. Accept the fact that some judges are not going to like what you have done. They will disagree with the subject or the style or you, personally. Chalk that one up to experience. If most of your judges didn't like the same thing, you may want to examine the reason. There may be a truth lurking there somewhere. Warning!! Forensic story...

    FORENSIC STORY: We once had a selection on the team that female judges loved, and male judges hated. We dropped it.

2. Accept the fact that some judges may find a truth that you and your coach overlooked. If this happens, rejoice. Add it to your 'bag of tricks'. Use it to illuminate your selection.

3. Remember that these ballots are usually not personal attacks on you. They are honest assessments of what that judge saw, based on their perceptions, in that one round. It wasn't a "world election".

4. **Ignore the most disturbing ballots**: the ones that bear a cryptic message in the center of a nice clean ballot. It usually reads, "GOOD JOB - 6th place". Just let it go.

The best way to use ballots:

1. As you receive the critiques, you might ask your coach, with as little hostility as possible, to review any serious questions about the information on them [things that will keep you from sleeping until they are settled]. Otherwise:

2. Before the next coaching session you may want to generate proposed solutions to the problems noted on the ballots. Much to your surprise, you may discover that someone else has not only identified that nagging problem you couldn't locate, but has a solution.

3. Then at your next coaching session, bring those ballots. Review them with your coach and decide what action, if any, needs to be taken. Don't be surprised if your coach chooses to ignore some items. Trust your coach.

WORKING FORENSICS: A Competitor's Guide

4. If you get the mark of the beast (6-6-6) in finals, remember that approximately 90% of the competitors in that event didn't even get to finals -- so put it in perspective and get on with your life! We don't mean to be cruel. We know that you may begin to feel the beginnings of self-esteem crumble. DO NOT PERSONALIZE. It might cheer you, in some really weird way, to know that some excellent competitors have been given The Mark.

    Too, some rounds are so wonderful that it is inevitable for good guys to get tough rankings.

    Take what you can learn from those ballots. You might even begin to revise on the ride home. Then before the next tournament, rehearse until you are absolutely wonderful. Challenge yourself to move from that spot where you were. Become a learning machine, and don't forget to allow some time for the change to show. You will be rewarded by a new confidence and a really nice feeling of accomplishment as you see your skills continue to blossom and develop.

VIII.

STATE OF MIND

MENTAL TOUGHNESS

Do things happen to you? Or do you happen to them? If you are drifting from event to event in your life, going where the tide takes you, then you are passively living. Passive living will get you from day to day, but achievement will be an accident not a mile marker. Some people tend to wander through life, watching achievers with envy or despair, wondering why things seem to work out for them and not for "pitiful me".

The truth is, those achievers have more than luck, they have a plan, a goal and they are aggressively working toward that goal. They have mental toughness. So can you. The surprising news is that you are in control of your destiny. You make the choices that determine your future. Your goals, thoughts and actions can determine your success.

Study after study has proven that goal oriented people have a higher rate of achievement than non-goal oriented people. So get a life. Get a goal. The first step is:

SET PERSONAL GOALS and focus your attention on attaining them.
How to start? While you relax in a nice quiet place, **IMAGINE ACHIEVING THOSE GOALS**. Take long deep breaths with your eyes closed. Imagine the details of achieving your goals. Be as detailed as possible. When you have imagined yourself having gone through all of the steps, spend five or six minutes studying the outcome. Fix it in your mind.

Then **STEP INTO THE PICTURE**. Really see yourself as having obtained your goal. Try it on for size. Really enjoy this stage. See how it feels. Know that it belongs to you. Claim it.

NOW REVIEW THE PLANS. Walk through every step mentally. Question the reasons for and the validity of each step. Visualize each step in detail and how it will help you get where you want to be. Find the mental state that will be most helpful to you. Then assume that state. Now go out and do step one.

Then RECALL. As you reach each step in real life, briefly remember its value to your goal. Focus on achieving that result. Visualize the goal being achieved.

While this may sound a little bizarre, the technique (normally referred to as 'visualization') has been used effectively in everything from tennis to cancer treatment. And it will work for speech competitors too. It has to do with accepting the resolve to triumph. Of course, it sounds easy, but it's not!
You may find you have lots of things in your life that get in the way. Do you have relationships that are negative? Do the people around you give you support and encouragement, or do they tell you can't achieve your goals or that the goals aren't important?

If you are involved in situations that drain you or deplete you, ask yourself why you continue that association. Surround yourself with people who empower you. Unload the ones that keep you form reaching for more.

Make decisions based on achieving your goals. Consider how you spend your time, what you choose to read, to watch. Think about how you think. If you notice your thoughts, you may discover that you are not using them to your advantage. In fact, many of us use our thoughts to stop us rather than to move us ahead. Do you eagerly anticipate challenge or expect defeat? Get rid of "Wouldn't, Can't, Won't". They are words that get in your way. Actually "I Can't" is a false self-limiting belief.

Anything you want to do that can be done by someone, can probably be done by you. It may take discipline, or time or training. More than anything, **it comes down to how badly you want it.** All the things people want are there to claim, to the people dedicated enough to claim them. What will you be willing to give up to gain the goal? How disciplined are you willing to become?

But if you say and believe that you can't do something...you probably won't be able to. When you accept the "I Can't" you are preventing accomplishment. It becomes a get-nowhere belief for which you seek self-defeating experiences to confirm your position. It keeps you from testing yourself, from breaking the limitations you put on yourself.

Substitute "I will". Tell yourself that you're more capable, more able, more superior than you had believed. You are then making yourself mentally tough, more able to accomplish. You are deciding not to let your past undermine your present participation in life.

When you catch yourself thinking negative thoughts, stop immediately and substitute a success thought. Focus every morning on the attitude you need that day and adopt it, energetically, enthusiastically.

Stop living randomly and start life with a sense of purpose to have personal success.

THE FRAMEWORK OF WINNING: ATTITUDE
or
HARDWARE HUNGER

In forensics, as in life, the key to success is in attitude. If your attitude is good, everything will seem good. If your attitude is bad, everything will seem...well...bad. A wise person once said that "Some people are gonna win today, some people are gonna lose...that doesn't mean that the winners are the best people, it just means that on that day, with that judge, that person was selected." A great number of people have trouble understanding that philosophy. They were led to believe that the only good person in any contest goes home with first place. They aren't even happy with the second place. They are destined to be very unhappy. So, we need to talk about the forensic competitor's attitude toward hardware.

Perhaps the hardest thing to understand about competition is the philosophy of hardware [trophies, plaques, medals] and what it means. First of all, those trophies are not especially valuable pieces of plastic. They have no real value, in and of themselves. The value they have is in what they represent to you, the competitor. Some unlucky people think that pitiful piece of plastic is what forensics is all about.

Behold we will tell you a mystery! Those people have missed the point. **Very, very few people take home trophies.** Even though the majority do not have hardware, no one needs to go home a loser. Every person who competes has been able to stretch their self a little taller by sharpening their skills for competition. Some worked harder and learned more. That is the real difference -- not the difference of trophy-haves versus trophy-have-nots.

A side note: it has often been observed that it is impossible to tell the outcome of contests until they happen. There is no surefire formula that says, "This plus this will always equal a trophy". No guarantees. Even having the most hours of rehearsal does not buy you the first place trophy. (It does, however, give you confidence and comfort in your rounds.)

Our experience has been that if you focus on the trophy, it seems to get between you and what should be your real goal--improvement. While you focus on one, you can't see the other. Did you read the poem at the beginning of this book?

In all honesty, part of the trophy-hungry attitude may stem from coaches. It seems very easy for coaches to give mixed messages about hardware. While we know our feelings are not necessarily those of all coaches, we would like to try to let you look at how we honestly feel about hardware.

We simply don't care whether our students win a trophy or not. The hardware means nothing to us. Oh, in the short term, we think it looks pretty--while we get to look at it. But, sooner or later it goes home in someone's suitcase. It is something we don't have to have in order to make our lives complete. Students, however, are another matter. We are very fond of students. We want them to know how good they are and how special. Year after year, we see some of them measure themselves by the "trophy yardstick." Some trick themselves into believing that they want the trophy for their coach or their mom. But, that is just a smoke screen. They want the hardware for themselves, to give themselves a measure of their worth. It is a very inaccurate way to measure. Yet, every year we watch a student or two, who want to prove their value by winning hardware. What usually happens is that they either break their hearts or loose their tempers on a regular basis. No one can measure themselves that way. People are worth more than a silly hunk of plastic!

But, no matter how many times we try to tell them, they continue to measure their worth by the hardware standard. The hunger grows and assumes an unnatural importance. As coaches, we care about the students and hope that they are able to satisfy their need for confirmation. We want them to have what they need for themselves....so....We sometimes begin to want that trophy......for them. Maybe that is where the mixed message sneaks in.

Competition is bait that gets you to do more for yourself than you would ever do on your own. Sometimes it's hard to keep everything in perspective. Even for coaches. **Attitude** in competition is everything. It is like the little girl with the curl right in the middle of her forehead. When it is good, it is very, very good. When it is bad, it is horrid.

WHEN DREAMS COME TRUE
or
THE FORENSIC GOD

The minute they come into view, you can tell that they are different. When they rise from their chair and walk to the front, a hush falls over the audience. As they begin, the audience is sitting up, leaning forward. They know that this one is going to be wonderful. They are in the presence of a FORENSIC GOD!

What makes a forensic god? What road do they follow? Well, to begin with, **total commitment** is a passion and a joy for them. They are committed - not to winning, but to improving. They believe in the importance of their speeches. They love their literature and want you to love it too.

They begin to find material early and eagerly. They always want more input, more polish. Get them in for coaching? They are there every time the door opens. They value the work, the getting there, the growth. BEHOLD, a mighty mystery: This is why they "lose" with grace and "win" with humility. They know that what they seek is not at the awards assembly.

They are easy to spot. Every time you see them at tournament they are genuinely happy to see you. They are glad that you "came to the party." They really love it when you both make the out rounds. Even if they aren't in the out rounds, they are truly glad that you are. They come to watch you and are the best audience you ever had. "Petty" is not in their vocabulary. Jealousy is something they purged from their system long ago. That isn't part of the fun.

Forensic gods always <u>seem</u> to be having fun at tournament. That is because the <u>are</u> having fun! They are full of energy, excited and ready to go. They are prepared--for anything. They look sharp--no wrinkles, no droop (you probably think they don't even sweat!). They smile a lot because, for them, this is not work. They did the work before they got here. Of course they are not the only ones that work hard. There are the other ones --- the fakes.

Oh, the world is full of false forensic gods. They think we can't see beneath their facade. But we can. When a forensic god is real, you can _feel_ it. It is like a surge of electricity, when they come to the front of the room. They "claim" that space for 7-10 minutes -- not with bravado or intimidation but with old fashioned love: for the words and for the work.

Believe it or not, these people exist. They are not a myth, nor a figment of a coach's imagination. They are the true competitors, the champions. Join their ranks. <u>Anyone</u> can be a forensic god. They will welcome you to the clan. It isn't a closed society. All you have to do is click your heels three times, begin at the beginning, and follow the yellow brick road.

TOUGH TALK
NEGOTIATING THE NEGATIVES

Can we talk? The good news (in case you haven't been paying attention), is that forensic isn't about winning and losing, its about learning and improving. The bad news is that forensic competition is still about winning and losing. Therefore, you may need some advice to help you understand the paradox, and to help you learn and grow in the face of emotionally stressful situations. Maybe this will help.

1. **Learn to accept criticism.** Criticism[82] is simply the honest opinion of your work by others. Learning to accept criticism is a vital skill because you <u>will</u> get lots of it. You will be analyzed, criticized and remodeled vocally, physically, mentally and maybe even spiritually. You will hear from coaches, teachers, teammates, non-forensic folk, parents and judges. Everyone, in fact, who hears you perform. It is a waste of your time and theirs, for you to defend every word and nuance. You want and need input, while you still have time to correct your work. Invite it. Listen politely, take notes, smile. If you don't understand the criticism or if it is an issue dear to your heart, as politely and as non-defensively as you can, ask for more information/clarification. Welcome it. Then go home and consider the value of what you have heard. Use whatever you think is valid. If in doubt, consult your coach. But, don't waste time by defending your choice. Accepting criticism is like taking a pill. You can accept it, hold it in your hand, look at it, ask about it, and then decide if you are going to swallow it. Give special thought, however, before rejecting the suggestions of your coach. In this case they are the doctor of choice.

2. **Learn to live with disappointment.** Disappointment is the flip side of excitement. If you're normal, you will get some of both. When it is your turn to experience disappointment.... cheer up. We know that sounds stupid and perhaps a little simplistic. But, it really is the best way to handle disappointment. Standing up has always been more difficult than falling down. In disappointment, it is easy to project a cloud of gloom and by doing so, obscure the lessons you have learned. Try to develop an attitude of challenge rather than self-pity. Nip jealousy in the bud. Support those teammates who need you. Be proud of your <u>team</u> effort. Be extremely proud of doing the best your were capable of. Be pleased to have learned lessons that you will be able to use to do even better next time. This is extremely important in building an attitude of confidence.

3. **Accept the fact that nerves are a competition inevitability.** Everyone is nervous: competitors, coaches, hosts, probably the custodian. The trick is to <u>use</u> the energy generated by the nervousness in your performance. Preparation is the key to defeating, or at least lowering the intensity of the jitters. Of course you'll have some butterflies, but they can be harnessed to work <u>for</u> you. Deep breathing will steady your mind, your voice, and occasionally your knees. Concentrate on what you have to communicate. Give the sharing of ideas your full attention. Shift the focus <u>away from yourself</u>. Then <u>get up</u>, because the most nervous moment is before you leave your chair. You've worked hard. You <u>are</u> ready. Relax and communicate. Lose yourself in communicating.

---

[82]Look it up in the lexicon for further clues.

4. **Don't judge a judge by his cover.** Judging judges is a favorite tournament activity. It is not a particularly helpful activity. If you decide, for any reason, that a judge hates you, what happens is that you get extra nervous when you stand before that judge, which in turn means that you will probably get yet another negative ballot from that judge. And so it goes. Instead, try to form at least a smiling acquaintance with that feared and dreaded judge. Study their ballots for clues about their criteria for good performance. Self-talk yourself into dazzling them at the next opportunity. Then do it.

    Let's face it. Sometimes judges are rude and insensitive. Those rare exceptions actually do read newspapers, drink coffee, or look out the window while you are competing. But you know what? They still have to give someone first place....and it could be you. Don't despair, sometimes these jokers are pretty good at reading the paper while judging competitors. Accept the fact that judges are a necessary part of competing. Accept it as part of your challenge to make each judge feel compelled to listen to you. Demand their attention. Then, don't worry. You did your job. Trust them to do theirs.

5. **Don't judge your own performance.** Just don't! Very few people can accurately determine how good they were in relation to the other performers. As sure as you tell yourself, "I know I was better than Snidely Cutthroat with that tired old piece on the love affairs of ants", that tired old piece will beat you. The reverse is not any better. The performance of your forensic idol may have brought tears to your eyes while it just bored the judge to tears. It is much easier to enjoy everyone's performance and do the best you can, without judging. Enjoy.

    Forensic story: A competitor of our acquaintance, once decided that he had done so poorly in his first round that he simply didn't show up for his next round. Reading the ballots on the way home, he discovered that he had taken first place in his first round. Sad, but true. Let this be a lesson to you, little grasshopper.

6. **Remember that trophy poisoning is lethal.** Trophy winning is sometimes harder than trophy losing. When someone has worked hard and finally brought home some hardware, the whole team should be happy. When someone wins hardware and gloats, the team is unhappy. When someone wins hardware and struts, any member of the team could become a lethal weapon. It is considered poor form to whine about losing one event as you hold four trophies in your arms -- especially in front of teammates who have no hardware. Understand? Being a good, sensitive person when you have a trophy in your hand is as important as being a good winner without a trophy in your hand. Compassion goes a long way. Trophy owners are still part of the team...no more, no less.

7. **"Psyching yourself" is an acquired skill.** People can psyche themselves up, down and probably a couple of other directions. It is never good to feed yourself negative messages about yourself... If you do that, stop it right this minute. Tell yourself "I'm going to be on time today" or "I'm well prepared and polished." Feed yourself positives!! Tell yourself how ready you are. <u>Out loud</u>, tell yourself how much you love your work and how you want to present it at its best because of that. Remind yourself that this activity has given you pleasure. Know that the pay off of all this work is the privilege of sharing! If you have done enough preparation, you can believe this self-talk. When the negative voices start, tell them to be quiet. Use the performances of other competitors to get you going - to energize your performance. Use their energy to fuel you. Use their good performances to excite you into doing your best work ever. You owe it to those wonderful writers you represent...especially if one of them is you.

8. **Remember that Mental Readiness is the key**. It is when you put it all together (preparation, positive thinking, self-talk, prayer, and attitude) that competition comes alive. Forget <u>yourself</u> in the moment of performing. Your performance will seem effortless as all the preparation, both mental and communicative, pay off.

APPENDIX FOR COACHES

COLLEGIATE FORENSIC ORGANIZATIONS

Often new coaches need to know about forensic organizations. Thanks to the Council of Forensic Organizations and especially to the efforts of Dr. Sharon Porter of Northern Arizona University, who compiled the Collegiate Forensic Directory, here is a list of organizations.

Only organizations that operate on a national level and host national competitive forensic tournaments on the college level are included in this listing. (Note: The contact people listed were 'current' in 1990. We are assuming they would still have knowledge concerning their organization.)

AMERICAN DEBATE ASSOCIATION - ADA: was founded to foster the growth of 'reasonable' policy debate. Decline seemed to characterize participation rates at most policy debate tournaments during the 1980's. Given this problem the charter members of the ADA set out to find a solution to the decline. The reasons most often cited related to excesses in certain types of behaviors exhibited by debaters and judges in policy debate. The ADA then set about to re-establish control over the activity of policy debate with the goal of diminishing the excesses. A decision was made to concentrate upon behaviors which could be uniformly curtailed to preserve fairness. Eventually, a set of rules was designed and adopted to curb those excesses. Example rules are: requiring that full citations be read on all evidence presented in the round, eliminating the reading of evidence by the judge at the conclusion of a round, eliminating the use of profanity in debates, encouraging the use of reasonable communicative behavior in rounds. The organization monitors the behavior of judges to determine compliance, but most adhere given a commitment to improve policy debate. Contact - Warren Decker, Communication Dept., George Mason University, Fairfax, VA 22030, (703) 323-3579

AMERICAN PARLIAMENTARY DEBATE ASSOCIATION - APDA: Parliamentary debate is extemporaneous, off-topic, and modeled loosely on a house of Parliament. In each round, a team, know as the "Government" is assigned a resolution, usually taken from a quotation, and has ten minutes to construct an affirmative case. A second two-person team, the "Opposition," opposes the case. No research or further preparation time is allowed. Parliamentary debate is the International style of debate and a world tournament is held annually. contact - Howard Robbins, Johns Hopkins University, Baltimore, MD, (301) 243-9331.

CROSS EXAMINATION DEBATE ASSOCIATION - CEDA: CEDA, founded in 1971, is the largest intercollegiate debate organization in the United States. CEDA was created to promote a form of debate that strikes a balance among analysis, delivery, and the use of evidence. The association encourages students to learn about debate by holding novice divisions at most sanctioned tournaments, and the mission of the organization is to promote excellence in education as well as competition. CEDA designates an official topic that is debated nationwide for each semester. Although recent topics have been propositions of judgment rather than policy, it is the style of debate rather than the nature of the topic that distinguishes CEDA. The Association also confers school sweepstakes awards on outstanding programs and hosts a National Championship Tournament that is open to all member schools. Contact - Ann Gill, Speech Communication, 302 Eddy, Colorado State University, Fort Collins, CO 80523, (303) 491-1107

DELTA SIGMA RHO - TAU KAPPA ALPHA DSR-TKA: A member of the National Association of College Honor Societies, this society is organized and operated exclusively for educational purposes. The specific purposes are: (1) To promote interest in, and to award suitable recognition for excellence in forensics and original speaking; and (2) To foster respect for, and an appreciation of, freedom of speech as a vital element of society. The society sponsors annual national regional conferences at which students discuss and debate current vital national issues. A National Student Council involves undergraduate members in the operation of the society. Annual awards are made to the Speaker of the Year, who exemplifies the characteristics of "effective, intelligent, and responsible communication in a democracy", to Distinguished Alumni and to the winners in the National Forensic League nationwide high school tournament. Contact - David Waite, Dept. of Speech, Butler University, Indianapolis, IN 46208, (317) 283-2626.

NATIONAL DEBATE TOURNAMENT - NDT: Sponsored by the American Forensic Association, the NDT encourages the growth of programs of excellence in forensic education in institutions of higher education in the United States, conducts a National Debate Tournament which is equally committed to encouraging the opportunity for quality debate for students of all institutions of higher education by maximizing the number and geographical representation of participating schools, encourages the highest standards of debate excellence by maximizing the competitive quality of participating schools, and encourages the highest standards of educational excellence by conducting a tournament consistent with the educational objectives of intercollegiate forensics competition. Published transcripts of the Final Round and the corresponding judges' critiques contribute to an enhanced understanding of debate practice and theory. Contact - Cori Dauber, Dept. of Speech and theatre, 1117 Cathedral of Learning, University of Pittsburgh, Pittsburgh, PA 15260, (412) 526-0895/5959.

NATIONAL FORENSIC ASSOCIATION - NFA: The NFA provides its nearly 150 institutional members with a wide range of professional, educational and competitive activities. Based on the associations philosophy of broad student participation and open competition, the NFA sponsors the Individual Events National Championship Tournament, the oldest and largest national individual events tournament in intercollegiate forensics. The National Forensic Journal is a juried quarterly publication which provides an outlet for research involving individual events, debate, pedagogy and theory as it relates to interscholastic and intercollegiate forensics. NFA offers institutional, individual and student memberships. Contact - Edward Harris, Jr., Dept. of Communication/journalism, Suffolk University, Boston, MA 02114, (617) 573-8236.

NATIONAL INDIVIDUAL EVENTS TOURNAMENT - NIET: Sponsored by the AFA, the NIET encourages the growth of programs of excellence in forensic education in institutions of higher education in the United States, conducts a National Individual Events Tournament which is equally committed to encouraging the opportunity for quality individual events for students of all institutions of higher education by maximizing the number and geographical representation of participating schools, encourages the highest standards of individual events excellence by maximizing the competitive quality of participating schools, and encourages the highest standards of educational excellence by conducting a tournament consistent with the educational objectives of intercollegiate forensics competition. Individual events consists of public speaking events as well as oral performance of literature. Published transcripts of original speaking events and the corresponding judges' critiques contribute to an understanding of individual events practice and theory. Contact - Michael Nicolai, 112 Harvey Hall, University of Wisconsin-Stout, Menomonie, WI 54751, (715) 232-2309.

PHI RHO PI - PRP: PRP is the only forensic honorary devoted to junior and community colleges. Established over 60 years ago by Sylvia Mariner, it is one of the oldest national forensic organizations. Annually, Phi Rho Pi hosts a national tournament with Interpreters' Theatre, CEDA debate (both team and Lincoln-Douglas), NDT debate (both team and Lincoln-Douglas), and eleven individual events. The tournament is usually held during the first week of April. One of the unique features of the tournament is that all semi-finalists receive plaques. Over 200 awards are presented each year including sweepstakes in both open and limited school categories. Contact - M'Liss Hindman, P.O. Box 9020, Tyler Junior College, Tyler, TX 75711, (903) 510-2206.

PI KAPPA DELTA - PKD: PKD is a national honorary forensic organization for intercollegiate debaters, competitive individual speakers, non-classroom audience speakers, and instructors teaching courses in oral communication at four year colleges or universities. The membership of PKD is composed of individuals united in the ideal of free speech -- the art of persuasion, beautiful and just. For nearly a century, PKD members through research, leadership, and service have nurtured, encouraged, and promoted higher ethics and increased proficiency in the use of the spoken work as a means of clarifying, guiding, and protecting the democratic processes of our American heritage. Contact - Robert Littlefield, Box 5462, University Station, North Dakota State University, Fargo, ND 58015, (710) 237-7783.

NOTE TO COACHES: HOW TO USE THESE FORMS

The forms in this section are some that we have found useful to us in coaching. We find that, next to the designated forensic bulletin board, they are some of our most helpful tools. We created this section because many of the forms are referred to in this text. As coach, you might be asked about them. Here is a brief description of how we use each:

PROGRESS CHART (SIGN-IN SHEET):

This form has a three-fold purpose.

1. We put it up on our forensic bulletin board and require students to sign up and indicate the events they have selected for <u>each</u> tournament. In that way, we don't make any assumptions. We feel that they feel more committed by making this public declaration. And they can constantly check to remind themselves of that declaration.

2. We indicate the progress of the student's events by placing red marks around their check marks as we hear them in coaching sessions:

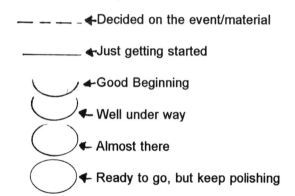

3. The students can readily see how they are faring in comparison to their teammates. This becomes a source of pride and an incentive to stay with the "herd". The rush to complete the circle is fun to watch.

The "entry restrictions" blank includes information such as the number of events per pattern that a competitor is allowed to enter or the number of entries a team is restricted to in any given event.

Note: Obviously, the patterns will change at every tournament. Simply adapt the form.

COACHING SCHEDULE:

Each week we post one schedule on our forensics bulletin board for each available coach. We mark out any time that we will not be available and then encourage students to sign-up for coaching in the remaining time slots. We ask that students only sign for a half hour per day, per coach, unless they have special permission.

PREPARATION SCHEDULE:

The preparation schedule is simply a schedule that we post before every tournament. We carefully consider the due dates of the completion of the phases and allow enough time for students to complete those phases (especially if they are novices) We know it helps students to have deadlines that are adhered to. It also helps them plan their own time use.

ACADEMIC STATUS:

We believe that students should be encouraged to maintain a good grade point average. Therefore, usually once, sometimes twice a semester, we require that these forms be hand carried by the students to all of their instructors. It is essential that a deadline for their return be included. We have found the reports very helpful in keeping good relations with non-speech faculty, and in reinforcing to students that we are serious about grades.

FORENSIC PERSONAL EVALUATION:

At the end of the year we always find there are many things we wanted to tell our students, but never had the opportunity. These things are performance related, interpersonal, goal oriented, and sometimes very personal -- everything from hygiene to confidence; from "Keep in there" to "Don't you dare". So, we invented this form. WARNING: They are very time consuming to fill out. But from the feedback we've gotten from our students, we feel they are very beneficial. The trick is that both you and the student understand that the evaluation will be honest: The unvarnished truth...painful or not. We do them only at the student's request. They are picked up or mailed after the end of school. We get a lot of feedback from students who have actually built their futures around discoveries made through these forms. You could easily adapt them to your style.

FORENSICS SIGN-UP & PROGRESS SHEET

PLEASE CHECK EVENTS IN WHICH YOU ARE INTERESTED AND/OR WORKING.

TOURNAMENT:_____ DATES: _____

ENTRY RESTRICTIONS:_____

pattern>>	A	A	A	B	B	B	B	C	C	C	C
contestant	pro	inf	imp	poi	per	ext	duo	ads	ca	poe	di

COACHING SCHEDULE

COACH:_____ WEEK OF:_____

TIME	MONDAY	TUESDAY	WEDNESDAY	THURSDAY	FRIDAY
8:00 AM					
8:45 AM					
10:00 AM					
11:00 AM					

CONTINUE AND/OR ORGANIZE IN TIME/DAY INCREMENTS AS YOU CHOOSE

_____

PREPARATION SCHEDULE

TOURNAMENT:_____

To help you get ready for forensic competition, we suggest you follow this six PHASE plan. We have given you "deadlines" for each PHASE, so that you will know if you are "ahead" or "behind" in becoming "Competition Ready." Check the worksheets for each of your events for more specific direction.

"ASAP"   PHASE 1:   Know which events you plan to enter

DATE_____   PHASE 2:   All materials for Interpretation events should have been found; Rough draft or outline for speeches should be completed

DATE_____   PHASE 3:   Cut to time for Interp. pieces, Second draft cut closer to time for speeches; Extemp file well under way of being ready for travel.

DATE_____   PHASE 4:   Continue to Work

DATE_____   PHASE 5:   Intros and materials in folders for Interp.; Final draft times and begin to prepare visual aids for speeches (if necessary.) BY THIS DATE, A COACH MUST HAVE HEARD EVERY EVENT THAT WILL COMPETE AT THIS TOURNAMENT.

DATE_____   PHASE 6:   Polish and put on video tape

One of the coaches must have heard you perform all of your pieces by the date of PHASE 5 if you want to be considered eligible to attend the tournament. This is non-negotiable. The coach has an entry deadline to meet. To be chosen, you must also have "signed up" on the sheet that will be posted on the Forensic Board, stating your name and the events you wish to enter, then come in for coaching times.

If you have already gotten your events (or at least some of them) together (i.e. you have competed with them previously this year) then you need to be doing the following on your own:

1. Continuing to analyze them for deeper meaning (this means speeches, too. Or research additional information to make your speech stronger, or to respond to data learned on ballots.)
2. Put your performances on video again and again and watch them to learn and correct your mistakes.
3. Perform for classes (English, History, Speech/Theatre ones.)

WORKING FORENSICS: A Competitor's Guide

STUDENT/COMPETITOR ACADEMIC STATUS REPORT

Forensic Students:

You must take the responsibility of getting this form (NEXT PAGE) completed for each of your classes. We have a copy of your course load, so do NOT omit any of your classes! Please get the forms filled out as soon as possible:

The deadline is: _____

We will not consider taking anyone unless we have their completed form by that date.

The sooner we have your form - the sooner we will all know who is going to join us at tournaments.

STUDENT/COMPETITOR ACADEMIC STATUS REPORT

We are considering taking (student):_____

to (tournament):_____

This student has qualified in the performance area, but before we can make the final determination of their qualifications, we must know their course status. Thank you for your cooperation in helping us make that decision.

Date issued:_____ Date due:_____

INSTRUCTOR:_____ CLASS:_____

ABSENCES:_____ TARDIES:_____ UNEXCUSED ABSENCES:_____

NUMBER OF UNCOMPLETED ASSIGNMENTS:_____

QUALITY OF CLASS PARTICIPATION:_____

ATTENTIVENESS:_____

CURRENT ACADEMIC STANDING: (GPA TO DATE)_____

COMMENTS:_____

_____

INSTRUCTOR:_____ CLASS:_____

ABSENCES:_____ TARDIES:_____ UNEXCUSED ABSENCES:_____

NUMBER OF UNCOMPLETED ASSIGNMENTS:_____

QUALITY OF CLASS PARTICIPATION:_____

ATTENTIVENESS:_____

CURRENT ACADEMIC STANDING: (GPA TO DATE)_____

COMMENTS:_____

_____

FORENSIC PERSONAL EVALUATION

NAME:_____

SPRING OF _____

The purpose of this evaluation is to provide you with an assessment based on our observations. It is to help you realize areas in which you have grown and areas in which you still need growth. This is designed as a self-help tool and we hope you will receive this constructive criticism in the positive manner in which it is given.

TALENT

Potential: _____ Realized _____ Unrealized

Work Habits:

Professionalism:

Dependability:

Willingness to accept responsibility:

Is the student constantly challenging self to be the best he/she can be?

Use of voice:

Use of body:

Use of analysis:

Use of time:

Is the student as willing to work in support roles as they are willing to work in positions of leadership?

Overall Assessment of Talent:

_____ Progressing _____ Stagnating _____ Regressing

INTERPERSONAL SKILLS:

Maintains good student/teacher relationships? If not, why not?

Interacts well with peers? If not, why not?

Understands appropriate behavior?

Effective listener?

Is able to make and maintain friendships?

Is able to learn from own mistakes?

Allows personal habits to interfere with work habits?

Leadership ability?

Can the student objectively criticize others?

Can the student accept criticism?

Is the student realistic in their expectations of others?

STUDY SKILLS

Superior   Good   Average   Below Average Needs Work

8   7   6   5   4   3   2   1   0

SELF-CONFIDENCE

Too Much   Just Right   Not Enough

8 7 6   5   4   3   2   1   0

OVERALL COMMENTS:

THE LEXICON

LEXICON

This section has a heck of a lot more in it than just definitions. It is full of snippets of information that are not found elsewhere in this book. The terms are usually "defined" as they relate to forensics.

In this lexicon "Refer" designates a document outside the lexicon, whereas "See" designates another item within the lexicon.

abstract
A type of topic or idea. In general, it refers to things that cannot be perceived by the human senses, i.e. love, patriotism. Refer to "INFORMATIVE SPEAKING"

adequate coaching
Coaching of all events as often as possible by a coach prior to each tournament.

ADS
After Dinner Speaking. A tournament event. A speech in which laughter is the main product, but the speech has a serious purpose and structure. It is **NOT** stand-up comedy. Also known as STE or Speaking to Entertain. Refer to "SPEAKING TO ENTERTAIN".

After Dinner Speaking
See "ADS".

ahead of the pace
A phrase used to refer to those who are ahead of schedule, or who are farther along in the steps of preparation toward a stellar performance than the rest of the group.

allusions
In literature, it refers to something in this piece of literature that refers to something from another piece of literature or history or mythology. An example might be Thoreau's referring to the **Iliad** when he wrote about the fighting of red and black ants. He didn't say. "...like the heroes of the **Iliad**". He alluded to it.

analyzing
The tearing apart and examination of literature. Good analysis is one of the basic building blocks of a superb performance.

analyzing the audience
Anticipating the composition of the audience (i.e. knowledge level, background, age, etc.) in order to effectively tailor a speech topic and content for them. Refer to "HOW TO WRITE A SPEECH".

anecdote
A personal story used to illustrate a point, used to get or hold the attention of an audience.

articulation
Producing speech sound that is easy to understand...clear, definite and correct.

artistic license
   Altering literature slightly in order to make it fit the situation without altering the author's intent.

assisted practice
   Practice with a critiquing audience that is not a coach (such as an experienced competitor. Refer to "PRACTICE PRACTICES".

attendance
   Being present and on time for classes. Lack of attendance will cause you to be dropped from classes, left out of the tournament squad, and might cause severe allergies.

audience
   The person/people who watch you perform. Your audience may be a single judge at contest, fellow contestants, faculty, or any one that happens to be in the hall when you are practicing.

audience contact
   Awareness of the audience; the inclusion of the audience. Direct eye contact with the audience.

audio taping
   Using a audio tape recorder. A good technique for practicing speeches and/or pieces. Refer to "PRACTICE PRACTICES".

audition
   Simply put, it is a try-out. Your day-to-day living is an audition. Everyone is watching your attitudes, sense of responsibility, willingness, class work. As for forensics, there may be "actual" try-outs for the squad or tournament.

audition pieces
   Usually short (1 1/2 or 2 minutes) cuttings used to show the skills of an actor wishing a role, a scholarship, or admittance to a school.

author/title
   For tournaments, the intro and transitions that introduce new material must give the title of the piece and the author. It will be important to state the adaptor and the title of the original work in some cases: "...as adapted for stage by George Gull from the novel Black Elk Speaks by Black Elk..."

awards assembly
   At the end of tournaments there is an assembly of contestants and coaches. It should be obvious that the purpose of this gathering is to find out who gets the hardware. It may not be so obvious that there is a specific code of behavior. Refer to "TOURNAMENT BEHAVIOR" ....film at 11:00.

awards etiquette
   The rules that govern behavior during an awards assembly. Refer to "TOURNAMENT BEHAVIOR".

balanced cutting
   This term is usually used in reference to Duo Interp. In a cutting for two, the division of words, emotional levels, etc. which gives a feeling that both are equally involved, or a cutting in which one character does not appear to be showcased at the expense of the other character.

behind the pace
    The opposite of "ahead of the pace". Refers to not being where you should be in relation to other competitors in preparing material/speeches for tournaments.

being cast
    Getting a role in a show. Sometimes a role will exclude you from some tournament participation, sometimes not. Check it out each time, before you audition for the play, so you will make a considered decision.

bibliography
    A list of the sources from which a speech writer has taken the facts of the speech. Look in your English manuals for the proper way to do them. A good competitor knows what info goes into a bibliography BEFORE doing the research.

blocking
    A theatrical term which means the design of the actor's movement during a play. It is also used to plot movement in an interp event.

body language
    Refers to the "statement" being made by your body and the expression on your face.

borrowing
    The taking and using of other people's property. The responsibility for such action is to be taken very seriously. It is NEVER done by good folks without specific permission. Borrowing involves trust: given and cherished.

brainstorm(ing)
    A technique that aids imagination, thinking, creativity by listing of ANYTHING that comes to mind on a given topic. No judgement is allowed. This allows the free flow of thought and creativity. It can be done by one or a group.

breaking
    Does **not** refer to bones. Short for "breaking into". Advancing from preliminary round(s) into the elimination level of competition. This is a good thing. It may be breaking into quarters, semi's, or finals. Unlike many high school tournaments, in college you may perform several times before you know who goes into semi's.

    Note: Parents tend to panic over the phone calls that announce "I just broke...". Help them out.

breaking in
    See "breaking".

breaking out
    See "breaking".

budget
    This term refers to the amount of money allocated to our work. The budget may keep coaches from taking everyone they would like to take to a tournament. The budget can be one of our worst enemies -- or one of our best friends.

build
A term used in both theatre and forensics. It refers to rising action or increased intensity pointed toward one specific point. The creating of emotional tension.

C.A.
See "Communication Analysis". A tournament speaking event. The easy definition: proving why a communication act (art, movies, old speeches, commercials) works or doesn't work, by comparing the communication act to someone's communication theory. Example: "Why do people buy tabloids such as **The National Inquirer**? Well, according to Do-Da Jones, people are prone to buy papers that (list 6 criteria). **The National Inquirer** and other such papers (list examples of Jones's 6 criteria) meet/don't meet these criteria." Refer to "COMMUNICATION ANALYSIS".

canned intros/speeches
Pre-written introductions and/or speeches which may be used by unethical competitors in impromptu or extemporaneous speaking. Boo!!! Hiss!!!

CATS
Short for catalog case. Those humongous pregnant-looking briefcase-like things used by debaters and extempers. Also called cat cases, ox boxes, the files.

character placement
A focusing technique used by interpers to help the audience keep track of multiple characters in a piece. Refer to "FOCUS IN INTERPRETATIVE EVENTS".

character study/analysis
One process by which interpers develop interesting and believable roles and thereby become better interpers. This goes for actors as well.

charts
One of many kinds of visual aids used to accentuate information in a speech. They are usually used for statistics. Refer to "VISUAL AIDS".

chit-chat
Harmless, non-judgmental kinds of conversation.

chronological
In time order: first to last, usually.

citing sources
Giving credit to the source of your information in a speech. Example: "According to Alexander Dumas of the Musketeer Gazette, August 21st issue, this is the only cause..."

climax
The point toward which action/intensity peaks in a selection/scene/play.

clothes at tournament
Classy, stylish, comfortable, stain-resistant, non-wrinkling, durable attire. Refer to "PACKING LIKE A PROFESSIONAL COMPETITOR".

coach
The person who controls much of your life: i.e. who decides who will be your roomie; who tells you how to live, breath, eat; who is often your best friend and worst nightmare all rolled into one. The faculty members who work to make you the best that you can be in this bizarre world of competitive forensics.

coached practice
Performing contest events with a coach as audience for the purpose of receiving criticism and positive reinforcement.

coaching
The act of helping to achieve polish.

coaching session
See "coached practice"

collage
From the French for pasted. Taking bits and pieces, pasting them on to a base and forming a picture. Refer to "PROGRAM ORAL INTERPRETATION".

color coding
The use of color to distinguish between and among differing items. Interpers often use colored highlighters to mark different "voices"/characters in a piece. This is color coding your characters.

Communication Analysis
See "CA".

communication happening
Same as "communication act". See "Communication Analysis".

companion piece
Literary material to complement or "go with" material you have for an event. It could contrast or show another angle. It is used to give as much variety as possible.

Companion Reading
Reading to be done to amplify the material you are currently reading in the manual. It is kinda like pre-read stuff.

competition
See "contest" and "tournament".

competition clothes
These clothes are usually packable, comfortable, professional looking, "match" your pieces, and live in a suitcase most of their lives. Refer to "PACKING LIKE A PROFESSIONAL COMPETITOR".

competition readiness
That state of preparedness where the material is polished and pleasing to both you and your coach. Refer to "CRITERIA FOR TOURNAMENT PARTICIPATION".

competitor
Any person entered in competition at tournament.

concrete
Refers to those things which can be detected by the 5 senses. For instance: a speech topic can be concrete: quilting, microsurgery, lasers. Refer to "INFORMATIVE SPEAKING".

conflict patterns
Events which compete at the same time at a given tournament. Information about these are available when the invitation arrives. See "pattern".

contest
See "tournament" or "competition".

contest clothes
See "competition clothes".

conversational
In a style that sounds like normal person-to-person talking/conversing, as opposed to a more formal/stylized "performance" way of speaking.

costume
This seems pretty obvious. It is mentioned because some events at some contests allow costumes; some specifically forbid costumes. Most plays, however, use them.

coached rehearsal
See "coached practice".

consistency
Doing something the same way every time. Competitors work and pray for consistency of time and quality performance level.

cover sheets
Blank poster or sheets of paper that hide a VA until you wish the audience to see it. When you want all the attention on you, you must cover the VA.

criteria
Requirements of an event, of tournament participation, of an essay paper...the standards for an assignment...the items that are the basis of judgement.

critical analysis
Opinions about literature which include such things as meanings, ways to interpret, background information about author and/or piece. The library has whole sections of published critical analysis.

criticism
In our world, it is advice given to help understanding of literature, performance, polish. It should be given tactfully, gently, honestly. It should be taken in view of other criticism (in other words, don't let ONE opinion kill all the other)

critiques (cri [like in critic] teeks')
Written criticism of a performance.
At contest: the judge(s) written comments made while you perform. They write them on your ballot. You can not see them until after the contest. Even then you must often wait until your coach gives them to you. Usually these are reviewed with coaches at the next coaching session. The quality varies, but most of the time "...attention must be paid..."
At school: It the same as above but this time it is your coach or your instructor (if you are in a speech or interp class). Your grade for performance is usually written on them.

cross enter (XE)
To enter more than one event in the same time slot. Usually done at the contestant's own risk. It is very normal to be XE in 2 events per pattern. It is occasionally possible to XE up to four events in a time slot, but this is certainly not recommended.
NOTE: Not all contests allow you to cross enter. If XE at a contest, you check out your speaker positions (check with others if in a team or duo event). Then you go to your event rooms and sign-in (name and "XE"). Then you go to the event that you do first, perform, excuse yourself, leave, and go on to the next. If you don't make it in time, tough blubber. Anyone doing this needs an accurate watch and a cool head.

cross reference
When doing research you may come across a title, name, or term that you had not thought or known of. When you then look up this new thing, you are doing a cross reference.

cross-ex debate
A type of debate which allows for cross examination or direct questioning of your opponent.

cums
Short for accumulated score. The hope and desire is to have low cum. Example: three rounds with a first place in each equals a 3 cum. Get it? Note: Some tournaments clean your cum totals and start over at finals. Some decide winners on the basis of total cums, from 1st round through finals.

cut
To arrange, assemble, and/or delete material for the purposes of a forensic program. Refer to "HOW TO CUT".

cutting
(v.) The act of making a piece short enough or (n.) the piece that you have cut. Ex.: "Have you finished cutting your cutting?"

DE
Same as double enter/entry.

deadlines
Dates and hours before which things are to be completed. In other words, your outline may be due by Friday, or your intros must be done before you get on the bus. Check out the Forensic Bulletin Board for these little-trials-of-life.

Sentences uttered by dorks when trying to hit on a smart competitors.

debate
A tournament event. Actually 2 or 3 events, as there are several forms of debate. Debate involves intensive research, logical organization of ideas and the ability to think and speak on your feet. It requires a lot of dedication to do well, but the personal rewards are many.

declaring a major
Official-like thing done at registration. You fill in the blank labeled **major** with a field like **Speech**. The number of "declared" majors usually figures in the amount of money allotted programs/departments.

DI
See "Dramatic Interpretation".

diction
A term which refers to the degree of clarity of enunciation/articulation.

disqualified
Thrown out of the event because of a rule violation. There are few things that can disqualify a contestant. Some of them are: plagiarism, going over time, spitting on a judge (this one is unofficial).

documentation
Research data/official sources for the information/facts in a speech.

double enter (XE)
To enter two events in the same time slot/pattern. See "cross enter".

down stage
A theatrical term meaning that half of the stage away from the back wall, close to the audience.

Dramatic Interpretation
A tournament event that uses "dramatic" material. It is often plays, teleplays, or screenplays. Refer to "DRAMATIC INTERPRETATION".

draw
A term used by impromptu and extemp speakers. It refers to receiving/drawing the topic choices for a round of low-preparation speaking.

dropping
Giving up on a class -- forever or just temporarily. This is not the same as just not showing up until the instructor gives up on you. A number of these will jeopardize your eligibility. Watch it. It also is used when you are performing an event you had previously planned. let your coach know as soon as possible if you plan to "drop" and event.

duo
See "Duo Dramatic Interpretation". Might also refer to frequently seen couples.

Duo Dramatic Interpretation
A tournament event using 2 people interpreting dramatic literature. Some might say that this is like sleeping with your socks on, as it is acting without blocking. It uses dramatic material (plays usually), scripts. The focus is off-stage and movement is limited. Refer to "DUO DRAMATIC INTERPRETATION".

duo interp
See "Duo Dramatic Interpretation".

easels
Little tri-legged stands used to hold up VA posters. Should be light weight and easy to assemble. You carry them with you.

empathy
If sympathy is feeling "for" someone, empathy is feeling "with" someone...empathy makes you cry when E.T. goes home because YOU will miss him.

extemp
Short for Extemporaneous Speaking.

extemp draw
See "draw".

extemp draw room
The place designated at a tournament contest for extemp speech prep and for draw of topics for extemp speakers. Also known as prep room. This is where you leave your extemp files during a tournament.

extemp files
The information compilation used by extempers. Heavy stuff to tote. Must be kept up to date.

extemper
One who competes in Extemporaneous Speaking.

Extemporaneous Speaking
A speaking event at tournament. Competitors should be "up" on current events, and glib. Refer to "EXTEMPORANEOUS SPEAKING".

eye contact
Looking directly at a person as opposed to through or past them. When eyes meet in "real" contact. A thing that professional competitors do in speeches and intros, especially.

Facts on File
A publication of pertinent information often used by extempers. They are usually kept in libraries.

finalist(s)
A competitor that has made it through all of the preliminary rounds in an event.

finals

This is the last round in each event at tournament. From these rounds come the first, second, third place winners. These are always terribly early, terribly late, or terribly soon after posting. They test your endurance and your ability to function under any circumstances.

As far as the rest of the academic world is concerned, this is the brain-busting tests held at the end of each semester in each class. Smart forensic folks plan ahead for them.

six step plan

The simplified version of preparation of events for contest. Refer to "THE SIX STEP PLAN FOR......".

flashlights

One of those tools that are valuable when on the road to tournament. Squads travel a lot at night. They rehearse and revise on the way. You will be 'noticed' for not having one when its time to work and you will be embarrassed if yours doesn't have working batteries.

flights

See "pattern".

flow

A term used to describe the movement from one piece to another in a program. Flow should be smooth. The audience should feel as if this was meant to be done this way, as if this were the way it was originally written. Refer to "PROGRAM ORAL INTERPRETATION".

In debate it refers to the way the people keep notes on the debate.

flow of action

A term used mostly when talking about cutting. The story should not seem to jerk around or jump. In other words, the audience should not be aware that you have taken things out.

fluency

The quality of effortless speech.

folder

The notebook or ring binder in which your pieces are kept. Sometimes called your script. Refer to "THE PHYSICAL SCRIPT".

food money

Contestants are sometimes given paltry sums of cash with which to buy food while at contest. It should be noted that most schools do pay for travel, fees, lodging-- but food money is usually hard to come by--be grateful if you get any.

forensics

A term used to describe the things we do at tournaments. Competitive speech and dramatic activities such as Prose Interpretation, Persuasive Speaking, and many more.

forensics board

The bulletin board on which all information for forensics is posted.

forensics coach
A person that critiques, guides, and manipulates your skills in order to help you be the best that you can be.

forensic stories
True tales from the past told by coaches or seasoned competitors to illustrate points. There is an endless supply of them--both good and bad.

forensics squad
The enthusiastic and prepared group that goes to forensic tournaments.

free time
A myth.

frenzies
A feeling of frayed nerves and panic.

full slate
When a competitor has entered the maximum allowed at a tournament they are said to have a full slate.

genre
Kind or type of literature.

gesturing
Movement of hands, arms, and/or body while giving a speech or interping.

getting in
Same idea as breaking. Refers to getting in to semi's, finals, etc. Whether in or out, breaking or getting in -- you've done well!

getting out
See "breaking".

golden rule of forensics
"Listen to others as you would have them listen to you."

GPA
Short for grade point average. GPA is more important than you sometimes think.

hand signals
Used in extemp and impromptu events. The technique may vary. The judge will let the contestant know non-verbally how much time is remaining. This is generally done by holding up a number of fingers to equal the number of minutes remaining.

handouts
Usually they are xeroxed sheets with important information on things related to specific tournaments, trips, classes, etc. Oh, Boy! Will you get the handouts. You thought the book would be the end of it. But, Noooooo. Might we suggest that you get a binder for the permanent ones.

hardware
 The trophies, medals, plaques, etc. won at tournaments. The plastic and imitation marble that some people use to measure their worth in the world of forensics.

heart of the piece
 The emotional center of your literature. The heart of a piece is just that. If you cut out the heart the piece is dead.

"he saids"
 Sometimes called the tag lines. After a character is established in a piece, these tag lines can usually be cut.

heads-up competing
 In most rounds there are several (5-6) competitors. But, in Interpreters' Theatre and debate the competition is one-on-one or heads-up.

highlighting
 The practice of using a see-through marker to denote lines in a book or script. Refer to "THE PHYSICAL SCRIPT".

hypothetical situation
 A made-up situation used to illustrate a point.

IE
 Stands for Individual Events as opposed to team events. Evenso, at most tournaments Duo Interp is an IE. Go figure!

IEer
 A person who does individual events.

illustrations
 Drawings used for visual aids. Should be well rendered. Refer to "VISUAL AIDS".

 Also refers to examples that one can use in a speech -- ones that are very vivid.

imagery
 The creation of mental pictures through the effective interpretation of words. Involves "seeing" those pictures yourself.

Impromptu
 Same as "Impromptu Speaking".

Impromptu Speaking
 A tournament event in which the contestant is given a choice of topics (usually quotes) and then must prepare <u>and</u> give a speech within 7 minutes. Refer to "IMPROMPTU SPEAKING".

improvise
 To make it up as you go along. Usually frowned upon in prepared events.

improvisation
Same as improvise.

individual events
A class of events in which individuals compete, both speaking and interpretative. It should be noted that Duo Interpretation counts as an individual event.

individuality
The ability to be different. The quality of being a person who looks around and then makes up his/her own mind.

The uniqueness brought to something by an individual just because of who that individual is.

Informative Speaking
A tournament speaking event in which the speaker gives relevant information through explanation and description rather than trying to than persuade the audience. Refer to "INFORMATIVE SPEAKING".

Informative
Short for "Informative Speaking".

interpers
People who do interpretative events. It is different from speakers--who do speaking events such as informative, extemp, debate.

interpreters
Same as interpers.

Interpreters' Theatre
A group event available at a limited number of tournaments. This is a theater performance of any kind of material which develops a theme or story line. It is done without costume, props or sets. This event is wildly exciting and innovative in its presentation. Same as Readers' Theatre.

interpretive movement
Limited body and off-stage focus type of movement allowable in interp events.

internal clock
That instinct (that is developed with experience) which lets you know how much time is left.

intro
An interper's introduction of the work(s) to an audience. This must include title(s) and authors. It sets the mood and explains anything that the audience needs to know. They are usually short and may be informative. Refer to "INTRODUCTIONS AND TRANSITIONS FOR INTERPRETATIVE EVENTS".

The beginning of any speech. Refer to "THE SIX STEPS....".

introduction
See "intro".

IT (eye tee)
See "Interpreters' Theatre".

jelling
A term used to describe a program, speech, or piece that is beginning to take shape or fall into place. Also one that is close to its final form.

judge(s)
A person(s) who sits in a stodgy classroom and decides the fate of frenzied competitors. For competitors with the right attitude it is a person who gives helpful hints and assesses the quality of the performance of this person with this material on this day. Then they compare that assessment to those competitors in the same round. In most rounds competitors will have one judge. In elimination rounds there will usually be three (a panel). The people who decide the round. They are, more often than not, coaches of other squads. Sometimes they are graduate students and/or paid judges. Whoever they are, treat them like knowledgeable revered royalty. They will have power over you, whatever their training. Remember, if you are good, everyone should know it!

judge's attitude
The mood and/or experience of a judge. A subjective thing over which competitors have no control.

judges/judging panel
A group of people who decide the round. In elimination rounds there are often 3 judges and occasionally 5. See "judge(s)".

judging philosophy for debate
The judges of debate are required at some tournaments (requested at other) to state their philosophy/ideas about debate before the round begins. Then it is the competitors' job to adjust to that preference.

jumps/skips
Used to describe what sometimes happens when big chunks are cut from a piece. The audience can feel lost or disoriented when the holes in the story are not bridged well. Refer to "HOW TO CUT".

LD
Stands for Lincoln-Douglas Debate.

Legs
No, not hose. It is a qualifying system that competitors use in order to qualify for the AFA National Championship Tournament. Based on the number of entrants in an event, legs are given for places attained in the tourney. Sometimes everyone in finals get legs in that event. Sometimes only first place gets a leg in that event.

To qualify for a National tournament (under this system) a student is required to get legs with a total of 9 or less in 3 tournaments. You must qualify each event separately. This fact causes ulcers. If you got a leg with a 4th place and a leg with a 3rd place, you would have to get a 1st or 2nd leg in a 3rd tournament to qualify that event. If you got a 3rd, you would exceed the total of 9. Placing at an AFA district tournament also qualifies a competitor (under this qualifying system).

lexicon
A dictionary of specialized terms. One that gives more than just definitions, etc. You are reading one.

library
Not what it is, but where. There are 2 major types available: educational and public. The library personnel will help you find information, etc. if you ask. They love to save stressed out people. In addition, there are many private libraries and your department probably has a pretty good one. If you are allowed to borrow from the private faculty libraries and do not return the books: THEY WILL TAKE YOUR FIRSTBORN CHILD OR ARRANGE IT SO THAT YOU NEVER HAVE ONE.

lifting
A term used to describe the taking of only a part of a piece of material.

light piece
A piece of material that has humor, wit, comedy, or one with subject matter that is not earth shattering. Bombeck is usually light while Umberto Eco is usually heavy.

Lincoln-Douglas
See "Lincoln-Douglas Debate".

Lincoln-Douglas Debate
A tournament event where debaters argue one-on-one in either policy or value topics. Frequently called LD.

linking material
A term used to describe the technique of making the various pieces in a program seem to go together. Refer to "PROGRAM ORAL INTERPRETATION".

logical sequence
A term used to describe the ordering of ideas in a speech. It could be large to small, least important to most important, etc.

major
The central focus of your college career. Your principal educational interest. Not a life-long unchangeable thing. But, a thing upon which budgets for departments may be measured. Support your department by declaring a major. See "declaring a major".

make-up work
Class work that is not done at the proper time because of absence (tournament leave, we hope). This should be completed as soon as possible or even ahead of time. Since you know what is due and when it is due, it is possible to "make-up" work ahead of time. Going to tournament IS NOT a viable excuse for being in trouble with your class work. Plan.

manuscript
Your clean, up-to-date, typed version of your contest material.

marking the script
Placing notes, highlighting, interp marks, etc. in the material that you are interping. Refer to "THE PHYSICAL SCRIPT".

master tape
A video tape on which the performances are recorded. Refer to "PRACTICE PRACTICES".

mastery of material
Knowing every nook and cranny of every syllable and pause in your material for contest, and being consistent and comfortable in the way you perform them.

material
The literature and research data used for tournament pieces.

materials for tournament
The stuff needed to perform at tournament. When going to tournament it is your responsibility to make sure you have your script(s), your visual aids, your easel, your files, etc. Be sure your intro and transitions are written out and are in your folders, as well. It is a good idea to make an extra copy of all of your material (just in case) and give it to your coach!

maturity
Growing up. A quality that comes with self acceptance and confidence. The knowing that you are acting in a socially acceptable way. Professional adult actions and reactions.

mechanical practice
Practicing with the use of audio and video equipment. Refer to "PRACTICE PRACTICES".

mid-term
A term used to describe the point in the middle of the semester. Many instructors give their infamous mid-term exams at this time. It is also used to refer to the end of semester one. Pre-Christmas break. It is also used to describe a cumulative test given at the end of semester one or the fall semester.

minor characters
Characters that are not at the core of the story. Those characters that can steal a story but not make a story, sometimes connected to a subplot.

mirror practice
Using mirrors to help refine off-stage focus and to correct negative body language. Refer to "PRACTICE PRACTICES".

missing classes
A negative side-effect of forensics, that should be controlled. There are ways of off setting the effects. Talk to your teachers early and often. Remember that you are responsible for initiating any missed work. Also remember that good attendance in your classes becomes mandatory if you want to miss additional classes to attend tournaments. A bit of advice: Keeping good attendance (NO MISSED CLASSES) is very important.

Mixed
Short for Mixed Genre Interpretation--an old name for Program Oral Interpretation. This event uses a program format derived from more than one genre (poetry, prose, drama) combined around a central theme. Refer to "PROGRAM ORAL INTERPRETATION".

monologue
A solo piece. A "speech" given by one character. May be to a character, to the audience, or to themselves.

mosaic
A picture composed of tiny pieces. Used to describe Mixed Genre. Refer to "PROGRAM ORAL INTERPRETATION".

motivation
The reason (physical or psychological) for doing or saying something. That which spurs the character into action.

narration
The words and lines from a piece of literature that are not spoken by the characters. The part that describes. In interpretation the speaker of these words (frequently the narrator) becomes a character and must therefore be developed as any other character must. Refer to "DRAMATIC INTERPRETATION".

narrative poetry
Poetry in which the main objective is to tell a story.

new babies
A term used to describe novice competitors.

note cards
Regular old note cards used by speakers at tournaments. Usually 3" X 5" but it can vary. Check each tournament for particulars. Note: Some extempers use these.

novice
One with little or no experience.

octas
An elimination round. Used more with debaters than anyone else (i.e. 16 teams advance meaning 8 debates going on in the octa round). This level precedes quarters, which come before semi's, which come before finals.

off-stage focus
A technique in which the people interping do not make direct eye contact or physical contact with each other. They "make contact" with an imagined other. See "focus".

OI
Short for Oral Interpretation. POI by another name.

ombudsman
A person who is chosen at some tournaments to be the referee. This person is usually the final arbitrator in all arguments regarding rules and the breaking of them. He or she is usually well respected.

on-stage focus
   The opposite of off-stage focus. A technique in which the people interping make direct eye contact with each other. (This focus is not used except in introductions of Duo Interpretation and occasionally in IT.)

one clap system
   Awards assemblies are notoriously long. So, the one clap system was developed. Instead of applauding for each winner, the audience gives them ONE loud clap. It is not used at all tournaments, but it should be.

opaque projector
   A machine which allows a drawing to be projected on a wall or any perpendicular surface. By adjusting the projection, a picture can be enlarged and then traced to use as a VA.

Oral Interpretation
   A general term used to describe what we do with literature at contests. Specifically it is a synonym for POI. Refer to "PROGRAM ORAL INTERPRETATION".

order of material
   In a program the order of the material can be as important as the material itself. Flow and the power of the pieces are deciding factors. Refer to "PROGRAM ORAL INTERPRETATION".

out of print
   A term used to describe books that are no longer being printed. This means that finding another copy can be nearly impossible. At best, you may find a used one. That is one reason why the return of books is so important.

out rounds
   The same as elimination rounds. Any round from octas to finals. If you are in out rounds, you have been chosen to advance in competition.

outline
   An organized list that is the plan or layout of anything that you are about to write. In our case, that is a speech.

outside world
   Any place that is not connected with your school. Not in the academic world.

over (time)
   You are over (or your piece is) when it runs past the time limit set for the event. This is avoidable and therefore inexcusable. It is referred to as "beating yourself". Time often and carefully. And don't try new tricks in rounds. They may cost time.

overall average
   Take current average of each class and then total these averages. Divide by number of classes and get your overall average. This must be a minimum of a "C" to be eligible for contests at most schools.

overused material
Material that has been used for tournament to the point that the judge will yawn all the way through or, worse yet, tune you out. The quality doesn't matter. It's like TV re-runs in the summer.

ox box
See "CATS".

pacing
The varying of the speed with which you talk.

packing
Stuffing your stuff into whatever to travel. There is an art to doing it well. Refer to "PACKING LIKE A PROFESSIONAL COMPETITOR".

page turning
A detail that needs to be mastered. Generally an interper should turn the page in such a way that the act of turning does not draw attention to itself.

pagination
The configuring of the lines on a printed page. You can adjust the lines so that you don't have to turn the page in a place that is distracting.

panics, the
Another word for "frenzies". If you have 'em, breathe deeply, stop thinking negatively, and them think positively.

parenthetical expressions
Phrases that are like extra thoughts and which are often set apart by parentheses or commas. Example: "He got on the camel, which is one of the animals one never wishes to get on, and left for the oasis."

patrons
Those people that support your program. Those people that support your program with scholarships. Real VIPs.

pattern
The group(s) of events scheduled to be performed in the same time slots. They are usually designated by letters: Pattern A, Pattern B. In other words, Poetry, Extemp, Debate, and Informative Speaking may all be going on at the same time and therefore form a pattern. Some tournaments refer to them as flights.

partying
Something smart competitors do NOT do until after tournament. Refer to "TOURNAMENT BEHAVIOR".

passing grades
"C" average or above.

pauses
The silent time spent in thought or reaction. Do not be afraid of these when interping or speaking (if you are consistently undertime).

periodical guide
A set of reference books in the library. They are published periodically and tell you where to find articles (by subject matter) in varying magazines. There are instructions on their use in the front of the guides. Or you could ask the librarian for help.

persuasive
Same as Persuasive Speaking.

How you have to be toward certain coaching faculty should you miss your scheduled practice session.

Persuasive Speaking
A tournament speaking event. Its purpose is to convince or to activate. Refer to "PERSUASIVE SPEAKING".

Phi Rho Pi
A national 2-year college forensic association that hosts a large tournament every spring semester.

picket fence
An extraordinary occurrence. When a contestant ends up with all 1st places in preliminary and final rounds. 11111111 looks like a picket fence. Understand? Rare and to be applauded!

pieces
Literature used as material for contests. Note that pieces are single. Programs are made up of pieces. Selections.

pitch
The "music" of your speaking voice. The "notes" of your speech pattern, usually described as "low" or "high".

plagiarism
Stealing other peoples words and using them as if they were yours. This can warrant disqualification at tournament and worse (it is against the law).

POI
See "Oral Interpretation". A synonym for Mixed and Oral Interpretation

poetry
Literature which is not prose.

Poetry
Short for Poetry Interpretation. See "Poetry Interpretation".

poetry index
A set of reference books in the library that will help you find poems by subject matter, poet, title, and by first line. The listings change some from year to year, which means that some are deleted and can only be found in prior volumes. The instructions for their use are in the front on each index/book.

Poetry Interpretation
A tournament event. Poem or poems are interpreted from a script. Refer to "POETRY INTERPRETATION".

polish
To shine up all the material. The process by which all the rough spots are removed and the performance is made to shine. Like all high gloss finishes, it is achieved through lots of hard, consistent work.

post
The verb form of postings.

postings
The lists of groupings for contests. These are placed in some conspicuous place at the tournament. They list the rounds, rooms, judges, speaker order, times of events, who advances (if a semi or final posting). The verb form is post: "Have they posted semi's yet?"

power match
In "out rounds", when powerful competitors are placed in the same round to speed the elimination process. Putting the best against each other. It is used primarily in debate and rarely, if ever, in individual event tournaments. You will hear lots of rumors about power matching -- it's best to ignore them.

power protect
When strong/weak competitors are placed together in rounds. (Titans vs. Underlings). This is also used primarily in debate.

powers that be
Anyone that has power over another. In forensics, the coach is the "powers that be" for squad members; the school administrators are the "powers that be" for coaches.

practice/rehearse
The action that adds polish. Refer to "PRACTICE PRACTICES".

practice rooms
These are rooms designated for practice or rehearsal. Some facilities have many such closet sized rooms for use by the students, usually music students. They are usually small, quiet and private -- perfect for forensic practice. Refer to "PRACTICE PRACTICES".

pre-intro
A brief "preview" of your selection before the introduction. Kind of like the pre-credit action in a movie or TV show.

pre-timing
> The practice of timing before you cut in order to estimate the percentage needed to be cut. Refer to "HOW TO CUT".

prep
> Short for preparation. Used in conjunction with the "writing" of speeches by extempers and impromptu speakers.

prep room
> The designated place for drawing of topics and prep of extemp speeches. Where all the extemp junk is kept during a contest. Refer to "EXTEMPORANEOUS SPEAKING".

preview
> A part of a speech introduction which forecasts the contents. The points in brief.

production schedule
> The schedule for the production of a show (regular stage play or IT). It includes deadlines for crews, rehearsal times, tech times, etc. Sometimes the production times/schedule will interfere with a person's being able to attend a tournament.

professionalism
> A quality that will take you a long way at tournament. It is behavior that says "I take this seriously." It is rational behavior that tends to be productive and without "childish" reaction. This is not to be thought of as stodgy or severe.

program
> The compiling of individual pieces of literature with intros and transitions for the purpose of interpreting. One is a piece, two or more is a program. Refers to material arranged around a theme.

progress of pieces
> Refers to the evolution of one's contest stuff. The linking of levels of polish. Where you are in the process.

promptness
> A MUST if one is to be considered a "professional". The quality of being on time or early to a scheduled event, appointment, rehearsal, etc.

pronunciation
> Having to do with how the word is supposed to be articulated when it is spoken. A voice and diction class will help with this one.

prose
> Same as Prose Interpretation

Prose Interpretation
> A tournament event. Refer to "PROSE INTERPRETATION".

protecting
> Same as power protecting

punching up
A term used when talking about adding zip to blah areas of a speech. This is not a violent sport.

punctuality
Being on time or early. A continual lack of punctuality is cause for extreme action. Lack of punctuality could cost you a slot on the team, a round, or place.

pushing (for humor, etc.)
The act of shoving something down an audience's throat. This is usually done by competitors who lack practice and confidence in themselves and/or their material. If no one laughs, they push. Bad choice.

quads
Another term for quarter finals.

qualifying
Becoming eligible. Fulfilling the requirements to attend a tournament. Refer to "CRITERIA FOR TOURNAMENT PARTICIPATION".

qualifying rounds
In college tournaments, you perform/speak 2 or more times before determining the elimination rounds (out rounds). These early rounds are qualifiers or qualifying rounds. Preliminary rounds.

qualifying student
A student who has met all of the criteria for eligibility to go to contest. These include such things as readiness of material, grades, attendance, etc. Refer to "CRITERIA FOR TOURNAMENT PARTICIPATION".

quarters
like semesters, except the school year is divided into 4 sections: fall, winter, spring, summer.

quarter finals
The round before semi-finals. It is used/needed mostly in debate. It involves 8 teams debating.

rank
Each judge in each round will score you by rate and rank. Your rank in the round is your place in that round only. These are 1st - 6th. There is only one 1st, 2nd, and 3rd. There is more than one fourth at some contests. These ranks determine a contestant's cum. If in 2 rounds you were ranked 2nd and then 3rd, your cum rank would be 5.

rate
Each judge in each round will score you in two ways. They will list your place in the round, your rank, (1st-6th). They will also <u>rate</u> you with speaker points. Example: 24 and a 2nd place. Usually 25 is the highest with the ballots usually indicating that 20-25 equals a Superior performance. The rates are sometimes used to decide things when the cums are tied. In a tough round, you could get a 4th and a Superior rating. Or, in a weak round, you could get a 2nd and a Fair rating.

Refers to the speed with which you speak.

Reader's or Readers'
Short for Reader's Theatre.

Readers' Theatre
A tournament team event. It is kinda like POI for a group.

refer
In this lexicon "Refer" designates a document outside the lexicon. Whereas "See" designates another item within the lexicon.

Regionals (Regional qualifier)
For many this tournament, or one like it, is used as a dress rehearsal for a national championship. And/or it is used by many to qualify students to go to a national championship.

rendering
A drawing.

research
Looking for information (usually in a library) on a given topic.

restatement
Saying the same thing again or saying it again in different words. Used for emphasis in speeches. Refer to "HOW TO WRITE A SPEECH".

rewrites
The most important thing that one does in the process of speech writing. It is necessary and common. One does it often.

rhetorical question
A question asked to which no answer is necessary or wanted. It provokes thought. Example: "Is every person in America qualified to be President of the United States?" Refer to "HOW TO WRITE A SPEECH".

rhythmic structure
In poetry it refers to the repeated pattern of rhythm in a poem. The thing that can put you to sleep, if you aren't careful. Refer to "POETRY INTERPRETATION".

roomies
Groups of competitors that share a space in some far away motel room for the purpose of non-sexual co-habitation. Refer to "ROOMIES".

rough draft
The first written attempt at your speech. It is the most difficult step. There is no better way to do it than to just do it, knowing that it is not supposed to be anywhere near perfect and may not even be too coherent. Refer to "HOW TO WRITE A SPEECH". See "rewrite".

rough spots
Places in a cutting or program or speech that cause the audience to stumble while listening.

roster
A list of who is going to a given tournament and in what events each is entered.

round
Is composed of a number of competitors (usually 6) in a room with a judge who listens while each competitor performs, in turn, their entry in a particular event. At the college level you have two or three rounds in events before the elimination round participants are chosen. In small tournaments do not be surprised if you compete against your own teammates or if you compete against the same person in more than one round. Do be surprised if you get the same judge in the same event. Tell your coach before the round starts. Maybe they can fix it...maybe not.

RT
Short for Readers' Theatre.

run through
A rehearsal in which a play is run without interruption in sequence (as it will be in performance). Occasionally, used to refer to I.E. rehearsal.

rules
The restraints of the event. They sometimes change a smidgen from tournament to tournament. Therefore, be sure to check.

scene
A piece of a story, play, etc. It usually has its own beginning, middle, and end.

scholarships
Money given to a person to be used for school expenses. How they are given, how "cashed", how awarded, earned, etc. varies.

school #
At each tournament your squad will have an assigned number that designates your school. The use of numbers instead of school names is supposed to keep a judge from letting prejudice sway their judgement. It is also easier than writing the whole name of your school all the time. The number will change from tourney to tourney.

scoring
A combination of rate and rank. Not a sexual reference.

scout
(v.) To look for good students that might make a contribution to a particular school's forensic/theatre program. Universities scout from the community colleges at tournaments.
(n.) The person looking for good competitors to go to their school. The person looking over a region or squad for trend or style--or material.

script
Your folder with your pieces/events in it. This should NEVER leave your grasp. It should have your name, phone, and school name inside it. It is usually black and small. It is never packed while you travel. IT people have two.

Script also refers to the pages of material in the folder. Refer to "THE PHYSICAL SCRIPT".

scripted
Refers to events that are "read"; have a script.
It sometimes refers to having typed up a pretty clean copy of your speech.

season
School year beginning to school year ending. Thus a season may be 1990-91, encompassing two year designations.

seasoned competitor
A person who has been there, who has competed, who has gotten their folder wet (so to speak). It implies a person that knows the in and outs.

section
A portion of the whole.

A group of contestants that compete against each other in a given round. Sometimes called a panel.

(v.) To decide which contestants will be in a round.

sectionizing/sectioning
The act of creating the sections for a round from those entered. This act is performed by the tournament staff.

see
In this lexicon "See" designates another item within the lexicon. Whereas, "Refer" designates a document outside the lexicon.

selection criteria
The guidelines used to determine what material will be appropriate for the event.

selections
Another name for piece/material/literature for contest.

semesters
The two halves of a school year. The first one is fall; the second one is spring. (There are also 2 summer semesters, designated as first session and second session.)

semi's
The elimination level before finals. A super place to be.

setting the mood/the stage
Term used to describe how an interper gets the audience ready to listen to the piece. Word choice, tone of voice, information about the time before we begin the story, etc. all contribute to this, as does the introduction.

sign posting
Putting up verbal signs to guide the listener through a speech. Kinda like transitions in interp. Includes preview and summary.

signing-in
The act of putting your name on the blackboard in a round. Something you especially do if you are cross-entered (XE). At college tournaments in most regions there is a roll-call of sorts. On the board there is a blank numbered list. When you arrive, you sign-in and add school number and/or contestant number. If XE you add XE at the end of your name. This lets the judge know that you are coming and/or going. A typical board may look like this when you enter the room:

OI Rd 2
1. Meyer 13 XE
2.
3. Kester 12
4. Williams 5 TE
5.
6. Tate 21

You would know that Meyer from school 13 is cross entered and may or may not be there. You need to sign-in your slot (2 or 5, whichever it is). Kester from school 12 is there. Williams may or not be there but is being braggy by indicating that he is triple entered. Tate from school 21 is there.

sign-up sheets
Forms hung at the door of some faculty on which a student can schedule themselves for coaching. Use this often. Refer to "PRACTICE PRACTICES".

short story index
A group of reference books in the library that list by title and by author the books in which short stories are published (anthologies). They are updated periodically which means that some titles are deleted each time. These may be found by looking in earlier volumes.

sing-song poetry
Poetry in which the rhyme and rhythm is so strong and regular that it sounds like a little song. Not too good for contests, generally.

skips/jumps
See "jumps/skips".

slicks
Clear plastic "sleeves" that the pages of your script are slid into. Keeps things clean and tidy. Not all people like them. They are not mandatory. Some people don't like the glare of them, but they are an 'in' thing. They do help protect your pages from wear and tear. Refer to "THE PHYSICAL SCRIPT".

social relevance
Something that speeches too often lack. Significance of the issue. In other words, how does all of this relate to society or me as a member of society? Why is this important?

solitary practice
Rehearsing or practicing by ones self. Most practice is done this way. Refer to "PRACTICE PRACTICES".

sources
The documented material from which you have taken facts for a speech.

space order
One way to organize the information in a speech. Example: explaining from inside out the workings of a motor. Refer to "HOW TO WRITE A SPEECH".

speaker
Any contestant/competitor at any tournament. It doesn't matter the event. It is a generic term, you don't have to do speeches to be one (i.e. speaker order).

speaker points
Rating points. In debate these are used to give awards for Best Speaker or Top Speaker.

speaker position
The order of the speakers in a round. If your position is 1, you go first. EXCEPT when at a round with XE. Then it is anyone's guess. Courtesy lets XEs go first. This means that if you are not XE and a XE is waiting to perform, you could offer to let them go first. Some people are superstitious about their speaker position. There is a myth that speaker order matters. People win from every position. Forget it.

Speaking to Entertain
The same as ADS. Refer to "SPEAKING TO ENTERTAIN".

speechie
A nickname for a forensics person.

split ballot
When judged by more than one judge during a round it is possible for each judge to rate and rank you differently. Example: Judge Jones gives you 1st and 20; Judge Smith gives you 6th and 19; Judge White gives you 3rd and 22. Your ballot is split all to heck. You get 10/61 for the round. It is therefore possible for someone to win in this round with three 2nd places. If you get upset because you got 1st, 3rd, and 5th and then lose the round, may we suggest you get an attitude adjustment. Stuff happens. Live with it. Also, remember that if you got split in the round, others did too.

spontaneous sounding
"First time" quality. Saying something in such a way as to not sound as though you have practiced it 10,000,000 times. The illusion of the first time.

stacked round
The round is stacked when a competitor has a handpicked audience whose goal is negative (for everyone except the one who picked them). This could be a group who intended to NOT laugh at the other speakers in this STE round. Bad behavior. Shame on them.

standing and sitting
A concept which involves emphasis on all aspects of behavior in a round, other than performance. Emphasis on having a confident bearing, courteous conduct, etc. This really requires a show and tell lecture to make it clear. Ask your coach.

stanza
    A distinct section of a poem.

STE
    Short for Speaking to Entertain. Same as ADS. See "Speaking to Entertain".

stop watch
    A mechanical demon that keeps telling you that your piece is too long or that your speech is too short.

style
    A unique and wonderful way of performing. If you lack style you perform like cardboard, you speak like those little styrofoam peanuts used in packing stuff.

subtext
    The thoughts under the words. What a character has in their heart and mind when the words come out of their mouth. Reading/feeling between the lines.

subtlety
    An understated, sophisticated way of informing the audience. It is under-playing the moment. Overdoing it is not necessary. A quiet voice is often the loudest.

summary
    The restatement of ideas (main points) in the conclusion of a speech.

super tool
    Video. Refer to "PRACTICE PRACTICES".

supporting the team
    This implies helping others, going to watch others when you have a round off, being a good audience during practice, helping teammates perfect their performance, etc.

sweepstakes
    A team win. It is a determined by the cumulative score of all contestants from a school. The sweepstakes awards are especially nice because they are won by the whole team.

    It is not unusual to have several kinds of sweepstakes given and several places given with each kind. There could be sweepstakes for interp events only; for debate only; for small school interp. The list has permutation possibilities out the kazoo. But, the big mamoo is always 1st place overall sweepstakes. Some regional and national tourneys have sweepstakes that are determined by cums that go back to the beginning of time. Your score from many years prior would help win the then current sweepstake award. Nice, huh!

    An individual competitor cumulative-points-win. At some contests, the speakers that accumulates the most points are given sweepstakes awards. It is based of the score of all of the events a person enters.

swing tournament
Two tournaments, in two different locations, that occur back to back. They give tournament sweeps (per tourney) and an overall sweepstake for the swing. These are extremely taxing but rewarding (lots of experience with less expense on your squad's budget).

T-Day
Short for travel day. The day you leave for tournament.

tag lines
In this manual we use the term to describe the "he said" kind of lines in prose.

It also means the last line of a story, speech, scene, or act.

TE
Short for Triple entered/entry. Used on the board by bragging people. WE prefer the use of XE, for cross entered....period. It could be called being gracefully understated.

team entry
One of two types of entry: individual or team.

team events
Those events such as team debate, group improv, IT, discussion.

team player attitude
A term used to define a person that considers the team before his or herself, most of the time. Refer to "CRITERIA FOR TOURNAMENT PARTICIPATION".

tentative tournament schedule
One never knows, until the formal invitation comes, exactly when most of the tournaments will be held. However, they usually fall at about the same time each season. Therefore, your calendar will have to be flexible if you use these dates. The invitation usually arrives later than is convenient.

theme
The main point or idea of a program. POI and IT always have a theme. Other events are also thematic, if they have more than one piece.

time slot
The period of time in which a group of events takes place. For example: "3-4:30 o'clock is the time slot in which Prose, DI, Duet, Extemp are taking place."

title/author
Introductions and transitions are used (among other things) to tell the audience the title of the work and who wrote it. That is pretty self-evident. The thing to be noted here is that sometimes you need not just the author, but the adaptor. You may need the screen play writer and the 'original work' writer. Look carefully at the version from which you are working. Make it clear to the audience (judge) who may only be familiar with one source.

time order
　　This refers to ordering ideas in a speech according to a which comes first sequence. This kind of order is often evolved when you are explaining how to do something, how to make something, how something works, or how something happened. Refer to "HOW TO WRITE A SPEECH".

time signals
　　signs given by judges to denote time remaining. Used in debate, impromptu, and extemp events. Vary from judge to judge. Usually a hand signal of some sort to let competitors know how much time they have left. If the judge does not explain the kind of signal they will be using, a competitor should politely ask the judge before beginning to perform.

timing
　　Refers to seeing how long you take to do your event. Get a stop watch and time (include the intro). Stop at the close of the folder or the end of the speech.

　　It also refers to that mystical element of humor that can kill a piece or event. You know that old saying that "in comedy timing is everything?" Its true. Knowing when to speak or pause is vital in humor. Take heart. It can be learned and it can get better.

topic
　　The subject of the speech.

topic order
　　Refers to a way of ordering the ideas in a speech based on such things as going from general to specific, least important to most important, or some other logical order that is at the discretion of the speaker. Refer to "HOW TO WRITE A SPEECH".

tournament
　　Contest or competition. A time and place at which one competes in forensics events. Tournament begins when you arrive at the hotel and lasts till you leave. Refer to "TOURNAMENT BEHAVIOR".

tournament behavior
　　Something that you should take VERY seriously. Refer to "TOURNAMENT BEHAVIOR"

tournament restrictions
　　Rules that may change from one tournament to another. They may cause coaches and competitors to have to adapt.
　　Examples: It may be that the tournament will only allow 2 entries in a certain event. It may mean that at this tournament you cannot enter both prose and poetry.

transition
　　The idea bridge between pieces in a program. The purpose of transitions is like that of the intro and, in addition, they are the "link". Refer to "INTRODUCTIONS AND TRANSITIONS FOR INTERPRETATIVE EVENTS".

　　Also words, phrases or sentences that smoothly lead from one idea to another in a speech.

triple enter
    Entering three events that all are in the same pattern; that all occur in the same time span. Takes much preparation and energy. Take vitamins and be rested or drop one event.

trophies
    See "hardware".

typing the script
    Refer to "THE PHYSICAL SCRIPT".

undertone
    A kind of loose translation might be the feeling hidden under the words. The mood.

unique
    One of a kind.

universality
    Term used to refer to something that appeals to most people because it is common to all: love, hate, fear, friends, health, etc.

VA
    See "Visual Aids".

VA case
    Huge black or brown, poster-board size, flattish cases for carrying VAs. Your name, etc. is on the INSIDE. Refer to "VISUAL AIDS".

variety
    Changing intensities; highs and lows; shades of color; mood differences. A quality of good interp. Without variety, a piece is boring.

VD
    Short for Voice and Diction Class at many schools. Not a social disease.

versions
    Some literature comes in versions. Example: <u>Hello, Dolly!</u>, the musical, started as a short story, then became a one-act play, then a full play, then a movie, then a musical, then a musical movie. They all have different name and adapters, but they are essentially the same story.

    Also, you may have more than one version of any speech, piece or program you are doing. For instance: a short version or a long version, or a clean version and a dirty version. Never get rid of a version. You may have to go back to it. Keep a note on each so that you will know which version is which.

vertical file
    A reference tool in the library. It is usually a set of file cabinets in which very current stuff can be found. It is in alphabetical order and contains news clippings, magazine articles, papers, etc. filed by subjects.

video
A very useful tool. It will be most valuable if you make many and watch them with a coach. Refer to "PRACTICE PRACTICES".

video tape
See "video".

virgin ears
If a person has not heard your speech/piece they are said to have virgin ears. Virgin ears may "catch" something that those familiar with the piece/speech have missed because they are so familiar with it.

virgin eyes
Same as virgin ears only visual deprivation. Not as common, but may be very useful for visual aids or blocking in a duo.

visual aids
Signs, posters, things, etc. used to illustrate, enhance or make clearer your speech. Used frequently in informative speeches. Sometimes in other speaking events. They should be super neat and professional. Refer to "VISUAL AIDS".

visualization
The art of "seeing" while you interpret. Thinking of memories in your mind projected on an invisible screen in front of you.

vitamins
Part of a good health plan. Contests go to the prepared and the healthy ones with stamina -- vitamins help.

voices
Another word for characters. Characters, including the narrator, often have different voices to help differentiate them for the audience. Good voices must have full characterization behind them to make them believable. This is why the term characters works better than "voices".

volume
The loudness or softness. One of the most important things a champion competitor must learn is how to fill a room without blowing out the walls. The volume must fit the room.

winner
The one who reached their goal, did their absolute best, gave it their all. This is not to be confused with the people who take home hardware. Although, they are sometimes the same.

work process
the individual style of attaining goals.

worksheets
Step-by-step procedures for each individual event.

INDEX

INDEX

This is a limited index. No reference has been noted for items within worksheets, appendix or the lexicon.

attendance
    as criteria for tournament 4
    informing teachers of absence 259
    tolerance by teachers of absences 224
    effect of absences 246
    excused absence sheet 252
attitude
    The Need to Win xii
    as criterion for tournament participation 4
    as part of tradition 15
    in the round 267
    as the secret of winning 273
    as part of mental toughness 279
    toward hardware 280-281
    and negotiating the negative 284-286
audience
    analysis of 23
    consideration in selecting topic 23, 299
    composition of at tourney 23
    and practice 26
    and the use of visual aids 32-33
    and use of script 143
    considerations in intros and transitions 144-145
    considerations with focus 148-151
    considerations with practice 240-243
    being an audience 265, 270
ballot
    using as learning tools 275-276
behavior
    at the tournament 265
    in the round 267
bibliography
    noting information for 227
    needs for speeches 24, 27
borrowing
    from coaches 17
    house rules 18
    and visual aids 33
    from roomies 254
    ethics 257
communication analysis
    event rules (AFA) 7
    general event description 74-75
    worksheet phases 2-6 76-86

calendar
- how to assemble and use ... 223-224
- back-timing ... 223, 225

coaches
- offices ... 16
- gestures of caring for ... 17
- needs of ... 17

coaching time ... 16

checklists
- pre-travel ... 252-253
- emergency supplies ... 255

clothes for tournament ... 254-255, 261, 269

criteria
- for tournament participation ... 4
- for a national tournament ... 9
- for selecting speech topic ... 29
- looked for by judges in speaking events ... 34
- for interp material ... 132
- for picking a partner ... 194
- looked for by judges in interp events ... 152

cutting
- how to ... 137-139
- what to consider ... 137
- the cutting copy ... 138
- rules of thumb ... 139
- after the first cut ... 139
- when to put in folder ... 241

delivery ... 31-32

dramatic interpretation
- events rules (AFA) ... 8
- general event description ... 181-182
- worksheets phases 2-6 ... 183-192

draw
- extemp prep/draw room at tourney ... 90
- how extemp draw is done at tourney ... 90
- time considerations of extemp draw ... 90
- impromptu topic draw at tourney ... 108, 109

drugs
- medications ... 247, 250
- and school policies ... 264

duo dramatic interpretation
- event rules (AFA) ... 8
- focus considerations ... 150
- picking a duo partner ... 194
- general events description ... 193
- worksheets phases 2-6 ... 195-204

emergency
- supplies ... 250, 256
- while traveling in caravan ... 260
- problem during tourney ... 268

energy
- as it applies to success ... 246
- and food ... 246, 249, 251
- use of energy at tourney ... 246, 268, 270, 282, 286
- and body signals ... 249
- patterns of energy ... 249

ethics
- at tourney ... 274

events
- rules ... 7-8
- how to choose ... 9-10

extemporaneous speaking
- rules ... 7
- partners/ extemp-mates ... 89
- files set-up and maintenance ... 102-104
- secrets of winning ... 102
- organizing ... 102
- topic sources for tourney ... 102
- weekly work for files ... 103
- topic outlines ... 104
- publications ... 105
- extemp games ... 106-107
- organizational ideas ... 122-125
- general events description ... 89
- worksheets phases 2-6 ... 94-101

extemp draw ... 90
extemp files ... 102-104
final edit check ... 228, 229
focus
- on the topic of speech ... 24
- marking in script ... 142
- and creation of character ... 147
- in interpretation ... 148-151
- defined ... 148
- on-stage focus ... 149
- inward focus ... 149
- direct focus ... 149
- considerations in duo ... 150
- cross focus ... 150
- off-stage focus ... 150
- on-script focus ... 151
- practice ... 245
- on goals ... 278-279
- and trophy hunger ... 280

forensic god ... 282-283

goals
- putting riders on goals ... 221
- defining goals ... 222
- sub-goals ... 222
- timetables for goals ... 222
- as a part of mental toughness ... 278-279

grades
- as tournament criteria ... 4
- and time management ... 221
- study helps ... 226-234

health
- general information ... 246-248
- while at tournament ... 249-250
- food/diet ... 251
- medications ... 250

impromptu speaking
- event rules (AFA) ... 7
- impromptu games ... 120-121
- organizational ideas ... 122-125
- general event description ... 108
- worksheets phases 2-6 ... 110-119

informative speaking
- event rules (AFA) ... 7
- general event description ... 37
- worksheets phases 2-6 ... 38-48

internal clock ... 92

introductions
- as part of speech writing ... 24
- what judges look for ... 34, 152
- for interp events ... 144-145
- and focus ... 149
- with DI (special note) ... 182
- memorizing ... 236

literary merit
- as part of rules ... 7-8
- defined ... 135-136

out rounds
- making it to out rounds ... 270-271
- not making to out rounds ... 272-273
- forensic god attitude ... 282

overtime
- if cutting is ... 139

rules, events ... 7-8

packing
- general information ... 254-155
- emergency supplies ... 256
- keeping it all together ... 258, 259

persuasive speaking
    event rules (AFA) 7
    general event description 49
    worksheets phases 2-6 50-60

philosophy
    of forensics vii
    toward trophies 280

poetry interpretation
    event rules (AFA) 7
    general event description 167
    worksheets phases 2-6 168-180

practice
    and your speech 26
    and visual aids 32
    and the extemp file 104
    focus practice 150
    consideration of partners and time 194
    and memorizing 236-238
    in general 240-245
    solitary practice 242
    mechanical 242
    assisted practice 243
    coached practice 243
    odds and ends about practice 245

prep times
    for extemp 89, 90, 91
    for impromptu 108, 109

program oral interpretation
    event rules (Phi Rho Pi) 8
    general event description 205-206
    worksheets phases 2-6 207-217

prose interpretation
    event rules (AFA) 8
    general event description 155
    worksheets phases 2-6 156-166

punctuality/being on time
    and your classes 230, 246
    in extemp 90, 91
    at tournament 279, 280, 288, 290
    and travel 282, 285

roomies
    behavior 257
    pre-planned sharing 254
    in general 257-258

signing-in 266

speaking to entertain
    event rules (AFA) 7
    general event description 61
    worksheets phases 2-6 62-73

stress
- controlling 246
- relieving 247-248

time limits for events 7-8

time management
- in general 221-222
- calendar 223-224

timetable for selection process 5

timing
- pre-timing 139
- and reading aloud 140

topic
- in impromptu and extemp rules 7
- selecting topic for speeches 24
- researching topic for speech 25, 28
- how to find speech topic 29
- criteria for speech topic 30
- significance 34
- for informative speech 37
- for persuasive speech 49
- for STE 61
- for CA 74
- for extemp speech 91, 92
- for impromptu speech 109, 110

traditions 15-16

transitions
- as part of POI rules 8
- in organization of speech 26
- in the cutting 138, 140
- considerations in pagination 142
- and script use 143
- in general for interp events 145-146
- and direct focus 150
- criteria in performance for interp events 153
- memorizing 237, 238, 239
- weaving 215

travel
- considerations in scheduling classes 224
- effects on health 246, 249, 271
- before you go 252-253, 259
- dress 254, 269
- supplies for working 252
- general information 259-262
- traveling in caravan 260
- when you arrive 260
- going home 261

trophies/hardware
    no reason to do forensic 2
    display 14
    ownership 14
    how to receive at assembly 269
    hardware hunger 280-281
    trophy poisoning 285
tutor 37, 224, 232
videotaping
    as concerns visual aids 26
    and mechanical practice 242
visual aids
    general information 32-33
    definition 32
    using visual aids 32-33
    producing visual aids 33

1. Of course the exception is us and your course.